Skills for Study

LEVEL 3

Craig Fletcher

Series editor: Ian Smallwood

CAMBRIDGE
UNIVERSITY PRESS
www.cambridge.org

CAMBRIDGE
UNIVERSITY PRESS

University Printing House, Cambridge CB2 8BS, United Kingdom

One Liberty Plaza, 20th Floor, New York, NY 10006, USA

477 Williamstown Road, Port Melbourne, VIC 3207, Australia

4843/24, 2nd Floor, Ansari Road, Daryaganj, Delhi – 110002, India

79 Anson Road, #06–04/06, Singapore 079906

Cambridge University Press is part of the University of Cambridge.

It furthers the University's mission by disseminating knowledge in the pursuit of education, learning and research at the highest international levels of excellence.

www.cambridge.org
Information on this title: www.cambridge.org/9781107686144

First published 2013
20 19 18 17 16 15 14 13 12 11 10 9 8 7

Printed in Great Britain by CPI Group (UK) Ltd, Croydon CR0 4YY

A catalogue record for this publication is available from the British Library

ISBN 978-1-107-68614-4 Paperback

Acknowledgements
The authors and publishers acknowledge the following sources of copyright material and are grateful for the permissions granted. While every effort has been made, it has not always been possible to identify the sources of all the material used, or to trace all copyright holders. If any omissions are brought to our notice, we will be happy to include the appropriate acknowledgements on reprinting.

Publisher acknowledgements
Urbaneye for extracts 4a & 4b on p.149 taken from On the Threshold to Urban Panopticon? Analysing the Employment of CCTV in European Cities and Assessing its Social and Political Impacts – Final Report to the European Union. Technical University of Berlin, 2004. Reproduced with permission.

Author acknowledgements
The authoring team would like to thank Clare Sheridan, Nik White, Ian Morrison and the editorial team at Cambridge for their constant help and support throughout the whole project. We also offer our grateful acknowledgement to David Allen for his thoughtful advice and feedback, and to Fred Gooch, Sarah Clark and Neil McSweeney for their invaluable contributions to the manuscripts. Finally, we would like to thank all ELT and academic skills staff and students across Kaplan International Colleges for their assistance in trialling the materials during development and for their valuable feedback and suggestions.

Photo acknowledgements
p.4 t-b ©ktsimage/istockphotos.com, ©Andrey Pavlov/ istock, ©Image_Source/istockphoto.com, ©mattjeacockistock; p.7 ©ktsimage/istockphotos.com; p.9 t ©Catherine Yeulet/ istockphoto, c Courtesy of One Laptop Per Child -OLPC-, b ©Caro/Alamy; p.39 b ©Images in the Wild/istockphoto.com; p.42 and p.43 ©Randolph Pamphrey/istockphoto.com; p.44 ©graytln/istockphoto.com; p.63 ©Andrey Pavlov/istock; p.65 a ©NASA, b ©NASA; p.99 ©brytta/istockphoto.com; p.112 ©Image_Source/istockphoto.com; p.119 ©David Joyner/ istockphoto.com; p.125 ©Martin McCarthy/istockphoto.com; p.131 ©Philipp Baer/istockphoto.com; p.154 ©mattjeacockistock

Design and illustrations by Hart McLeod, Cambridge

Skills for study Contents

Map of the book

	Part A **Understanding spoken information**	**Part B** **Understanding written information**
1 **An electronic world** 	Understanding disciplinary differences in listening aims Understanding the difference between informative and persuasive speech Reviewing your notes after listening Using Cornell notes	Recognizing types of text in different disciplines Understanding academic arguments Recognizing the development of arguments Identifying persuasion in texts
▶ **UNIT TASK** Communications technology and culture		
2 **New frontiers**	Identifying the speaker's stance on a topic Recognizing and responding to bias Being an active audience member in a presentation	Identifying arguments in texts Evaluating arguments Recognizing assumptions Developing a response to arguments
▶ **UNIT TASK** Ethno-tourism		
3 **The individual in society**	Evaluating the strength of a speaker's claim Recognizing speculative claims and why people use them Judging speculations as you listen Investigating claims through questions	Identifying logical flaws in the relationship of ideas Understanding necessary and sufficient conditions Understanding correlation and causation
▶ **UNIT TASK** Biometrics		
4 **Choices** 	Listening for logical flaws Listening for logical conclusions Reviewing your active listening skills	Identifying arguments 'against the person' Identifying 'you too' arguments Identifying circular arguments Identifying weak analogies Identifying the use of limited options
▶ **UNIT TASK** Decision-making		

Review
Good study practice checklists
Appendices

Part C Investigating	Part D Reporting in speech	Part E Reporting in writing
Defining critical thinking Using critical thinking in your studies Assessing your own critical thinking skills Recognizing factors that can interfere with critical thinking Understanding how and why writers use citations	Identifying the purpose of a presentation Using software to create effective presentation visuals Making presentations with persuasive content Delivering presentations persuasively Creating and delivering a successful group presentation	Matching structure and purpose in writing Writing a suitable introduction Using citations in writing Using citations in different academic disciplines
Developing your own stance on a topic Using logic and reasoning Evaluating and selecting sources	Incorporating graphics into a presentation Improving the quality of your graphics Acknowledging sources in a presentation	Structuring an argument-based essay Structuring an essay to incorporate counterarguments Supporting your argument effectively
Taking notes which are relevant to an assignment Synthesizing information from your notes Referencing sources correctly in synthesized notes Reflecting on notes to help clarify your ideas	Identifying your purpose in giving a presentation Presenting an oral summary of research Including alternative points of view in a presentation	Synthesizing sources in writing Incorporating quotations into writing Incorporating paraphrase into writing Understanding plagiarism and patchwriting Using hedging
Understanding more about independent learning Analyzing your own independence as a learner	Drawing suitable conclusions in a presentation Speculating on findings Making recommendations Preparing and rehearsing for a presentation	Writing a suitable conclusion Proofreading written work Reviewing written work for logical flaws Editing written work for logical flaws Reflecting on completed work

Introduction
Thinking in
higher education

A   Before you start to use this book, complete the questionnaire about the various types of mental and critical processes that are important to success in higher education. Decide how strongly you agree or disagree with each statement by ticking (✓) the column (1–5) which best describes your opinion according to this scale. Do not worry about giving 'correct' answers, as this exercise is designed to help you reflect on the way you approach your studies.

1 = strongly disagree
2 = disagree
3 = neither agree nor disagree
4 = agree
5 = strongly agree

Using and interpreting data	1	2	3	4	5
1 The most important skill for success in an English-speaking higher education institution is being fluent in the language.					
2 Critical thinking is not important for my subject.					
3 Memorizing facts, concepts and details is essential to my success in higher education.					
4 Critical thinking is much more important for subjects in the social sciences and humanities than for those in STEM (Science, Technology, Engineering and Mathematics).					
5 The most important task for a higher education student is to learn the information that the tutor or lecturer gives them.					
6 I should critically evaluate the information I hear when listening to lectures.					
7 I should carefully consider the accuracy of the information in every text I read.					
8 I should question the logic, methods and claims in everything I read or hear.					
9 I should be able to generate original ideas when completing projects and assignments in my subject.					

B   Higher education students need to think critically about their studies. Use your own ideas to complete the definition of 'critical thinking', then compare your ideas with a partner. You will come back to this page to review your ideas later in the course.

Notes
Critical thinking is

Unit 1 An electronic world

Unit overview

Part	This part will help you to ...	By improving your ability to ...
A	Listen more effectively in lectures	• understand disciplinary differences in listening aims • understand the difference between informative and persuasive speech • review your notes after listening • use Cornell notes
B	Become familiar with different types of written text	• recognize types of text in different disciplines • understand academic arguments • recognize the development of arguments • identify persuasion in texts
C	Develop critical thinking skills	• define critical thinking • use critical thinking in your studies • assess your own critical thinking skills • recognize factors that can interfere with critical thinking • understand how and why writers use citations
D	Prepare effective oral presentations	• identify the purpose of a presentation • use software to create effective presentation visuals • make presentations with persuasive content • deliver presentations persuasively • create and deliver a successful group presentation
E	Develop essay writing skills	• match structure and purpose in writing • write a suitable introduction • use citations in writing • use citations in different academic disciplines

Understanding spoken information

By the end of Part A you will be able to:

- understand disciplinary differences in listening aims
- understand the difference between informative and persuasive speech
- review your notes after listening
- use Cornell notes.

1 Disciplinary differences in listening aims

1a Work in pairs. Take turns to say what subject(s) you are planning to study in your higher education course. Discuss the reasons for your choice.

1b Work in pairs. This diagram shows a common classification of higher education subjects into four categories: *pure, applied, hard* and *soft* fields. Say which category you think your subject belongs to.

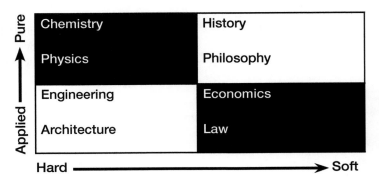

	Pure	
	Chemistry	History
	Physics	Philosophy
	Engineering	Economics
Applied	Architecture	Law

Hard ⟶ Soft

1c Work in pairs. Discuss what the different characteristics of each category might be. Then use your ideas to complete the table.

Classification	Characteristics
1 Hard	
2 Soft	
3 Pure	
4 Applied	

1d Now listen to a lecturer in education explaining the four categories. As you listen, add any key points to the notes you made in 1c.

1e Work in groups. Compare your notes on the differences between the categories and then use your notes to discuss these questions about your subject.

1 How should you prepare before you attend a lecture?

2 What kind of information can you expect to learn in a lecture?

3 How important is it to think critically about the content of a lecture you hear?

4 What general approaches to learning will be most useful for your studies?

5 What specific approaches do you think will be most important for success?

2 The difference between informative and persuasive speech

2a Work in pairs. Discuss the extent to which you agree or disagree with these statements about the Internet.

The Internet ...

- has revolutionized global communications

- is a valuable tool for education

- is an essential part of work and study in the modern world

- can be accessed by almost everyone today.

2b Work in pairs. Read these quotes about the digital divide. Then write notes on p.10 about what you think 'the digital divide' means.

'It is dangerously destabilizing to have half the world on the cutting edge of technology while the other half struggles on the bare edge of survival.'
Bill Clinton

'There are three aspects to bridging the digital divide, the three Cs – computer, connectivity and content. You have to get all three right to increase penetration of computing devices.'
N. Balakrishnan

'Many people see technology as the problem behind the so-called digital divide. Others see it as the solution. Technology is neither. It must operate in conjunction with business, economic, political and social systems.'
Carly Fiorina

Notes

▶
1.2

2c Listen to three extracts about the digital divide. For each extract (A–C), write notes in the table about:

1 the source of the extract (e.g. *a lecture, a TV advertisement, a radio broadcast, etc.*)

2 any new ways of defining the digital divide

3 whether the purpose of the extract is to:

a *inform* the listener

b *persuade* the listener to accept a claim

Notes on the digital divide	
Extract A:	
Extract B:	
Extract C:	

The purpose of some higher education lectures is only to deliver information. You are not expected to decide whether or not you agree or disagree with the speaker's views when their purpose is *informative*. However, sometimes the speaker's purpose is *persuasive*. In these cases, the speaker will explain ideas and present information in a way that attempts to make their audience agree with a particular point of view (this is particularly common in 'soft' subjects). Sometimes a lecture may be both informative and persuasive.

2d Consider the ten speakers in these situations. Decide whether the speaker would be more likely to talk in an *informative* or *persuasive* way (or both). Then compare your ideas with a partner.

1 A chemistry lecturer giving a lab demonstration.

2 A journalist making a TV news report.

3 A course tutor leading a group seminar.

4 A lecturer giving an introductory lecture on sociology.

5 A lecturer presenting the results of their own recent research.

6 A student discussing ideas for a research project he/she is working on with three other students on his/her course.

7 A student giving a presentation about the causes and effects of the digital divide.

8 A science student discussing the content of her poster presentation at a conference on computer security.

9 A manager giving a business presentation for an improved technology to company directors.

10 A government minister giving a speech to parliament.

2e Work in pairs. Which techniques could the relevant speakers in 2d use to persuade their audience? Write notes in this table.

Techniques for persuading an audience
Intonation / way of speaking:
Type of language used:
Supporting information and material:

2f Work in groups. Think about the differences between hard and soft subjects which you examined in 1c. Do you think the type of subject (hard or soft) influences the method(s) the speaker might use to persuade an audience? Discuss your ideas.

2g Read this paragraph about Internet use. What problem is the writer describing?

Increasing numbers of people around the world use the Internet for things like watching TV or movies, or even listening to radio broadcasts. These activities were previously performed with other technology. Some scientists claim that watching TV or listening to the radio over the Internet actually uses more energy than it would to use a regular TV set or radio.

2h Imagine that you are going to join a group discussion about the topic in 2g. First of all, decide your feelings about it. These questions may help you.

- Do you believe the scientists' claims?
- Do you have any information about this subject already?
- Even if using the Internet in this way uses more energy, how serious is this issue?

1.3

2i Listen to extracts from two different lectures to learn more information on Internet use and power consumption. Write notes on the lectures and then decide whether the aim of each one is to inform or to persuade.

Notes
Lecture 1:
Lecture 2:

2j Work in pairs. Discuss the questions.

1 Which lecture (if either) could be used to support your own opinion on the topic?

2 Have you changed your original ideas on the topic after listening to the lectures? If so, why?

2k Listen again and make a note of which persuasive techniques from 2e are used.

2l Look at the transcript for the two lectures in **Appendix 1**. Can you identify any words or phrases or any supporting information and material the speakers use to persuade their audience? Add them to your notes in 2i.

3 Reviewing your notes after listening

> Always take time to review the notes you have made during a lecture, seminar or lab session to help you make sure you have understood the key information. You should do this as soon as possible after the lecture / seminar / lab session has finished. Reviewing your notes after listening helps you to quickly identify gaps in your knowledge or understanding. If you do not review your notes soon after listening, you may not be able to fully understand what you have written later.
>
> Reviewing your notes can also be useful to ask yourself how information from a particular lecture or class fits into the course that you are studying.

3a Work in pairs. Compare the notes you made while listening to the two lectures in 2i and answer the questions.

1 How useful are your partner's notes for discussing the topic of Internet use and power consumption?

2 Did your partner make notes on any information that you did not?

3 Could your partner improve their note-taking style? How?

3b Look at your notes again and answer these questions.

1 Did you manage to take notes on everything?

2 Is there anything which is still unclear?

3 Is there anything that you need to find out more about?

4 Did you include any references that you could check in the library?

> As well as reviewing your notes to check that they are accurate and cover all the key information, you can also use your notes to think about your *attitude* and *personal responses* to the information you have heard. This means:
>
> - taking a careful, reflective attitude to any claims the speaker has made or information they have presented
>
> - questioning the speaker's opinions and deciding whether the information that you have heard matches your own opinion
>
> - considering (or questioning) the methods or theories that you have heard.
>
> Considering, reflecting on and questioning claims and information you have heard does not always mean disagreeing with it. The purpose is to identify points that you need to investigate more carefully.

1.4

3c Listen to three people describing the benefits of critically reviewing their notes. Write notes next to the speakers' names.

Notes
Clare:
Manjit:
Fran:

3d Read a student's notes on Lecture 1 in 2i about the effects of Internet use. Then answer these questions.

1 Can you see any problems with the style of these notes?

2 Do you think the student has missed any important information?

3 What is the student's opinion on the topic?

4 Do you agree with the points made in the notes?

Energy Consumption – watching TV etc online

Internet use ↑ rapid.
∴ electric. demand ↑

2007+ = Many people watch
TV etc online / radio.

Dedicated home radio. (??)

Desktop = 100 - 150 W
Laptop = ½
TV = 74 W

(But) not just end user
 Data centres use much
  power.
(61 bn kwh in 2006/80 bn 2010)
 other things besides TV.

Intern. worse than TV/rad.
 for energy use.

3e Look back at your own notes on Lecture One. Are they still understandable?

3f Use your own notes to complete the column to the right of the student's notes in 3e with your comments, ideas or questions. Use these points to help you.

- the type of data
- the writer's opinion
- any problems you can see with the information
- your own opinion
- where the information came from

3g Compare the comments you made in 3f with a partner.

3h Now look at the same student's notes, in which the right column has been completed, and answer these questions.

1 What problems did the student find with the data given in Lecture 1?

2 Which of the speaker's claims did the student disagree with?

3 Overall, what is the student's opinion about the ideas in Lecture 1?

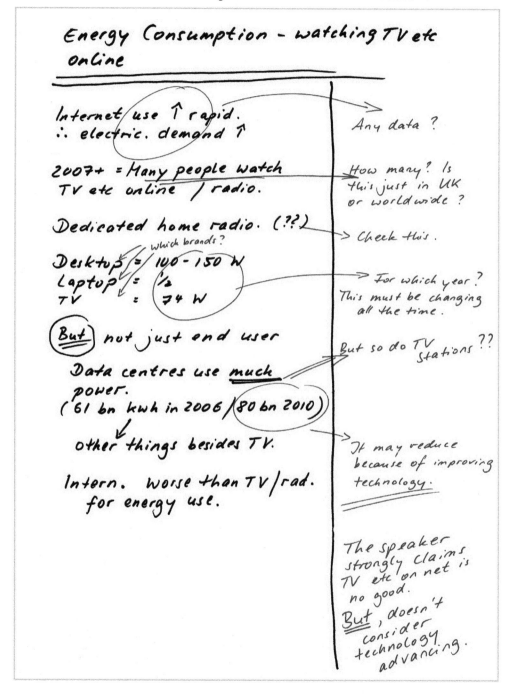

3i Compare the student's notes with your own in 3g. Did you have the same ideas?

3j What is your opinion of the content of the lecture after looking at the student's notes? Compare your ideas with a partner.

4 Using Cornell notes

Cornell notes refer to a note-taking system developed in the 1950s by a professor at Cornell University in the US. This note-taking style is designed to:

- help you memorize key information
- encourage you to think critically and reflect on material you have heard in lectures, seminars or lab sessions.

The notes below are used in 4a–c on p.17.

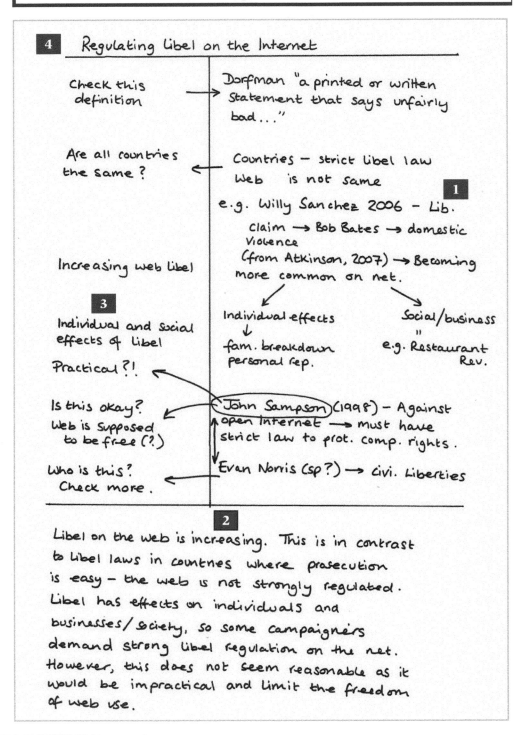

4a Work in pairs. Read the excerpts of Cornell notes on p.16 and discuss what the purpose of each section (1–4) might be.

4b Read this text on how to use Cornell notes. Match each paragraph (A–D) with a numbered section (1–4) of the notes on p.16.

How to use Cornell notes

A Write useful information such as the title, speaker or author, and date, in the box at the top. Draw a line to make another box at the end of the notes, then draw a vertical line to create two columns in the main body of the notes. Make sure the right-hand column is wider than the one on the left.

B In lectures or classes, use the large column on the right side to record notes.

C After a lecture or class, note key words in the left-hand column. Also, think of questions that you have about the information you heard, and note them here. You could also add your own comments or opinions. Cover the right-hand column, and look only at the key words and questions that you noted down. Try to recall as much as you can about the key points, or say your answers or opinions about these things out loud. If there is something that you are unable to comment on or don't understand, make a note that you need to check more about this in the library. Ask yourself how the information here is connected to other information you have learned in your course. Are there any problems with the information or claims? How can the information be applied to other situations? This is the stage when you really begin to think critically about what you have heard.

D Use the space at the end of your notes to write a brief summary in your own words. You should also add your own comments or opinions about the information in your summary. This helps you to understand the information, as well as memorize it. Review your notes regularly, to help you remember key information as well as develop a deeper understanding of the subject.

4c Work in small groups. Compare this style of taking notes with the method you currently use. What are the advantages and disadvantages of writing notes in this way?

> **UNIT TASK**   **Communications technology and culture**

As you study each unit of this book, you will be asked to work on different stages of a task related to the theme or topic of the unit. The Unit 1 task is on the theme of *The Internet and culture*. At the end of each part, you will be asked to complete a stage of the task as follows:

Part A: Listen to an introduction to the topic.

Part B: Read two texts about it.

Part C: Think critically about the topic.

Part D: Prepare and deliver a group presentation on the topic.

Part E: Write an essay with this title:

How has the spread of communications technology affected cultures around the world? Assess the extent to which the Internet is a medium for western culture alone.

a Work in small groups. Discuss your ideas about the essay title you are going to write about in Part E of this unit.

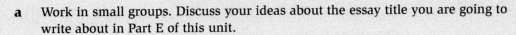

b Listen to an extract from a lecture about the relationship between communications technology and cultures around the world. As you listen, write notes to answer these questions.

1.5

1 What effect does the spread of communications technology, such as the Internet, have on different cultures around the world?

2 To what extent do you think that cultures are becoming more similar because of the spread of the Internet?

c Listen again. Use this space to take detailed Cornell-style notes on the topic.

d Spend some time reviewing your notes, adding comments and questions.

e Work in small groups. Compare your notes and discuss your ideas on the topic.

Go to the checklist on p.198 and read the tips relating to Unit 1 Part A.

Understanding written information

By the end of Part B you will be able to:

- recognize types of text in different disciplines
- understand academic arguments
- recognize the development of arguments
- identify persuasion in texts.

1 Recognizing types of text in different disciplines

In your higher education studies, you are expected to read information from a variety of different sources. Some types of text are usually only found in certain disciplines, while others (such as textbooks) are common to all.

1a Complete this table by writing the words for various text types in the correct column. Words can go in more than one column. Then compare your ideas with a partner.

dissertation   essay   guidelines   handbook
monograph   regulations   report   research article
textbook   thesis

Sciences	Social sciences and humanities	Your subject

1b Check your answers by reading this excerpt from an article in a communication studies journal.

Disciplinary differences in higher education

The past two decades have seen an increasing awareness of the subtleties and diversity of expression in different fields of study. Seminal studies such as Becher (1989) have clearly demonstrated the way different academic disciplines build, shape and express meaning. The traditional division of fields of study into hard and soft disciplines is reflected in the types of media through which written information is presented to students or, more precisely, the types of media which students are expected to look to for knowledge. The following paper will briefly outline some of the key distinctions between written text types used in differing categories of discipline following Biglan's (1973) framework, before making some tentative recommendations for use at an institutional level.

Before examining the hard–soft distinction, it may be instructive to consider the differences in text type at varying levels of study. At the undergraduate level, accepted, conventional written input tends to be the norm. Consequently, there is a greater amount of study using conventional textbooks which introduce classic concepts or key information in a non-contentious manner. These textbooks are characterized by containing little, if any, highly original or unorthodox theories. Monographs and research articles, which are often used to introduce original research and potentially unorthodox claims, tend to be introduced more at the senior undergraduate or postgraduate level.

The 'hard' scientific disciplines, therefore, most commonly use textbooks for core concepts, as well as manuals or handbooks which contain background information and instructions for lab work. As students advance from junior to senior, undergraduate- and then to postgraduate-level study, they may be expected to read more work in research journals or, in the case of postgraduate students, detailed research monographs.

Newman (2001) notes that monographs are used more frequently (and earlier for undergraduate students) in the 'soft' disciplines. This may be explained by the way that knowledge is constructed in the soft disciplines, with a greater focus on debate and individual claims, thus more of the student's study time is spent comparing various authors' theories and approaches to a specific topic. The use of monographs in this way may help to establish a framework of understanding about key debates, and also train students in critical thinking. For similar reasons, research articles and postgraduate theses more often find themselves on 'soft' discipline reading lists.

In soft applied subjects such as management or law, the use of reports of various kinds is common, as well as a slightly greater tendency to rely on textbooks rather than monographs, as is seen in pure soft disciplines. The use of course handbooks prepared by teaching staff, which contain abstracted 'key' information, is common across all disciplines.

2 Academic arguments

Each text that you read has been written with specific claims by its author. *Argument* is a common expression used to describe the author's purpose in academic contexts.

2a Work in pairs. How would you define an academic argument? Discuss your ideas and complete the definition. Then share your ideas in small groups.

Notes
An academic argument is …

2b Read the text and complete the table on p.21.

The decline of US economic power?

The US is the world's economic superpower. Its per capita GDP is nearly $50,000, compared to $34,000 in Japan, its closest economic rival, and just $500 in some third-world nations. The US has unrivalled trading power, and, in the dollar, has one of the most secure reserve currencies in history. However, recent events within US financial markets, combined with the emergence of new economic powers in the last decade, have led to a gradual erosion of US economic dominance.

The United States owes its powerful economic status in part to the creation of the Federal Reserve System in 1913, and particularly to the Bretton Woods agreement after World War Two, which saw the United States given a central role in the world economy, leading to its scendancy as the global reserve currency. Under the Bretton Woods system, the US has enjoyed unparalleled advantages which have added to its already considerable economic might. This period of prosperity and growth appears to have culminated in the bubble years of the early 21st century, which ended with the financial turmoil of 2008 (Brooking, 2009). Bankers and investors had overlooked the fact that the economic boom was being fuelled by highly risky speculative lending, the danger of which became clear after payment defaults led to a catastrophic loss of confidence which saw several major US banks collapse, or come so close to collapse that they needed unprecedented government bailouts. The cost of these rescue packages has been enormous, creating a mass of public debt which the US is no longer in a strong position to pay.

At the same time as the US has suffered internal financial turmoil, the emergence of strong economies in other nations has undermined US economic primacy. The last decade has seen the rapid growth of the Chinese and Indian economies, as well as the emergence of the Eurozone, which has the stated aim of challenging the US dollar as the world's reserve currency. In fact, the dollar's status as the reserve currency has played a part in this, with China, for instance, holding such massive dollar reserves (Ferguson, 2007) that the US is now considerably in China's debt. As emergent economies continue to grow off the back of manufacturing and high-tech skills, it seems likely that they will pose an increasing threat to American economic might.

The fading of American economic might may also be suggested in what some have called a 'reversing globalization' (Millner, 2009), which describes a gradual turning away from American-centred institutions in the first years of the 21st century. During the last half of the 20th century, the US was almost universally accepted as both a financial and cultural role model around the world. Its status as an economic superpower was assisted by US-centric institutions such as the IMF and World Bank, military might, the popularity of English, American entertainment icons and, until relatively recently, the English-dominated Internet. Recent trends suggest a turning away from this American-centred world to a more multi-polar one, with attendant effects upon US overseas trading power.

The US remains the world's principal economy and is likely to hold that position for some considerable time. Recent financial upsets at home, the emergence of competing economies and a turning away from the unipolar world of the late 20th century mean that America's economic dominance is no longer unquestioned.

Topic

Overall argument

Supporting arguments

3   Recognizing the development of arguments

The sources you read have a number of different functions. The functions described in 3a commonly appear in different sections of a text and can contribute to an author's argument.

3a   Look at the table and match the functions (1–7) with the text samples (a–g).

Function	Samples
1 Defining	**a** *First, the required amount of compound is heated in a test tube. Next, the heat is withdrawn and water is added. The final step is to observe the reaction between the compound and the water.*
2 Comparing	**b** *This instrument is long, slim and usually made of glass. One end is sealed and at the other end there is a bulb containing mercury. The tube is inscribed with a measuring scale.*
3 Describing an object or phenomenon	**c** *After careful evaluation of all the PCs within our cost schedule, I suggest that we purchase the new ProDesk from JCN. This machine is both functional and excellent value for money.*
4 Making an argument	**d** *This suggests that some element in the protein extract was causing the neuron cells to collapse and die, because no cells could survive more than 24 hours if the culture contained any protein extract.*
5 Describing a sequence or process	**e** *There is no doubt, then, that the development of the computer will have disastrous consequences for employment. Those who support the ever-increasing use of computers claim that they will release humans from boring work. This is doubtless true — but unemployment is likely to be rather more boring.*
6 Interpreting results	**f** *Asian classrooms appear to be dominated by the teacher, while those in the West seem to be oriented to meeting the needs of individual students.*
7 Recommending	**g** *Sometimes biological control, rather than insecticides, is used to keep insect pests in check. Biological control means the use of one living species to control another. This often provides a very effective solution to an urgent problem, but can have unexpected, negative consequences.*

3b   Check your answers with a partner. How did you decide which function each sample fulfilled?

3c   Decide which functions (1–7) can be found in each of these text types:

Guidelines   Research article   Essay

3d You are going to read three extracts from a text about video-conferencing technology. The author argues that video-conferencing technology can reduce the effects of status differences between staff members. Read each extract and identify the function(s) of each paragraph. Use the functions in 3a.

Text	Function of paragraph
1 It is necessary to reach a meaningful definition of high and low status within the workforce. Siebert's (1997, p.203) classic distinction draws the line between high and low status staff, depending on executive decision-making privilege. Moreno (2006), however, has offered a subtle alternative in which the status distinction is derived from staff intuitions. Therefore the working definition of what it is to be a 'high' status staff member is taken from the opinions of the staff in the workplace being studied.	
2 Siebert's definition has the advantage of being the commonly accepted one, having been used in a number of key studies into status effects. However, it suffers in our view from the necessity of further defining which decisions are 'executive'; many lower ranking staff enjoy decision-making powers but would not be recognized as 'high status' by their peers. In this regard, Moreno's definition seems to offer a clearer view of the reality of status distinctions within any given organization.	
3 In the present study we have chosen to follow Moreno's definition. 'High status' staff are therefore defined as being those within the organization who the staff members themselves perceive as holding executive decision-making privileges.	
4 18 business meetings were observed: 6 of the meetings were carried out face-to-face, 6 took place using a conventional telephone conference call link and the remaining 6 took place using PC video-conferencing software. The meetings were scheduled as part of routine work tasks within the organization. Participants were drawn from all levels of the company, and included a mix of both high and lower status staff members, though all were in theory entitled to participate. Participants in the face-to-face and video-conference meetings were asked to sit around a table and talk freely. In the case of the video-conference, staff at three separate locations participated in the same meeting. The participants in the phone meetings worked at individual desks spread throughout the company's offices worldwide. The meetings were recorded in full and later analyzed.	
5 The PC video-conferencing software was a commonly available workplace package. It combined video cameras enabling participants to see the entire roomful of staff at each of the other locations, as well as incorporating PC Tablet technology at each position around the table. The Tablets allowed each participant to view shared graphics and documents during the meeting, as well as focusing a built-in webcam on a particular speaker's face for close-ups when required.	

Text	Function of paragraph
6 As expected, higher status members tended to dominate the discussion in each of the three modes of contact. However, slight differences emerged in the extent to which they dominated the conversation in each of the modes. In conventional face-to-face meetings, higher status members talked for about 80% of the time during the meeting. This was approximately the same in the video-conferencing meetings, with an average of 75% of the time taken by contributions from high status staff members. In the phone conference, however, there was a much freer interaction by lower status participants and the percentage of the total speech-time taken by higher status staff fell to 61%.	
7 The results suggest that communications technology serves to mediate contact between higher and lower status staff members. The fact that lower status staff members participated most freely in a purely audio meeting clearly indicates that visual cues are important when assessing whether it is appropriate to speak. It seems that lower status staff members watch those high up for signs of the intent to speak, as well as approval of lower status contributions. In a telephone conference, with the absence of these cues, lower status staff feel more comfortable making contributions, while the higher status staff members themselves are more prepared to allow others the chance to speak.	

3e Compare your answers with a partner. How does each of the three extracts help to support the author's argument that telephone-conferencing technology helps to reduce the effects of status differences?

3f The paragraphs in the example student essays in **Appendices 2** and **3** have both been labelled (A–H). Work in pairs. Read one text each and identify the functions for the paragraphs in each text. Then summarize the text for your partner and explain your ideas about the function for each paragraph.

4 Identifying persuasion in texts

4a Work in pairs. First, re-read both texts in **Appendices 2** and **3**. Then discuss which text you think is:

1 informative

2 persuasive.

4b Complete the table by making notes on the typical features of information and persuasive texts.

Notes	
Features of informative texts	**Features of persuasive texts**

Persuasion is common in many text types. A writer's purpose in producing much academic writing is ultimately to persuade his or her readers to accept that what she/he has written is accurate, logical, true, or reasonable. However, the methods by which writers try to persuade their readers vary between disciplines. As a critical reader, it is important to be able to recognize the writer's purpose and evaluate the ways in which they are trying to persuade you.

4c Read the text in **Appendix 3** again. While you read, consider these questions. Then underline any language that you feel is intended to persuade you to agree with the author's argument.

   1 In what ways does the writer try to persuade the reader that email causes serious stress effects?

   2 In what ways does the author claim that email is the *greatest* cause of workplace stress?

   3 What is the author's purpose in claiming that email is more like a letter than a Post-it note? How does the author try to persuade the reader that this is reasonable?

4d Work in pairs. This table describes seven common techniques used in persuasive writing. First, read the techniques and their examples. Then discuss which ones are most likely to persuade you to accept an argument. Explain your reasons.

Technique	Example
1 Presenting evidence and examples to support the author's claims	Mobile phones are predicted to overtake PCs or laptops as the main platform by which consumers access web content. Service providers in Brazil, for instance, have noted a 3% year-on-year increase in mobile Internet access, at the same time as a slide in the number of users accessing from conventional computer platforms (Silva, 2007). It is reasonable to suppose that this pattern will be repeated in other nations.
2 Emphasizing consensus with other authors	Numerous studies (Bergson, 1988; Calderon & Watts, 1991; Baranwal, 2001, 2003a, 2003b) have demonstrated the link between Internet dependency and lower attention span.

Technique	Example
3 Using (large) numbers to demonstrate weight of evidence	Whereas Tycho (1997) considered only 12 cases, the current paper is based on findings from 143 interviews conducted with institute staff during the 1993–1997 period.
4 Using emotive vocabulary to convince the reader that something is true when, in fact, it may only be a theory	We sincerely hope that this paper will be understood for what it is: a call to arms. It is vital that government and the private sector cooperate to ensure that those who suffer in economically deprived areas of our own cities are offered the same chances for success and happiness as their more fortunate peers.
5 Appealing to common sense and reason	Tse and Pollock (2008) have proposed that the anomaly may be a signal fault, but this would clearly be impossible.
6 Extending easily acceptable propositions by applying them to less acceptable claims	The Internet has proven itself to be a powerful business tool, therefore it seems clear that providing Internet access to previously underdeveloped areas will contribute strongly to their economic development.
7 Using analogy to show similarities between ideas	The proposed police computer database would go much further than any previous legislation has allowed. It would be the same as allowing a government inspector to follow you everywhere you went.

4e Read the text in **Appendix 3** again. Draw a box around each part of the text which uses one of the techniques presented in 4d. Then label the parts with the number of the technique (1–7). Then compare your ideas with a partner.

4f Work in pairs. Read these three claims the author of **Appendix 3** makes. Discuss whether you think the author has done enough to persuade the reader to accept that these claims are true.

- Email is possibly the greatest cause of workplace stress.
- Email is like a letter, and needs the same types of politeness and content.
- The most serious email-related stressor is lack of salutations.

 **UNIT TASK** **Communications technology and culture**

a Remind yourself of the essay title for this unit task (p.17). Using Cornell-style notes, write notes on a separate piece of paper on the example essays (Texts A and B) in **Appendix 4**.

b Critically review your notes on the example essays. Then complete the tables below (A and B) for each text you read in **Appendix 4**.

Text A

Topic:

Overall argument:

Supporting arguments:

Summary of your response to the claims in this text:

Text B

Topic:

Overall argument:

Supporting arguments:

Summary of your response to the claims in this text:

Go to the checklist on p.198. Look again at the tips relating to Unit 1 Part A and tick (✓) those you have used in your studies. Read the tips relating to Unit 1 Part B.

Investigating

By the end of Part C you will be able to:
- define critical thinking
- use critical thinking in your studies
- assess your own critical thinking skills
- recognize factors that can interfere with critical thinking
- understand how and why writers use citations.

1 Defining critical thinking

1a Work in small groups. Re-read the definition of critical thinking you wrote on p.6, then share your opinions with your group. Decide together the best way to complete these notes.

Notes
Critical thinking involves:
Benefits of critical thinking:

1.6

1b Listen to three people describing what critical thinking involves and what the possible benefits are. Write notes next to the speakers' names. Add any relevant information to your notes in 1a.

Notes
David:
Natasha:
Zoe:

1c Work in pairs. This box lists a number of critical thinking skills. For each skill

(1–12), discuss how it can benefit you in *your own* field of study. If you think that any particular ability is not beneficial for your field of study, be prepared to justify your answer.

1 Being able to differentiate between apparently similar things	7 Doing independent research
2 Being able to identify variables in complex phenomena	8 Problem solving
3 Being analytical	9 Recognizing flaws in argument or methodology
4 Being observant	10 Thinking of original ideas
5 Being persuasive	11 Using judgement
6 Categorizing information	12 Using reasoning skills

2 Using critical thinking in your studies

2a Work in pairs. Read the essay title below. If you were given this as an assignment, decide what preparation you would need to do to write the essay. Consider:

- where you would find background information
- how you would generate and organize ideas.

Television viewing figures among 18–33 year-olds have been dropping steadily for four years. Identify the main causes of the decline and suggest ways in which viewership could be increased.

> If you have not done primary research on a topic, you will need to generate your opinions by reading, comparing and critically evaluating the work of other authors in the same area. For essay titles like the one in 2a, you are also required to make suggestions of your own (in this case, suggestions for ways in which viewership can be increased). This requires you to reach your own, independent conclusions.

2b Complete this flow chart, which shows five different stages in the development of an essay, by matching a stage (1–5) with the correct description (a–e). Then compare your answers with a partner.

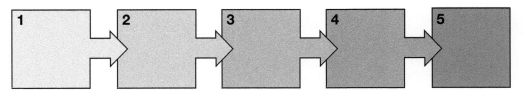

a Come to a temporary conclusion of your own based on the evidence you have read.

b Find the best evidence to support your conclusion, but be prepared to change if you discover that your temporary conclusion was incorrect.

c Plan the most logical argument to lead your audience to support your conclusions.

    d Read and evaluate the sources, identifying their arguments and the evidence they use to support them.

    e Search for the best sources of information to do background reading on the subject.

3 Assessing your own critical thinking skills

3a In this exercise, you are going to try five different tasks designed to help you evaluate different aspects of your critical thinking skills.

Task 1

Read this extract from an article on the topic of emails. Then decide which conclusion (A, B or C) is most appropriate.

The decline of the letter

The rise of email and a host of online communication systems mean that conventional letter-post delivery services are under pressure as never before. In the UK, the volume of post delivered has fallen 1 to 2% year-on-year since 2002, a fall which is closely paralleled in many of the G8 nations. Significantly, the fall-off in demand for post services is matched most closely in those countries which enjoy the best Internet access. Regular mail continues to be the rule where the Internet is not as reliable or easily accessible. Other services delivering larger packages have seen small declines in their business but are largely unaffected.

A

It is possible to conclude from this that the situation facing companies specializing in large package delivery will be secure for the foreseeable future, given the inability of email to send anything other than electronic documents.

B

As Internet communication becomes more widespread, with more users able to send and receive text from an ever-growing variety of devices, it seems likely that conventional letter-post will increasingly lose its importance to electronic alternatives.

C

Post services therefore look set to continue their decline, which will have a significant impact on employment conditions for postal workers throughout the developed world.

Task 2

Read about the methods used in three different studies into the response of computer users to a new 'ergonomic' keyboard. Then answer these questions.

    1 Which study has a method that is noticeably different from the other two?

    2 In what way is the method of this study different?

Study 1

300 respondents, divided equally by gender, were chosen by email invitation. The respondents completed a series of ten tasks, requiring three minutes each, using the new keyboard. After completing the tasks, they were asked to fill in an online questionnaire using Likert scales to rate their satisfaction, ease and physical comfort when operating the new computer keyboard.

Study 2

75 respondents were chosen by random selection of passersby at a booth in the Student Union. Participants were given a chance to use the new keyboard for a single writing task and then performed the same task using a conventional keyboard. They then answered a questionnaire comprising 14 closed questions investigating the comfort and ease of the new keyboard.

Study 3

Three respondents were chosen to participate in in-depth interviews which investigated their opinions of the new keyboard design. The participants were given the use of one of the new keyboards for a period of three weeks. At the end of the period the researchers discussed the respondents' opinions of the new keyboards in non-structured interviews which lasted approximately one hour. Follow-up interviews were conducted approximately a week later in order to clarify their answers.

Task 3

Organize the shapes into different categories, for instance 'triangles' or 'shapes with a thin border'. Try to arrange the shapes into as many different categories as possible. Each shape can appear in more than one category.

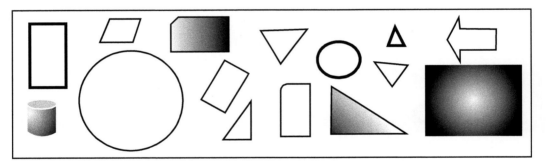

Task 4

Look at the information in this box. These have all been claimed as effects of the development of the Internet. How many different categories of effect can you find? (for instance, 'crime')

- Computer hacking
- Online shopping
- Internet addiction
- Free communication
- International business
- A decline in the sales of newspapers
- Minority groups able to reach a wide audience with their message

- The weakening of government control
- Faster international communication
- Social withdrawal
- Internet piracy
- Cosmopolitanism
- Easier political campaigning
- Fewer children doing exercise outdoors

Task 5

Read this description of the situation of the DVD industry in the early 21st century, then work in small groups to discuss the question that follows.

> Sales of DVDs reached their peak in the year 2007. Since then they have fallen consistently across the world, with a particular slump in late 2008 and 2009. Industry executives are pessimistic that the DVD market will recover strongly at all.

What combination of factors may have contributed to the decline in DVD sales?

3b Work in pairs. Compare your ideas and answers to the question above. Explain the reasons for the answers you chose.

3c Work in pairs. Look back at the elements of critical thinking in 1c. Then answer the questions.

1 Which of the critical thinking skills (1–12) did you need to complete Tasks 1–5?

2 Which activities were easiest and which did you find more difficult? Why?

4 Recognizing factors that can interfere with critical thinking

The aim of critical thinking in higher education is to help you base your academic opinions on sound investigation, logic and evidence, even if these appear to conflict with your own beliefs. A good critical thinker should always be ready to question the basis of their own beliefs.

4a Look at the list of factors which can interfere with critical thinking. Can you add any more to the list?

Factors that can interfere with critical thinking
1 Nationalist sentiment
2 Emotion
3 Chauvinism
4 Cultural beliefs
5 Unquestioned life–long assumptions

4b Match an example (A–E) with a factor (1–5) from 4a.

A

The choice of a woman for such a sensitive post must surely be questioned. Dr Edwards is a highly intelligent woman with more than twenty years of experience in the field, but the post of Chief Executive Officer of such an important corporation requires someone who is able to take cold, rational decisions.

B

Probably the greatest, and most devastating, health threat in the modern world is stress. It afflicts millions of people every year and, from my own painful experience of it, I can say that it is the most dreadful thing for a person to suffer.

C

Don't think I'm saying this just because I'm English, but Britain really is the best place for the Olympics; there's something about the special atmosphere that you only get in Britain – that special blend of creativity and vibrancy which is like nowhere else in the world.

D

Why do you talk to such a young baby like that? She can't even talk yet and she's certainly too young to understand what you're saying. Back in my home country we never talk to infants until they're old enough to understand – everyone knows it doesn't help their development to speak to them before that.

E

To avoid putting on weight, I make sure to avoid eating fatty foods like cheese and red meat. Instead, I eat lots of plain and simple food like bread, pasta and rice. It's much better for you.

5 How and why writers use citations

Writers use citations from other authors' work to support their own writing in a variety of different ways. Understanding why the writer is using a particular citation can help you read critically.

5a Each of the sentences below contains a citation. Match each sentence (1–3) with the correct function (A–C) of each citation. Then compare your answers with a partner.

1 The World Wide Web was invented by British scientist Tim Berners-Lee, who was working at CERN at the time (Boswell, 1996).

A Supporting a claim

2 It seems likely that mobile technologies will increasingly become the most popular method of accessing the Internet. A recent study by Chung (2007) demonstrates a clear preference for mobile technologies among the younger generation of 'new' Internet users.

B Giving background information

3 Jones and Macke (2004), however, take the opposing view that the changes in frequency are significant.

C Showing disagreement

5b Read this extract from a study about online security. What is the author's opinion on the most serious risk to personal information online?

> Recent studies into the risk to personal information on the Internet have claimed that one of the most significant security threats is deliberate theft of personal information, caused by spyware and phishing scams (Mazzi & Tills, 2007; Prewitt, 2009; Wharton & Maas, 2003). A different position about Internet threats can be found in Ison and Roth (2009), who argue that the risk from spyware and phishing is actually exaggerated. Many home Internet surfers feel that they are insufficiently knowledgeable to protect themselves against increasingly sophisticated attacks by online criminals. Poor awareness of how spyware operates has often been cited as a reason why people magnify its importance as a threat. In one study of 2000 home Internet users in the US (Pask, 2008, p.272), 87% of respondents had only the most general idea of how spyware actually worked, but 92% consider it 'a very serious threat'. Sensational media stories have likewise been reported as the source of this fear (Croft, 2008; Roth, 2007).
>
> Contrary to the position of Mazzi and Tills (ibid.) and others, our paper demonstrates that the perception of risk from spyware is indeed exaggerated by comparison with both the number and the severity of attacks. We argue that a considerably more serious risk is posed by misuse of personal information by companies or organizations that are actually in legal possession of one's information for business purposes.

5c Read the text again and answer the questions. Then check your answers with a partner.

1 Which other researchers have a different opinion from the author?

2 Which other writers' work supports the author's opinion?

3 What evidence supports the author's claims about spyware?

> **UNIT TASK**   **Communications technology and culture**

a Work in small groups. Remind yourself of the essay title for this unit task (p.17). To help you develop your ideas further, you are going to listen to a seminar in which the tutor is leading a discussion with three students about the positive and negative impacts of communications technology on cultures around the world.

Before you listen, brainstorm the advantages and disadvantages of the spread of communications technology.

b Listen to an extract from the seminar. Write notes about what each student says on the topic, and any justifications they give for their ideas, next to the speakers' names.

1.7

Notes

Lucy:

Simon:

Sergei:

c Consider each student's opinion and justifications. Add your own comments in the right-hand column, using these questions as a guide.

- Were any arguments made based on emotions and not evidence?
- Were the arguments made supported by reasons?
- Was any evidence given which was not strong enough to support the arguments?

d Consider your own position on this topic and answer the questions.

- Which points do you tend to agree with?
- Are there any points which you disagree with, even if the speaker provided evidence? If so, what are your reasons for disagreeing?

e Work in small groups. Discuss your answers to the questions in 6d. Give reasons for your answers.

 Go to the checklist on p.198–199. Look again at the tips relating to Unit 1 Parts A–B and tick (✓) those you have used in your studies. Read the tips relating to Unit 1 Part C on p.199.

Reporting in speech

By the end of Part D you will be able to:

- identify the purpose of a presentation
- use software to create effective presentation visuals
- make presentations with persuasive content
- deliver presentations persuasively
- create and deliver a successful group presentation.

1 Identifying the purpose of a presentation

> The purpose of any presentation is to persuade the listener that what you say is logical, true, and has authority. However, presentation types vary depending on how overtly persuasive they are, and the persuasive techniques they use. In some types of presentation, the speaker's purpose is clearly to persuade the audience to accept something, while others are more descriptive and/or informative. The explicit aim is always to transmit or demonstrate knowledge.

1a Work in pairs. Place the presentation types (a–f) along the line depending on how overtly persuasive they attempt to be.

a A presentation of academic research findings with an original claim

b A presentation of the results of a science project

c A report on a business project

d A sales presentation

e A training session

f An academic lecture to undergraduate students

Informative   Persuasive

1b Which types of presentation (a–f) are most common in your field of study?

1c Think about a presentation that you have given. What things did you do to make your message more persuasive? Write notes in the table.

Notes	
Preparation:	**Content:**
Visual aids:	**Delivery:**

2 Using software to create effective presentation visuals

2a Work in small groups and discuss these questions.

1 When was the last time you used presentation software?

2 How easy was it to use?

3 Did you have any problems using it (either while creating the visual aid, or during your presentation)?

4 How do you think software packages help to support spoken presentations?

5 What is the difference between the spoken and visual content of a presentation?

2b Read the tips in the table and tick (✓) the correct column (*Do* or *Don't*) according to your opinion. Tick the third column if your opinion depends on the type of visual or presentation. Then compare your answers with a partner.

Tip	Do	Don't	Depends
1 Include an image on every slide.			
2 Help your audience to understand complex ideas by reading the text directly from the slides.			
3 Impress your audience with complex diagrams and charts.			
4 Reduce text to key words and phrases.			
5 Keep one key idea per slide and give handouts with extra information if necessary.			
6 Speak to the screen so you share the same view as your audience.			
7 Use a lot of animation to catch attention.			
8 Only highlight key points on your slides. Give more detail in your speech.			
9 Keep the same fonts and backgrounds throughout the slideshow.			
10 Use a font colour which contrasts with the background colour.			
11 Use eye-catching visuals and graphics. It doesn't matter if they are relevant.			
12 Don't worry about mistakes in spelling or punctuation. Presentations aren't as formal as essays or reports.			
13 The minimum font size on a slide should be 30. Any smaller than that gets difficult to read.			

2c These two slides were made by two students for a presentation about biometrics. Read the slides to find out what 'biometrics' means.

Slide 1

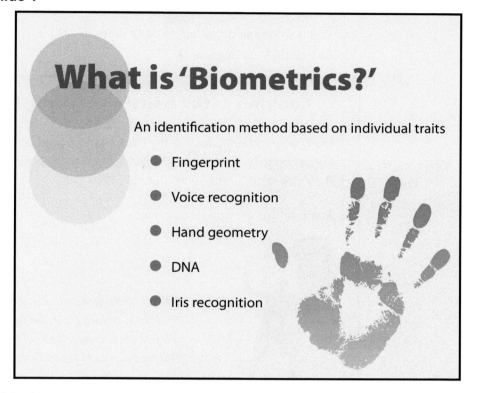

What is 'Biometrics?'

An identification method based on individual traits

- Fingerprint
- Voice recognition
- Hand geometry
- DNA
- Iris recognition

Slide 2

An answer to the question 'What is biometrics?'

It is a system for recognizing or identifying humans based on their innate human characteristics.

Biometrics includes
Using fingerprints, DNA, iris scans, hand or palm prints and a range of other methods for identifying people. This can be used for active law enforcement such as catching criminals, or for security access to private or sensitive areas. It is being used more and more often for tourists.

Biometrics facts
DNA and iris scans are used in the US Military and Federal Bureau of Investigation.
Most biometric systems have a very high accuracy (nearly 100%).
Many nations now use biometrics to scan visitors at the airport.

2d Work in small groups to complete these tasks.

    1 Use the tips in 2b to help you discuss which of the slides in 2c is more effective and why.

    2 The slide below is not effective.

      a Why is this slide not as effective as those in 2c?

      b How could it be improved?

Looking at the benefits of using biometrics

Many governments, such as the UK, Canada France, Spain, Korea and Italy want to use biometric identity cards for all of their citizens (Sharpe, 2009), But… !

Many people are opposed to this…

There are many benefits to using biometrics, however, such as easier identification. Biometrics can also be used for a variety of different purposes; for example, they could replace passports and get rid of the need to remember passwords or carry keys.

---

3   Making presentations with persuasive content

> The content of your presentation is the message or information that you want to communicate. The first step in creating persuasive content is thinking about who your audience will be, and what things are likely to persuade them that what you are saying is logical, true and has authority.

3a Work in pairs. Look at the information in the table and complete the third column with your own ideas.

Situation	Audience	Ways to make the content persuasive
1 A salesperson delivering a product presentation	The board of executives of a company	
2 A PhD candidate presenting doctoral research results	PhD supervisors and other academics	

3 A higher education student doing an assessed presentation about applications of new GPS technology	Classmates and teachers	
4 A presentation on workplace safety	New company staff members	

3b Match the presentation descriptions (A–D) with the situations in 3a (1–4). Then add the different ways that the speakers make the content persuasive to the third column in 3a.

A

The presenter used a PowerPoint slideshow to highlight the main points of the topic, using an overview–background–applications structure. She used citations and references to research by leading scholars in the field, before presenting a conclusion.

B

The presenter used a brightly coloured PowerPoint which displayed the specifications and images of the item, as well as comparisons with other similar items by competitors. He also introduced the results of performance tests by his company's R&D staff. At the end, he gave out free samples for people to try.

C

The presenter began with a series of government statistics about injuries and fatalities at work, then showed a series of deliberately gruesome pictures on PowerPoint to warn the audience about the dangers of carelessness. He passed around a document which explained people's legal responsibilities and, finally, told shocking stories of his own experience dealing with accidents in the company.

D

The presenter gave an overview of the key literature on the topic, citing key studies by other researchers. She then presented the findings from her own research and showed how they were comparable to the work done by others. She concluded by giving a summary of her main findings and explaining their implications.

3c Compare your answers with a partner. Then discuss these questions.

1 Which types of persuasion are you most likely to need in this course?

2 How about other courses that you are studying?

> One requirement of many student presentations is that you demonstrate understanding of a subject, as well as provide evidence to support your claims. In this way a presentation is similar to writing an essay.

3d Look at the list of possible presentation content features in this table. Tick (✓) the ones which you think are most important to persuade the audience in an academic presentation that the content is logical, true and has authority.

Features	✓
A clear structure	
Your own opinions	
A lot of text on PowerPoint slides	
Handouts with key and supplementary information	
Conclusions which are supported by the information in the main body	
Supporting evidence	
Stories from your own experience	
Citations and references	

3e Work in pairs. Look at these slides and the presentation content on the topic of technology overload. Then discuss these questions.

1 What is the student's main idea?
2 What evidence supports the main idea?
3 How satisfactory is this evidence? What could be done to improve it?
4 How well do the PowerPoint slides match the content of the presentation?
5 Does the information presented in the main body support the conclusion?

Slides	Presentation content
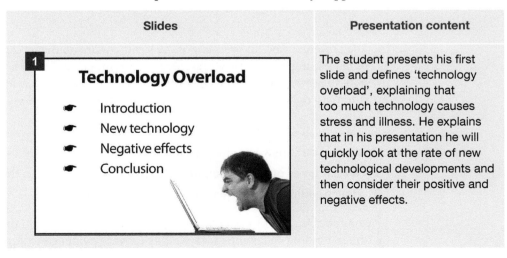	The student presents his first slide and defines 'technology overload', explaining that too much technology causes stress and illness. He explains that in his presentation he will quickly look at the rate of new technological developments and then consider their positive and negative effects.

2

Technology Overload

We are confronted with more types of technology than ever before.

- Internet applications and hardware
- Hi-tech gaming systems
- Sophisticated mobile technology

The student explains that more and more technology is becoming available to the average consumer. He quotes some statistics from a UK survey about which high-tech products people own.

3

Technological Milestones

Year	Milestone
1977	First home computer
2001	iPod launched
2006	Facebook launched
2009	iPhone 3GS launched

The student introduces some examples of technological developments to show how quickly new products are being developed. He explains the benefits of these different systems, including easier communications, more choice, and the availability of more information.

4

Negative effects

Indecision

▼

Stress

▼

Illness

"Illness is a fact of life in the modern world" (Benson, 2009)

The student explains that there are also negative effects. Too much choice causes indecision, which in turn leads to stress, according to a 2009 report by the British Association of Psychologists. The student claims that an obvious consequence of stress is more people getting ill.

5

Conclusion

Technology provides us with more distractions than ever before. This is leading to:

- More people suffering from stress caused by technology
- An increasing number of people choosing a 'simple' technology-free lifestyle

The student explains that more technology is leading to greater stress and illness. His final conclusion is that this is causing large numbers of people to reject technology and choose a simple lifestyle.

3f Work in pairs. Suggest ways to improve the slides in 3e. Make notes in the table below, and plan to add any extra slides if you think the presentation needs them.

Slide	Suggestion
1	
2	
3	
4	
5	

> The title of your presentation plays an important part in persuading your audience. It helps them to focus on the subject and any key issues; it lets them know what the content will be and what they can expect to hear; and it also gives clues about how much you have prepared in advance.

3g Work in pairs. Read a presentation brief. Then discuss which of these three titles would be most suitable.

Brief

Prepare a five-minute presentation about next-generation mobile phone technologies. Outline their operation, applications and benefits.

Possible titles

1 Next-generation mobile phones
2 Next-generation mobile phones: their operation and uses
3 The benefits and drawbacks of next-generation mobile phones

4 Delivering presentations persuasively

> The content of your presentation is the important information or message that you want to communicate to your audience. Another way to increase the impact of your presentation is to concentrate on your delivery.

4a Work in small groups. Discuss what *impact* means in the context of a presentation.

4b Work in pairs. Complete the table below by deciding whether each of the factors (1–12) has a positive (+) or a negative (–) effect in these three situations:

1 A formal presentation at a conference
2 A graded presentation as part of the assessment for a course
3 An ungraded presentation to classmates as part of a course

Factors affecting the impact of a presentation	Situation 1	Situation 2	Situation 3
1 Speaking for longer than the allowed time			
2 Finishing your talk too soon			
3 Not wearing formal clothes			
4 Speaking too quickly			
5 Using slang			
6 Speaking in a conversational way			
7 Speaking formally			
8 Pausing at appropriate moments during the talk			
9 Repeating ideas to reinforce them			
10 Making eye contact with the audience			
11 Asking rhetorical questions			
12 Stressing important words or ideas			

1.8

4c Listen to extracts from three different presentations and decide which one has the most impact. Then compare your ideas with a partner.

4d For each presentation, write notes on anything that had either a positive or negative effect on the impact of the talk.

Notes
Presentation 1
Presentation 2
Presentation 3

4e Work in pairs. Discuss any particular strong points in your own presentation style, as well as particular weak points that you feel you need to work on. Then take turns to make suggestions about how you could practise and improve on your weaker points.

4f Read this report about GPS (Global Positioning System). Then use the text to create a one-minute presentation on one of these two topics:

- The importance of GPS
- Threats to the GPS system

The end of GPS?

GPS, or Global Positioning System, is a service that uses satellites in orbit around the Earth to relay pinpoint information about one's location on the ground. It is run and maintained by an arm of the US government. Initially introduced in the early 1990s (Godwin, 2008), it has fast become an almost indispensable feature of modern life; travellers who have GPS systems in their cars and on mobile phones increasingly rely on it to help them find their way around. The GPS system is also used extensively in civilian air and sea navigation, as well as by the rescue services and scientists in a variety of fields. However, a recent study (Barrow & Holloman, 2009) indicates that the GPS system is in serious disrepair and predicts a possible total breakdown of the network in the near future.

The cause of the problem is the enormous expense of putting GPS satellites into orbit. Lack of funding has meant that the US has been unable to launch any new GPS satellites for several years (Dickinson, 2009, p.196) and has also been unable to repair ones that have already outlived their service lives.

Barrow and Holloman (ibid.) claim that the system is likely to suffer a complete failure within the next three years. Even if further investment can be found, it will be too late to put satellites into orbit. This would have serious effects on a modern world, which has come to rely on GPS. Though India, China, Russia and the EU are all developing their own alternatives to GPS (Nye, 2009), these are not predicted to be ready for widespread operation for at least ten to fifteen more years.

4g Work in small groups. Take turns to give your presentation to your group. Together, decide which presentation was most persuasive and why.

5 Creating and delivering a successful group presentation

5a What are the differences between individual and group presentations? Use your own experience of giving presentations on your own or with groups to complete the table.

	Notes	
	Strengths	**Weaknesses**
Individual presentations		
Group presentations		

> A key step in producing an effective group presentation is to get to know your group members and their different abilities as presenters.

5b Evaluate your own skills as a presenter by ticking (✓) the column 1–4 that is true for you for each of the fifteen statements about presentation style. Choose 1 if a statement is never true for you and 4 if it is always true.

What you do in a presentation	1	2	3	4
1 My presentations generally have clear objectives.				
2 I target the content at my audience.				
3 I organize my ideas clearly and logically.				
4 I have a strong opening that grabs attention right from the beginning.				
5 I use clear transitions between main points to guide my audience.				
6 I support my ideas with a variety of information, such as facts, figures, diagrams, etc.				
7 I refer to my sources and they strengthen my talk.				
8 I close my talk in a meaningful way.				
9 I make eye contact with all my audience throughout the presentation.				
10 I use hand gestures and other body language to help express my ideas.				
11 My visual aids are attractive and relevant.				
12 I speak in a lively and conversational style.				
13 I vary the tone of my voice and use pauses effectively to give emphasis to key words.				
14 I speak fluently and confidently.				
15 I am grammatically accurate when I speak.				

5c Work in small groups to compare your answers to 5b. Then discuss these questions.

1 What particular strengths in presentation skills do members of the group share?

2 Which areas would you need to focus on while practising your presentation so that all members were able to develop their skills?

Group presentations require teamwork to do effective research, preparation and rehearsal before the presentation, but they also require effective teamwork during the presentation itself. All members of a group are normally expected to speak during a group presentation and to hand over to one another when each person's speaking turn finishes. Turn-taking and handovers should be planned and practised.

5d Work in pairs. Put the typical stages of a group presentation (a–e) into the correct order (1–5).

Stages in a group oral presentation

a The coordinator introduces the topic of the talk.

b The first speaker introduces his/her section and talks about it. He/she then hands over to the second speaker. The second speaker introduces his/her section and talks about it. He/she then hands over to the third speaker. Other speakers continue as above.

c The coordinator explains how the talk will be divided and who will talk about each part. He/she confirms that there will be time for questions afterwards and then hands over to the first speaker.

d The coordinator sums up the talk and perhaps makes a conclusion. The audience is invited to ask questions.

e The coordinator introduces himself/herself and the other members of the group.

1.9

5e Listen to two presentations about GPS. Make a note of the claims and supporting information given in each presentation.

5f Listen again if necessary and answer these questions.

1 Which group has the more effective turn-taking and handover techniques?

2 In what way were they more effective?

5g Look at the examples of handover expressions below. Add each function from the box to the correct stage of the table. Then in groups try to think of other expressions you could use. Write them in the relevant section of the table.

Outlining the presentation organization
Starting and finishing an individual speaker section   Introducing group members
Introducing the topic   Concluding the presentation

Notes
Stage 1 function: Hello, I'm ... and I'd like to introduce other members of my group. This is ...

Stage 2 function:
Today, we are going to talk about ...
The topic of our talk this morning is ...

Stage 3 function:
Our presentation will be divided into ... parts.
We would like to divide our talk into ... sections.

The first part will be led by ... , who will talk about ...
... will talk about the first section.

After our talk we will be happy to answer questions.
Our talk will take about ... minutes and we will leave time for questions.

Stage 4 function:
Opening the section:

Hello, I'm ... . As ... said, I am going to talk about ...

Closing the section and handing over to the next speaker:

That's the end of my section of the presentation. Now I'm going to hand over to ... , who will talk about ...

Stage 5 function:

In our talk today we have ...

To sum up then, ...

I'd like to conclude by ...

Let me end by saying ...

If you have any questions, we will do our best to answer them.

Giving polite and helpful feedback to other group members is an important part of practising together. Feedback should be expressed in a way that makes it clear what could be done differently in future to improve the presentation.

Example

'I thought the presentation was really interesting, but the introduction section was very brief and I didn't get a clear idea about the central argument. In future, make sure you emphasize this more by speaking more slowly and clearly and checking everyone has understood.'

5h Read this statement. Then note down some guidelines to make your feedback more useful.

The purpose of giving feedback is to assist improvement and to give encouragement, rather than to punish.

Notes
Guidelines for useful feedback:

5i Work in pairs. Read eight examples of comments given during feedback on presentations. Complete the positive or negative column with a tick (✓) to show your answer.

	Feedback comments	Positive	Negative	Useful
1	'You spoke for too long and didn't pause at all, so it was difficult to follow what you were saying.'			
2	'The description of the data was unclear. None of us understood what you were trying to explain.'			
3	'Very good!'			
4	'What you said was very interesting. You highlighted the points that were relevant to us.'			
5	'The description of data could have been clearer. You should have shown the figures on the PowerPoint, for example.'			
6	'It was absolutely hopeless!'			
7	'It was really poor. It showed that you had not prepared properly.'			
8	'Not very good. Could have been better.'			

5j Decide which of the comments in 5i are useful (whether positive or negative) by writing Y for 'Yes' or N for 'No' in the last column of the table.

1.10

5k Listen to the second (better) group presentation. While you listen, write notes about any strengths and weaknesses in the table. Then compare your ideas in small groups.

Criteria	Strengths	Weaknesses
Content		
Organization		
Delivery		

5l Choose two points you think it would be most important to feed back to the second group you heard presenting. Write the feedback, taking care to be clear but polite.

> **UNIT TASK** **Communications technology and culture**

In this unit task, you will prepare and deliver a six- to eight-minute group presentation on this essay topic:

How has the spread of communications technology affected cultures around the world? Assess the extent to which the Internet is a medium for western culture alone.

a Work in groups of three or four. Work together to decide a group response to the essay topic. Then plan out how you will complete the task. You should consider these points.

- Your presentation should be six to eight minutes long.
- Each member of the group should take turns presenting.
- You should use visual aids to support your presentation.
- You will need to persuade your audience of your claims in a way that is academically appropriate (e.g. by giving evidence).

b In your group, practise your presentation together. Use this table to give feedback to each other.

Criteria	Strengths	Weaknesses
Content		
Organization		
Delivery		

Go to the checklist on p.198–199. Look again at the tips relating to Unit 1 Parts A–C and tick (✓) those you have used in your studies. Read the tips relating to Unit 1 Part D on p.199.

Reporting in writing

By the end of Part E you will be able to:

- match structure and purpose in writing
- write a suitable introduction
- use citations in writing
- use citations in different academic disciplines.

1 Matching structure and purpose in writing

> Classic essay structures, such as cause–effect, compare–contrast, and problem–solution, may actually be too basic for many writing assignments, which require more sophisticated structures. An important step in planning writing is to decide what classic structure features to include and the best way to arrange them.

1a Work in pairs. Read these two essay titles (1 and 2). Decide what each one is asking you to do.

1 *Examine the current uses of nanotechnology and evaluate possible future applications.*

2 *To what extent is success in the workplace affected by computer literacy?*

1b Now read two possible outlines (A and B) for each of the essay titles in 1a. Then decide which outline gives the best answer to each question.

Essay 1	
Outline A	**Outline B**
Introduction	Introduction
Claim – Nanotechnology has many potential medical applications. We should invest strongly in developing this technology in future.	Background + outline
Body	**Body**
Supporting argument 1 – Nanotechnology allows doctors to treat patients without surgery.	Current uses of nanotechnology 1 – medical Possible future medical applications – pros Possible future medical applications – cons
Supporting argument 2 – Nanotechnology has a higher rate of efficacy than other treatments.	Uses of nanotechnology 2 – industrial Possible future industrial applications – pros Possible future industrial applications – cons
Supporting argument 3 – Nanotechnology research is currently underfunded.	
Conclusion Summary of main points + restate main claim	**Conclusion** Summary of main points + general recommendations + author's opinion

Essay 2

Outline A	Outline B
Claim – Computer literacy has a great effect on workplace success.	**Claim** – There are many causes and effects of workplace success.
Body	**Body**
Supporting argument 1 – Computer literacy allows for a higher work output.	Causes of workplace success 1 – Training
Supporting argument 2 – Computer literate staff have more job opportunities.	Causes of workplace success 2 – Motivation
Supporting argument 3 – Staff working in jobs where computer literacy isn't necessary have lower incomes.	Causes of workplace success 3 – Computer literacy Effects of computer literacy – Higher salary, higher work output, more job opportunities
Conclusion Summary of main points + restate main claim	**Conclusion** Summary of main points + general recommendations + author's opinion

1c Discuss your ideas with a partner.

1d Read this answer to essay title 2 in 1a. Write notes on the function of each paragraph in the left-hand column.

Notes	
	To what extent is success in the workplace affected by computer literacy?

1 Computer literacy is commonly defined as 'the ability to understand how computers work and use specific software to perform tasks' (Harmon, 1998, p.116). Computers are rapidly coming to dominate work tasks across all industries and it is likely that this trend will continue into the future. Even jobs which were traditionally seen as involving manual labour (or at least not requiring computer skills) have begun to incorporate computers in support of certain tasks – such as delivery people who now routinely use handheld computer tablets to register deliveries made and the destinations that each driver must visit. It is likely that this trend will only intensify throughout the coming years. Computer literacy affects job success in a variety of different ways. These can be divided into two categories: computer literacy for core job skills and computer literacy to enhance job performance.

2 In those jobs for which computer use is expected, it may be referred to as a 'core job skill' (Matthews, 2003). In other words, without this skill it would be impossible to complete the job. This can be seen, for example, in much routine office work where staff are required to use word processing or spreadsheet software to create documents. It is also the case with some more specifically skilled jobs, such as automotive design or architecture, where skill with design software is necessary. This first type of computer literacy is arguably becoming a common feature of most jobs, whether they are based in fundamental word processing packages used across a range of industries or specialized computer packages tailored to use within a specific work environment. It is in this sense that computer literacy of some sort can be described as a fundamental 21st century job skill.

Notes

3 However, if we take 'success' to mean more than simply performing one's basic job requirements, computer literacy can be seen to be a powerful booster of work efficiency. Petit (2001, p.292) offers a view of true workplace success as *high* achievement – in other words, achieving something beyond satisfying basic job requirements. Taking this definition, we can see that a thorough understanding of all the features and uses of a software package can help someone to work more efficiently. For example, Harmon (ibid.) has shown that office workers who were taught to use all of the features of common word processing and office management packages to their fullest were able to improve work rates by up to 25%, as well as cutting down on excess printing and overtime.

4 From this it is possible to conclude that staff who are properly trained to make the most use of all features of common software packages can accomplish their work tasks with greater success as a result. Therefore, as computers come to be used more widely in almost all job types, it will be the responsibility of insightful managers not just to train staff to a basic standard, but to ensure that true computer literacy – familiarity and confidence with all aspects of the software needed for a task – is encouraged.

1e Work in pairs. Discuss how well this essay answers the original question.

2 Writing a suitable introduction

2a Read the following introduction from a text. Identify and underline as many examples of common features of essay introductions (a–f) as you can find.

a A definition of key vocabulary or ideas

b A statement focusing the reader's attention on the topic of the paper

c A statement of the aims of the essay

d A statement of the author's position (thesis statement)

e An outline of the structure of the essay

f Summary of background information to the topic

In the 21st century, computer systems and word processing packages have become an indispensable part of modern life. Commercial word processing software packages currently account for the vast majority of word processing software in use. According to Sherston (2003, p.54), over 85% of all digital text documents are created using commercial word processing applications. However, recent years have seen the growing popularity of 'open source' word processing packages (Guhlin, 2007), such as Open Office or Abiword. Open source refers to any software for which the source code is made freely available online, thus making payment to a copyright-holding company unnecessary. Open source word processing applications offer essentially the same functionalities as the commercial packages but are, of course, distributed for free. Some experts (see for instance Bateman, 2009) have argued that the quality of these free packages has now improved to the extent that they present a serious threat to commercial word processing software businesses. However, it seems likely that with more money to invest in development, commercial software producers will always be able to offer a superior product to the versions developed for free by keen volunteers. This essay will demonstrate that the features available in open source software packages often lag behind their commercial competitors by a year or more.

This paper begins with a review of the current commercial and free packages available, followed by an in-depth comparison of the functionality on offer in the leading free and commercial applications. The essay will conclude with a discussion of their relative merits and argue that the claim of technical superiority in commercial software is justified.

> Not all of the features mentioned in 2a need to be included in every type of introduction. In fact, it is common for essays in different academic fields to have their own styles of introduction.

2b Read the introductions from five different articles. Identify and underline any examples of the common features described in 2a. Then compare your answers with a partner.

1 Consumer-grade GPS (Global Positioning System) devices have been in common use for nearly two decades now. A range of GPS receivers are available to consumers, but the accuracy and dependability of these units varies with the surrounding landscape. Wing et al. (2005) report that some popular units differ from accurate readings by as much as 10 metres. The following paper reports the results of a study of the accuracy of a range of lower-priced GPS units in a variety of urban environments and finds only moderate variation from a confirmed accurate reading.

2 Some recent studies (e.g. Bardelli, 2007; Jones, 2008a) have questioned the effectiveness of open source word processing software packages. In answering this question two aspects must be considered. Firstly, whether the free versions offer the same range of features as commercial ones and, secondly, whether they offer the same affordance, which is defined here as ease of use. The first section of the essay is a comparison of two commonly used systems, one commercial and the other open source. This is followed by a discussion of their comparative merits. I will attempt to demonstrate that the differences in both features and affordance are negligible.

3 Virtual conferences are a powerful tool for business professionals and involve using information technology to overcome problems created by distance by allowing participants from all over the world to communicate in real time (Nagae, 2003). This essay outlines the main features of video-conferencing packages and concludes with a discussion of the benefits and limitations of this type of communication method. It will be argued that this innovative technology will continue both to facilitate and to shape the future of global business.

4 The Pioneer 10 and 11 space probes have long been known to report anomalous data (commonly known as the Pioneer Anomaly). This anomalous signal from the spacecraft is widely accepted (Low, 2006), but there is considerable disagreement about its cause. Possible explanations include gas leaks on board the spacecraft, as well as the distorting effects of heat radiation from several separate components within the craft. The current paper investigates the strength of the existing claims and aims to demonstrate that the anomaly is not sufficiently explained by existing theories. The paper concludes by presenting some brief ideas about areas for further investigation of the phenomenon.

5 Online peer-to-peer communities allow people with shared interests to gather virtually. This offers benefits for healthcare workers, who can use peer-to-peer technology to help patients with similar needs share their experiences, give advice, get answers to questions and offer practical and emotional support (Waller, 2004). Internet-based virtual e-health communities, which some estimates put as high as 30,000 in the UK (ibid.), can now be seen as a kind of mental health support tool. This paper will consider how effective these virtual communities are in supporting patients, and their ultimate impact on health outcomes.

2c Work in pairs to answer these questions.

    1 Which introductions (1–5) are from essays in:

      a hard science subjects?

      b soft subjects?

    2 Can you make any generalizations about the typical features of introductions depending on whether they are from hard science or soft subjects?

2d Look at the assignment title in the unit task on p.17. Write a draft introduction to the essay, including any features that you think are appropriate.

Notes
Draft introduction:

3 Using citations in writing

3a Work in pairs. Cover the box in 3b. Quickly try to recall the different ways in which citations can be used, which you looked at in Part C.

3b Match the types of citation (1–6) with the examples (a–f). Then check your answers with a partner.

Citation type	Example
1 Giving background information	a More than 30% of users suffer from carpal tunnel syndrome on a regular basis (Shantz, 2004, p.202).
2 Supporting a claim	b Based on the results of the current study, it seems likely that so-called 'Internet addiction' is not an actual addiction in the true sense. This accords with the position taken by Hobbes et al. (2003).
3 Showing disagreement	c The products were tested using the titration method (Walkley & Black, 1934).
4 Identifying the origin of a method or instrument	d In the current study 'power' will be defined as 'the ability to act effectively on persons or things' (Smith, 1960, p.18).
5 Giving another person's definition	e Since the start of the new millennium, personal computer ownership has increased in the developed world at a staggering rate (Drew, 2010).
6 Giving examples and data	f Diamond (1997) claims that computer security depends on individual behaviour rather than technical solutions. However, we take the view that the increasing sophistication of hacker attacks make strong technical security measures necessary.

3c Work in pairs. Discuss which types of citation you think are more common in soft subjects compared with hard subjects.

> There are three common ways of incorporating a citation into a text.
>
> Examples 1 and 2 below include the author citation in the grammar of the sentence. This is known as an *integral citation*. In 1, the author of the citation is the subject of the sentence; in 2, the author is part of an adverb phrase. Example 3 refers to the author of the citation in parentheses (brackets) outside the main body of the sentence. This is known as a *non-integral citation*. Although all three types of citation acknowledge the original source, they give a different emphasis (or prominence) to the author.
>
> ### Examples
>
> 1 Krantz (2001, p.221) suggests that the anomaly may be caused by human error.
> 2 According to Jackson (2009), personalized digital advertising will be commonplace within the next ten years.
> 3 Eco-tourism projects now account for 80% of all tourist business in the Andaman Islands (Suard, 2009, p.16).

3d Look at the text in **Appendix 3** again. Underline the citations in paragraphs A–D of the essay. Then answer these questions.

1 Which type of citation in 3b can you find examples of?
2 Can you find any patterns in the purpose of the citations and the way that they are written?

3e Read this essay title. What two tasks must you complete in order to answer the question?

Give an overview of the potential uses of personalized digital advertising and assess how realistic proposed personalized digital advertising systems are.

3f Work in pairs. Read these examples of how PDA (Personalized Digital Advertising) can be used. Then brainstorm some further possible uses, making notes of your ideas.

1 Internet browsers gather and record information about which websites you like to visit and then this information is used by your ISP to display adverts on your screen which are likely to be of interest to you.
2 Advertising billboards which can be programmed to scan your mobile phone to identify you as you walk by. After recognizing you, the billboard's computer can access electronic records about your shopping preferences and direct adverts directly at you, perhaps even calling you by your name.

3g Melody, a student, believes that personalized digital billboard advertising is technically impossible and unethical because, even if it were possible, it would be an invasion of people's privacy. Read the summaries of the opinions of five different writers on this topic and say which writer(s), if any, have:

a similar ideas to Melody and support her point of view
b similar ideas to your own point of view.

Writer and source	Summary
Kenji Tamura, 2009, p.23	PDA on billboards will become commonplace within five years.
Gillian Cameron, 2010, p.1712	PDA has been used by ISPs and web browser software since 2006.
Joyce Chen, 2006, p.401	PDA via electronic billboards is technically too difficult to achieve.
Simon Hartnoll, 2009, p.17	A survey of 1000 shoppers: 77% said that they would not want personal adverts targeted at them in public spaces.
Frederick Groscurth, 2008, p.369	A basic PDA billboard system is currently being trialled at a shopping centre in Tokyo.

3h Follow instructions 1–4 to write four short paragraphs.

1 You want to write some background information about PDA. Write one or two sentences, citing Groscurth and Cameron, to explain current uses of PDA.

Notes

PDA is a potential system of personalized advertising which uses analyses of electronic records of an individual's shopping habits to target personalized adverts at them.

2 You agree with Tamura's claim that PDA technology will be available soon, but disagree with his claim that it will only take five years. Write one or two sentences to express this, citing Chen.

Notes

3 You want to claim that most people do not like the idea of PDA being targeted at them. Write a sentence expressing this, citing Hartnoll to support your claim.

Notes

4 Joyce Chen is an influential writer on this topic and many people tend to agree with her views on the subject. However, you disagree with Chen. Write a sentence expressing your disagreement, citing Chen.

Notes

3i Work in pairs. Read and compare what you have written. Discuss the similarities and differences.

4 Using citations in different academic disciplines

4a Look at the following excerpts from two different journal articles which discuss different aspects of the social networking site Facebook. Decide which subject area the authors of each article might specialize in.

Text 1

It is perhaps surprising that Facebook has not yet demonstrated its full potential to the advertising industry. Globally, there are now nearly a billion Facebook users and according to research by eMarketer (2011), advertising revenue for the company will increase 100% this year, yielding nearly $3.9 billion. However, despite this dramatic growth, Facebook is using a results-based, low-key strategy for approaching potential advertisers. They are conscious that to justify a private valuation of $80 billion, and in preparation for the expected flotation of the company next year, they must demonstrate the effectiveness of their particular approach to ad design. 'So far, the most effective Facebook adverts are the ones which fit best into the existing layout of the site. They look like the rest of the content,' says Facebook's Ray Fleischmann (Statton, 2011).

However, this pitch has not yet worked on everyone. Advertising on Facebook converts views to actual clicks half as effectively as traditional web banner ads. And Facebook ads are 40 times less effective than Google search ads. It seems that the majority of commercial spending on Facebook has so far been spent trying to attract users to 'like' their product or brand page. Recent research by tech firm Content (2011) reports that less than 15% of advertising and marketing agents believe that Facebook can help an advertising campaign in any other way. The huge amount of traffic on Facebook also makes it difficult for experienced ad executives to decide how to interpret the numbers and translate them into sales. Senior Vice President of internet ad agency 320dpi Jane Lyons explains, 'The most common questions we get from clients these days when we run through the numbers of ad clicks, page "likes" and post shares relates to the way in which these figures might be expected to convert to hard sales. And, to be honest, we're not always certain ourselves.' (Smyth 2011).

Text 2

New creative possibilities have been made available to software developers by social networking sites like Facebook and Myspace (James, 2011). But the opportunities are inevitably accompanied by challenges. Application programming interfaces (APIs) allow apps to access and use the resources of the specific platform (e.g. Facebook) as well as some of the information uploaded by the user to their profile. This allows users to post widgets to their own profile as well as to share them with others. The user is prompted to give their permission when installing the app and is asked whether they are happy for the software to have access to their profile data. However, the prompt is rarely very specific and the user may not be entirely clear about exactly what data they are consenting to be shared (Haywood & Pareetha, 2012). This has led to concern about privacy on the social networks (Li, 2011). So developers are faced with the challenge of developing increasingly innovative and complex apps whilst at the same time maintaining the integrity of the personal data held by the sites. They must also consider the appropriate method for alerting the user to the need for their application to access some personal data in a way which is meaningful to the user. If they provide too much information the user may be less likely to grant permission. And if too little information is included in the prompt, then it may mislead the user about the extent of the access being granted (Harrison et al, 2010). As Facebook comes under increasing pressure to guarantee a level of security, this may make the difference between a successful application and a waste of a developer's time and effort.

4b Read the texts again. Draw a circle around citations which appear in the sentence. Underline citations which appear at the end of the sentence.

4c Work in pairs. Discuss which kinds of citations are more common for each type of writing.

4d Before the next lesson, find examples of writing from your discipline and see which kinds of citations are more common.

Communications technology and culture

Use all the work you have completed in Unit 1 on communications technology and culture to write an essay with this title:

How has the spread of communications technology affected cultures around the world? Assess the extent to which the Internet is a medium for western culture alone.

Your teacher will tell you how long the essay should be.

a Complete the table with your essay plan.

Title:		
Your main idea:		
Your supporting ideas:	**Evidence or citations:**	
	For	**Against**
1		
2		
3		
4		

b Write your answer to the essay title.

Remember:

- Use information from other sources to support your ideas.
- Use citations and a reference for each source you use.

Go to the checklist on p.198–199. Look again at the tips relating to Unit 1 Parts A–D and tick (✓) those you have used in your studies. Read the tips relating to Unit 1 Part E on p.199.

Unit 2   New frontiers

Unit overview

Part	This part will help you to ...	By improving your ability to ...
A	**Identify a speaker's position and aim**	• identify the speaker's stance on a topic • recognize and respond to bias • be an active audience member in a presentation
B	**Understand written information**	• identify arguments in texts • evaluate arguments • recognize assumptions • develop a response to arguments
C	**Clearly express and support your own stance on a topic**	• develop your own stance on a topic • use logic and reasoning • evaluate and select sources
D	**Create effective visual aids**	• incorporate graphics into a presentation • improve the quality of your graphics • acknowledge sources in a presentation
E	**Incorporate argument into your writing**	• structure an argument-based essay • structure an essay to incorporate counterarguments • support your argument effectively

Understanding spoken information

By the end of Part A you will be able to:

- identify the speaker's stance on a topic
- recognize and respond to bias
- be an active audience member in a presentation.

1 Identifying the speaker's stance on a topic

One key difference between a lecture on basic principles in a subject and a lecture in which the speaker is describing their own recent research is that a speaker presenting their own research has much more freedom to express their own opinions, which can help you to understand their attitude to the topic. The speaker's attitude towards information, their own opinions and the arguments that they are trying to persuade you of are known as the speaker's *stance* or *position*. Listening actively to recognize the speaker's stance on a topic is an important part of critical thinking.

1a Work in pairs. Discuss what it means when we say that a particular person 'belongs to a school of thought'. Then read this passage to check your answers.

Schools of thought often develop when there is disagreement in the academic community about a particular topic. Different academics will form groups with others who hold similar opinions, arguing against a 'school' with opposing ideas. A school of thought is said to exist when a number of academics involved in a certain topic agree about theories explaining the topic, or the methods used to investigate it. Agreement between the members of the school does not always have to be complete. It is important only that there are overall similarities in their approach to the subject. Schools of thought are sometimes identified with a name – such as 'The Copenhagen Interpretation' in physics, or the 'Marxist' school of thought in certain social science and humanities subjects.

1b Work in pairs and discuss these questions.

1 Which schools of thought are important in your field of study?

2 When you evaluate a speaker or writer's claims, how might knowing their school of thought be useful?

1c You are going to prepare for a lecture about the consequences of the disappearance of sea ice in the Arctic Ocean. First, read the information on p.65 and decide your own stance on the topic.

Figure 1: Arctic summertime ice coverage – 1979 and 2005

The ocean around the North Pole used to be entirely blocked by ice throughout most of the year. The region has effectively been off limits to commercial exploitation throughout recorded human history. That period of isolation may be coming to an end, as the permanent ice cover in the Arctic is rapidly diminishing; most scientists claim that this is a result of global warming.

Whatever the cause, the disappearance of sea ice in the Arctic Ocean is likely to have several significant consequences: the seabed is thought to contain substantial reserves of hydrocarbons and minerals which might become accessible if the thick ice cover vanishes. Commercial fishing may similarly benefit, as more ships sail further north to harvest the plentiful marine life without the danger of ice. Moreover, an ice-free Arctic region would allow cargo ships to pass between the Atlantic and Pacific oceans much more quickly than ever before, which will have important knock-on effects for global trade.

The commercial potential of an ice-free Arctic Ocean is enormous, but many scientists and environmental campaigners argue that the environment of the region, together with the animal and plant life there, are at risk from the changes which developing the region would bring.

1d Two schools of thought on this topic are represented in the two texts below. Read the texts. Do the schools differ in terms of *theory* or *method*?

The 'practicality' school

Stance:
The disappearance of the sea ice in the Arctic Ocean is a historic opportunity for a range of vital human commercial activities. The route across the Arctic Ocean will make trade between the Atlantic zone nations and Asia much faster and safer due to the typically calm waters of the Arctic Ocean. The potential profits from fishing and mineral exploitation are massive, as well as the many opportunities for tourism on cruise liners to a region never before available to ordinary holidaymakers. The protection of the existing Arctic ecosystem is an issue, but with strict regulation of activities in the region, it will be possible to protect the environment as well as exploit it for commercial profit.

The 'pristine Arctic' school

Stance:
The disappearance of the sea ice is disastrous for life and the environment in the Arctic. Local animals rely on the ice for their survival. The use of the Arctic Ocean for commercial enterprise such as mining and shipping will introduce human settlement into the high Arctic. This will lead to pollution and the destruction of Arctic animals' habitats. Moreover, development of the area will contribute to global warming, and an even faster destruction of the remaining sea ice.

1e Listen to the lecturer explain the situation in more detail. As you listen, write notes in the table.

The consequences of an ice-free Arctic Ocean
1 General topic information:
2 The lecturer's stance:

1f Work in pairs. Discuss whether you agree with the speaker's stance. Explain your reasons.

1g Listen to another speaker on the topic who is not clearly in either school. Decide which aspects this speaker has in common with each school and to what extent you agree or disagree with the speaker's point of view. Add more detail to your notes in part 1 of the table in 1e.

1h Work in pairs. Compare your notes with a partner. Answer these questions.

1 What is your own stance on the topic?

2 Do you strongly identify yourself with either of the two schools?

1i Work with another pair of students. Discuss your opinions about the implications of an ice-free Arctic Ocean.

2 Recognizing and responding to bias

2a Work in pairs. Review the section on factors that can interfere with critical thinking in Unit 1 Part C4 and discuss a possible definition for the word 'bias'.

2b Decide if each of these statements is True or False.

A person is biased …	True	False
1 if they adopt a position on a topic which will bring personal benefit to them		
2 when they adopt a strong position on a topic and will not consider contradictory evidence		
3 when they are emotional about a topic		
4 when they support their own nation in an argument		
5 when they maintain a strong position on a topic, even when they know that the position is not logical		
6 when they support their nation in an argument without considering alternative points of view.		

2c Work in pairs. Think back to the speeches you heard about the Arctic (Audio 2.1 and 2.2). Discuss whether this background information about each speaker makes it possible that information they have given is biased.

> **Speaker 1:**
> - is an economist who has written a book about the positive economic benefits of using Arctic shipping channels
> - has written articles strongly supporting the idea of strict safety regulations on all commercial operations in the Arctic
> - has written a book supporting the Canadian government's undersea land claims
> - serves as an advisor to a commercial fishing lobby group
> - is a supporter of an environmental conservation group.
>
> **Speaker 2:**
> - was a keynote speaker at a climate change conference, arguing that we must make drastic cuts in our carbon emissions in order to prevent climate change
> - has written a book strongly critical of nuclear policy
> - was part of a UN-funded research expedition to investigate the effects of global warming in the Arctic.

2d Compare your answers with another pair. Do you all agree on whether or not bias was evident in the two speeches?

2e Work in small groups and answer these questions.

   1 What criteria did you use to judge if what the two speakers said was biased?

   2 What steps can you take to ensure that you can detect bias when you are listening to a speech on a particular topic?

3 Being an active audience member in a presentation

> Being aware of the speaker's stance, and recognizing any potential bias, can help you to be a more active listener. This is particularly important when you are an audience member in a presentation. Listening to a presentation is different from listening to a lecture, in part because the presentation audience is often expected to ask questions on the topic at the end.

3a Work in pairs. Discuss what the purpose of asking questions in a presentation is.

3b Look at the list of possible reasons for asking a question in the first column of the table below (1–5). Match them with the example questions in the second column (a–e). More than one answer is possible.

Type of question	Example
1 Disputation (Challenging what the speaker has said)	**a** 'You mentioned that video-game technology is likely to develop to the point where players are wearing equipment that completely isolates them from the environment outside the game. I wonder if you could comment on how that would affect family life.'
2 Decision Aid (Helping you decide your opinion on the topic)	**b** 'The 2003 UN report on the development of space says that no military activity should be allowed there. How does this affect your claim that only trained military pilots are suitable astronauts?'
3 Clarification (Getting more information about something which is not understood)	**c** 'You mentioned that space travel is enormously expensive, but then you said that you still think it's possible for private companies. Don't you think it will be impossible if the cost is so high?'
4 Enquiry (Asking about the consequences of the information)	**d** 'I'm sorry, I didn't understand your point about computer developments. Did you mean that computers will be about ten times faster within a decade?'
5 Synthesis (Asking how the new information in the presentation connects to prior topic knowledge)	**e** 'I'm not sure I fully agree with your point on the negative impact of tourism in the Arctic. Do you have any more data about it?'

3c Read the following questions that you could ask yourself as you listen and that would help you to formulate questions to join in the discussion at the end of a presentation. Add three more questions.

Questions
1 What is the speaker's stance on the topic?
2 What evidence has the speaker presented?
3 Are there any problems with the evidence?
4 Is there anything that seems important which the speaker has not mentioned?
5 Is there any potential bias?
6
7
8

3d You are going to listen to a short presentation on the subject of space and private enterprise. Before you listen, read the following text and answer this question.

Do you think that space travel should be offered by the private sector, or should it be left to government space agencies?

Table 1: Space tourists

Tourist	Year	Reported cost ($m)	Duration (days)
Dennis Tito	2001	20	9
Mark Shuttleworth	2002	20	11
Gregory Olsen	2005	19	11
Anousheh Ansari	2006	20	12
Charles Simonyi	2007/2009	25/35	15/14
Richard Garriott	2008	30	12
Guy Laliberté	2009	35	12

Source: *NASA*

Since its beginnings in the 1950s, involvement in human space travel has been strictly limited to giant government agencies such as NASA in the US, the Federal Space Agency in Russia, or the National Space Administration in China. Human space travel has been seen as a venture so expensive and dangerous that only large governments could underwrite its costs and risks. However, increasing attention is now being paid to the idea of human space travel through private enterprise. The International Space Station has hosted a number of wealthy private tourists who paid a national space agency to train and transport them there for a short 'holiday' in space. More recently still, a number of private aerospace companies have been competing to create the first fully private space vehicles which could reach space at a fraction of the cost that government agency flights require.

3e Safety, cost and technical difficulty are often given as reasons why private companies should not become involved in human space flight. Write notes on your opinions of these aspects, and any other relevant aspects, in the second column of this table.

Aspect of topic	Your opinion before listening	Notes from presentation
Safety		
Cost		
Technical difficulty		
Any other ideas		

2.3

3f Work in pairs. Compare your notes. Give reasons for your opinions.

3g Listen to the presentation and write notes on the speaker's claims, together with any evidence they present, in the third column of the table on p.69.

3h Check your answers with a partner. Then discuss whether your opinion about private space travel matches that of the speaker.

3i Work in pairs and discuss the questions (1–3) for each section (A–F). Now listen to the presentation again. Then write a question for each section.

A   Evidence

1   What evidence did the speaker present for the claim that private companies can access space more cheaply than government agencies?

2   How suitable was this evidence?

3   If you do not think the evidence was suitable, write a question you could ask in the space below.

B   Clarification

1   What point did the speaker make about government responsibilities under the Outer Space Treaty?

2   How well did you understand the speaker's point?

3   If you need some clarification on the speaker's point, write a question you could ask in the space below.

C   Disputation

1   Did you disagree with any of the speaker's points?

2   What are your reasons for disagreeing?

3   If you did not agree, write a question you could ask in the space below.

D Decision aid

1 Are there any points that the speaker made which you cannot decide if you agree with or not?

2 What information could the speaker give that would help you decide?

3 If you need more information to aid you in making a decision, write a question you could ask in the space below.

E Synthesis

1 You learned in an earlier lecture that there is a dangerous amount of junk, like old satellites and debris, currently in orbit, which is already a big danger for existing space missions. How does this information compare to the speaker's claim that private companies could operate safely in space? Is it possible to synthesize the two pieces of apparently conflicting information?

2 Why would you ask a question in this case?

3 Write a question you could ask in the space below.

F Enquiry

1 Are there any aspects of the topic that you have thought of but which the speaker did not discuss?

2 Why would you ask a question in this situation?

3 Write a question you could ask in the space below.

> Your participation as an audience member does not end as soon as you have asked the question – rather, you need to listen and decide if the speaker's response answers your question satisfactorily or not, and then be prepared to ask more questions if need be.

3j Here are some questions asked by the audience at the end of the previous lecture about space development. Discuss what answers you think the lecturer might give to each one.

   1 'You mentioned that under the 1967 Outer Space Treaty, nobody can claim private property in space. Doesn't that mean that it is simply pointless for private companies to get involved in space exploration and things like mining, because they can't make any private claims?'

   2 'How can you claim that private companies are safer than governments, when no private space missions have been launched yet?'

   3 'Could you explain the point about government responsibility under the OST again? I didn't really understand it.'

   4 'I'm not convinced about the argument for private enterprise in space. I see your point, but ultimately, isn't it better if space exploration is kept as a non-profit thing? I mean, space should be for all of us – it shouldn't belong to anyone just to make a profit. Isn't it better if we leave the exploration to government scientists who are doing it for the sake of science, not profit?'

2.4

3k Listen to the questions and answers to see if your predictions were accurate.

3l Listen again. Make a note of the answers given. Use your notes to decide if the answer is satisfactory. If not, what follow-up question would you ask?

> **UNIT TASK** **Ethno-tourism**

The Unit 2 task is about ethno-tourism: adventure holidays in remote locations where the aim is to meet, or even make first contact with, previously isolated communities. This is a controversial issue because of claims that such contact is extremely harmful to tribal societies that are exposed to the modern world.

At the end of each part, you will be asked to complete a stage of the task as follows:

Part A: Listen to two introductory lectures on the topic.

Part B: Read two texts about it.

Part C: Think critically about the topic.

Part D: Prepare and deliver a group presentation on the topic.

Part E: Write an essay with this title:

Should ethno-tourism be encouraged?

In this section, you are going to listen to two lectures explaining the background of ethno-tourism, and outlining different arguments on the subject.

a Read this description of an ethno-tourism situation. Complete the table below with your ideas about the advantages and disadvantages of this situation for yourself, the tour company and the local community.

Imagine yourself taking a holiday in a remote part of the world. The resort that you are visiting has recently been built in an area where a local tribal society lives. The tribe never had contact with the outside world until last year and is cautious about contact with outsiders. The holiday brochure promises that besides regular holiday activities like spending time on the beach and shopping, you will also take a trip to visit the tribe and learn about their way of life. The brochure claims that this is a rare opportunity to be one of the first people to contact a stone-age tribe and help to bring them into the modern world.

	Advantages	Disadvantages
Yourself		
The tour company		
The local community		

b Work in pairs. Compare your ideas. Discuss briefly whether you think ethno-tourism should be encouraged in general.

2.5

c Listen to the two speakers. Make a note of their claims.

Claims
Speaker 1
Speaker 2

d Review your notes and answer these questions. Then discuss your ideas with a partner.

1 What points do both speakers agree on?

2 What points do the two speakers disagree on?

3 How big is the difference in the two speakers' stances on the topic?

Go to the checklist on p.199. Read the tips relating to Unit 2 Part A.

Understanding written information

By the end of Part B you will be able to:

- identify arguments in texts
- evaluate arguments
- recognize assumptions
- develop a response to arguments.

1   Identifying arguments in texts

An argument is both your main idea on the topic and the way you develop this idea to communicate it to others. It should be logically consistent and supported by reasons and evidence. An 'argument' that has no supporting reasons or evidence is not actually an argument at all, merely an opinion.

1a   Read these statements. Decide if you agree or disagree with them. Then work in pairs and compare your answers.

1   Video games are a waste of time.

2   Humans will colonize Mars some day.

3   Human history shows constant progress.

4   The human lifespan can probably be extended to 170 years or more.

5   Genetically modified food is the best solution for world hunger.

At the moment, by simply agreeing or disagreeing, you have expressed an **opinion**. To begin to make this into an **argument**, you need to add supporting reasons for your opinions. An argument is composed of a *main idea*, based on certain *premises*, and supported by *reasons* and *evidence*.

1b   Read this text. Identify the main idea.

According to Koskinnen (2008), around 80% of workers in developed nations need a computer for at least some of their work tasks. Koskinnen predicts that this figure will rise to nearly 100% inside a decade. Within ten years, company offices will look very different to the way they do today. The typical office space will look more like a stylish airport waiting lounge or coffee bar, with comfortable furnishings and relaxation spaces where employees can enjoy games or even take a nap. This will be because most people will be working from home using computers, so bosses will need to make the office space more enjoyable in order to attract employees.

1c   Which of these things does the writer ask us to accept? Write 'Yes' or 'No'.

1   All jobs can be done with computers.

2   Company offices will soon look very different.

3   Computer use will increase in the workplace.

4   All people have access to a computer at home.

5   People work at home because they prefer the environment.

The argument is based on what the writer believes is true: these beliefs are known as the premises of the argument. The premises are only what the writer believes – they may not in fact be correct. When reading critically, it is useful to question whether the writer's premises seem correct.

1d Consider the premises in 1c. Do you agree with them?

1e Read the short texts. Identify the author's main idea. Then make a note of the premises that it is based on in the second column of the table.

Text	Premises
1 Companies involved in creative industries such as software design need to arrange their offices in a way that enhances creativity. By removing single offices and cubicles and replacing them with an open-plan space in which no one has a fixed desk, you can encourage creativity and teamwork – everyone gets to contribute to the ideas, and the space itself supports a creative environment.	
2 As birth rates drop in the highly industrialized societies, the future workforce is shrinking and it is becoming necessary to find a way to replace the citizens lost from the workforce. The creation of advanced robots is a possible solution to this problem. Sufficiently advanced robots would be able to do certain jobs like cleaning, maintenance and hospitality services. This would leave the remaining human population free to concentrate on other work.	
3 With an ever-growing population and an ever-shrinking supply of fertile farmland, the world is facing a food crisis. One of the clearest solutions to this problem is the so-called 'Farmscraper' – a multi-level, high-rise building in which floor after floor of hydroponically grown food can be produced, right in the heart of Earth's biggest cities. This would enable city dwellers to enjoy an abundant supply of fresh, locally grown food.	
4 Within a decade we will probably see the return of the airship to our skies, replacing conventional commercial airliners, which consume an enormous amount of fuel and cause carbon pollution of the environment. Airship technology has come a long way since its early days in the 1930s and modern airships are environmentally friendly, comfortable and safe. A modern airship could carry up to 300 people across the Atlantic in about three days – somewhere between the speed of a modern airliner and the stately elegance of an ocean liner.	

1f Work in pairs and compare your answers, then discuss whether you agree with the author's main idea and premises or not.

1g Re-read the text in 1b and answer these questions.

1 What reasons does the author give for the claim that offices will be very different in ten years' time? Do these reasons support the main idea in the text?

2 What evidence is given as proof to support the claim? How relevant is the evidence?

1h Read this article from a news magazine and complete the table below.

The populations of the industrial nations are declining. This presents a significant economic problem for the future, as the workforce will decline with the population. Most of the nations facing this are attempting to fight the decline by encouraging immigration – people from regions of the world with lower economic prospects can take the place of workers in the industrialized nations and help to support the economy directly through their work, and through taxation. However, an innovative solution is being investigated in Japan, where semi-autonomous robots are being created to perform routine work. Opponents of the scheme claim that it will be impossible to implement successfully; the robots require a level of complexity that is currently beyond our technology and, in any case, it will be impossible to create enough robots to make the system worthwhile. However, the evidence seems to suggest that both of these issues can be overcome within the next decade and that robots will become a viable method of compensating for workforce decline.

Several robots are already at the advanced testing stage. These include a robot cleaner created by NishiCorp, which is already used in hotels and hospitals in Tokyo. NishiCorp's robot is capable of navigating corridors by itself, while disinfecting or vacuuming the floor and even polishing the walls. The robot can even manage stairs. Similarly, the Maruya chain of hotels has been using a robot receptionist since 2007. The receptionist is fixed to a chair and so cannot walk behind the front desk – instead it is located at a fixed point behind the counter. It looks, and has a basic range of movements, like a human, and is capable of responding to questions from hotel guests, as well as giving tourist advice about the area, handling check-ins and even dealing with complaints. The kind of robots which look completely human and, more importantly, behave in a completely human way, are still many years off, but these examples show that robots which are fully capable of doing specific jobs are already being used.

In answer to the claim that it will be impossible to create enough robots to cope with the decline in population, Seiji Yamada, the head of NishiCorp's design division, points out that several robotics companies are looking at the possibility of robotic self-assembly. A first generation of robots would be created by humans, but these initial robots would then be programmed to duplicate themselves, completing the assembly of a second generation of robots which in turn would be programmed to replicate themselves and so on. All that would be required from humans would be the creating of the first generation and after that the provision of raw materials for the robots to do their work. Yamada notes that this is still largely theoretical, but points to the recent P-N7 prototype created by NishiCorp, which is a very simple robot capable of self-replication. A similar project is being carried out in partnership between Tokyo University and MIT, which last year resulted in a first generation of, albeit very basic, robots managing to replicate themselves in a second generation.

Main idea/argument:		
Premises:		
Supporting reasons:		**Evidence:**
1		
2		

1i Work in pairs. Discuss how strong the writer's argument is.

2   Evaluating arguments

> An argument's strength depends on how accurate the author's premises, reasons and evidence are. As such, an important part of critical reading is to evaluate the author's arguments to decide if they are strong or not. Even the most famous authorities on a topic may have made an error in the construction of their argument.

2a   Work in pairs. Discuss and make a note of the things that you should take into account when evaluating the strength of an argument. Write your ideas in the space below.

How relevant is the evidence?

Are the premises realistic?

Is the author biased in some way?

2b   Read this extract from a journal article and answer these questions.

1   What is the main idea?

2   What premises is the argument based on?

3   How good are the supporting reasons?

4   What evidence is offered?

5   How well do the reasons support the conclusion?

6   Is there anything in the argument which is not relevant?

NASA has established a constant presence in space, with the permanently manned International Space Station, space-based satellites and probes, human spaceflight in near-Earth orbit, and even ambitious plans to return astronauts to the moon in the very near future and then on to a pioneering mission to Mars by the middle of this century. NASA's total yearly budget is approximately 13 billion dollars (Haskins, 2008). However, far from the popular perception that this is money well spent on exciting and innovative space research, the money itself gives little return in benefits and could almost certainly be put to better use dealing with more important issues on Earth. This is a particularly important issue as countries such as China and perhaps India look to spend money expanding their own presence in space.

50 years of US spaceflight have provided little direct benefit when compared to the costs associated with the venture. At the time of writing, the International Space Station is the highest profile space mission and certainly the one for which most scientific claims are made (Bose, 2009). However, the extent of actual scientific research generated by the station is limited. There have certainly been valuable projects carried out by the astronauts on the station, such as their contribution to an understanding of climate change and a range of medical projects which can feed back into advances in medical practice on Earth (Liu, 2009). It has been argued that approximately the same benefits could have been obtained by investing in scientific and medical research in existing, Earth-based universities (Jackson, 2010).

Similarly, the recently cancelled Space Shuttle programme, which for so long was celebrated for its contributions to science, was in fact often engaged in projects which were of little real benefit, and certainly did not justify the cost or danger of the flight. Examples of this include investigations into how flowers release their perfume in orbit, the way paint moves in zero gravity (Mackin, 2004) and studying the life-cycle of various insects in space (Howell, 2007). Such endeavours are of dubious scientific benefit and offer little return to the people funding them.

Besides the fact that research budgets have often been used poorly in space itself, there is a strong argument to be made that the whole venture of human spaceflight is overfunded and detracts from more worthwhile projects on Earth. A survey of the various terrestrial issues which present a serious threat to the health, life and well-being of Earth's population, and which are seriously underfunded, suggests that the money spent on space exploration could in fact be better spent here on Earth.

NASA's budget for human spaceflight, including programmes such as the International Space Station, is approximately 4 billion dollars a year (Haskins, 2008). This is the same amount of money that was promised by the leaders of the world's rich nations at the 2007 Rome Summit, intended to fund causes such as medical programmes in the world's poorest countries, as well as tackle the increasingly serious problem of world hunger. However, only a small fraction of this money has actually been delivered at the time of writing (Brassington, 2009). Research carried out at the London School of Economics found that a similar amount of money could pay for the creation of five hospitals, each of which could provide a city of a million inhabitants with state of the art healthcare (Ide & Lowell, 2008).

Another significant area in which the money could be better spent is offsetting the effects of human damage to the environment. 4 billion dollars a year could fund a proposed solar power system in China which would cater for all of Shanghai's power needs in an environmentally neutral way (Li, 2007). Economists in Australia have estimated that the cost of investing in environmentally neutral new power generation would be approximately similar. Of course, these nations do not contribute to NASA's budget and so it is hardly fair to claim that the US should consider itself responsible for funding other countries' environmental development. Nevertheless, these figures indicate what could be achieved even in the US by redirecting funds from space.

2c Review your list, from 2a, of things to bear in mind when evaluating an argument. Is there anything to add to the list?

3   Recognizing assumptions

> *Premises* are usually stated beliefs on which a writer builds an argument. Underlying the premises and argument are certain *assumptions*: the writer's unspoken or unstated beliefs about the world in general. These inform the premises that the argument is based on and, like the premises, may not always be correct or reasonable.

3a Read the three paragraphs (A–C). Identify:

1 what you think the writer's explicit idea is

2 any assumptions you believe the writer has but which are *not* stated in the text.

The first one has been done for you.

A
> The coming years will see remarkable and universal improvements in healthcare. This will be in the form of advances in nanotechnology – the creation of extremely small robots which can be programmed to carry out delicate tasks which humans are unable to do.

1   nanotechnology will lead to improved healthcare

2   assumes that 1) <u>everyone</u> has access to the <u>same</u> level of healthcare and that everyone will benefit from these advances 2) (probably) all new technologies will get to developing countries in time

B

I can't say I agree with claims about climate change – that our society may be destroyed by environmental damage. I mean, the forecasts say that this might happen within a couple of hundred years, but by then we will have colonized space, so it's not really all that important, is it? Our society will survive.

1

2

C

One of the key advantages of ethno-tourism is that the tribes which are contacted will be able to get the benefit of modern civilization – modern hospitals, education, housing. By bringing isolated tribes into the civilized world we give their children the opportunity to participate in the world.

1

2

3b Work in pairs. Compare your answers. Decide whether the assumptions are reasonable.

3c Read this newspaper article. What is the author's argument? Try to identify any hidden assumptions in the text. Then discuss your answers with a partner.

Video game advances threaten society

by John Holmes

The video games industry is worth approximately $48 billion USD (£30 billion) a year, similar to the revenue earned by Hollywood. This is remarkable when you consider that games industry revenues have increased 50% in the last three years and look set to continue rising. What's driving this boom in gaming? Three things, says Games Designers Conference organizer Ron Kricek: improvements in the quality and speed of games platforms, the spread of high-tech mobile technology, and a widening section of the population who are trying games for the first time.

Top-of-the-line games platforms already boast processing speeds in the range of 3 to 4 gigahertz, as well as powerful software which can render lifelike graphics and a certain level of artificial intelligence in the characters that one meets in a game. Experts predict an explosion in processing power in the next decade, anything between 10 and 100 gig systems, with software to match. But that's not the end of the story: at the most recent Games Designer's Conference delighted fans and developers were able to get a taste of the future of gaming – headsets which can 'read' the brainwaves of players and translate them into actions on the screen; cameras which can be mounted on top of screens and capture your movements as you play – no need for a Wii remote when the games console can simply capture your movements; even goggles which give the player complete – or near enough – immersion in a hyper-realistic game environment which only they can see.

All of this is great news for the army of gaming fans around the world – an army which is growing rapidly. Gone are the days when video games were the sole preserve of teenage boys – the popularity of the Wii, and its relatively simple games, demonstrated that just about everyone likes to play games of some sort, if given the chance. A large part of the growing games market is women, young children, and the elderly, and the industry is responding by creating more games tailored to their interests.

When you couple this with the revolution in mobile technology, it's possible to glimpse the future – and it's not a nice one. Imagine the scene on your morning commute to work – a carriage full of passengers, wearing goggles that wrap them in their own game fantasies, each absorbed in a virtual world while ignoring the world around them. As games platforms improve, people will be exposed to a more realistic, and more satisfying, gaming experience, and will inevitably want to spend more time in the fantasy worlds that the games offer. The result can only be the weakening of our societies, as real-world social bonds are ignored in favour of the imaginary pleasures of the game. In a world in which everyone is wrapped up in their own reality, real criminals will find it easier to prey on distracted people.

When the temptation to play games is so strong that we all – kids, parents, the elderly – want to spend our time in them, what happens to family life? What happens to exercise? We risk sacrificing a better future for humanity by allowing ourselves to be hypnotized by a make-believe world.

3d Now read excerpts from some letters (A–D) which readers of the newspaper have sent in response to the article. What assumptions can you identify in each person's letter?

Letter	Assumption
A Your article on 14th April (Video game advances threaten society) seemed to be nothing more than scaremongering by someone who's afraid of technology. If the predictions about the popularity of gaming are correct, we will see a society in which people have more in common with each other because of a shared love of gaming. That has to be a good thing.	
B I fail to see how an increase in computing power is going to lead to the breakdown of society, as John Holmes proposes. Video games may be becoming more popular for some sections of the population, but this will hardly affect serious-minded people.	
C I congratulate John Holmes on his insightful article on the dreadful effect that video games will have on our society. It's obvious that playing violent games makes people more inclined to be violent in daily life – the same thing happens with rap music. If it's true, as Holmes says, that more and more people are being seduced into playing these games, then I fear for the future.	
D As someone who loves exercise as well as being a keen video gamer, I take offence at John Holmes' suggestion that we will become a society of physical weaklings. He also completely overlooks one of the biggest changes in games over the last few years – that we no longer need games consoles because game technology can 'read' our body movements. There are lots of games involving physical activities, which help users to stay fit and healthy. In fact, the increase in gaming will probably lead to a society which is more active than before.	

3e Work in pairs. Compare your answers with a partner. Then work with another pair of students and discuss whether the assumptions are reasonable or not.

4 Developing a response to arguments

> Look back at the third stage of the flowchart in Unit 1 Part C2. The third stage in developing a critical position on a topic is coming to a temporary conclusion. This is the point you reach when you have completed some background reading on a topic and begun to form your own opinions about it. A good reader should remain open-minded at this stage and be prepared to change their opinions as a result of doing more research.

4a Work in small groups and discuss this question.

Are video games ever likely to become a mainstream pastime for people of all ages and social levels?

4b Write your own opinion in the Cornell notes format below. This will be your first (temporary) conclusion on the subject.

4c Now read the text on the topic on p.82, and answer these questions.

1 What is the author's position on the topic?

2 What reasons does the author advance to support his/her argument?

3 What evidence does the author present to support his/her reasoning?

4 To what extent does the writer's position match your own temporary conclusion on the subject?

5 How has reading this text affected your opinion on the subject? Discuss your position on the topic.

Things to come: video games

Video gaming is now a multi-billion-dollar-a-year industry (Abbot, 2009), yet the negative stereotype of the 'typical' video-games player – a lone (and possibly lonely) teenage boy remains in many quarters. This prejudice is changing only slowly as gaming becomes more popular with a broader audience, and many people are still resistant to the idea of gaming as a respectable activity for all ages and levels of society. However, within a decade, and possibly even sooner (Johanssen, 2010, p.12) we will see gaming become a mainstream activity, with broad social appeal. This will be a true revolution not unlike the mobile revolution of the early 2000s, unlocking a powerful range of human potentials which well-designed games can capture and enhance.

The key to this is, as Shales et al. (2004) point out, redefining our view of games. Whereas in the past we have often dismissed games as mere recreation, we will increasingly come to see gaming as a powerful learning tool and it is this that will be the secret of its appeal.

As Dahl (1994, p.270) and others have claimed, 'learning by doing' is one of the most successful methods by which people learn and remember new things. People respond intuitively to situations in which they can learn by doing and also by playing. An element of enjoyment in any learning situation makes it easier to accept the educational message, as well as incentivize us to learn more. So if people enjoy learning by playing, it seems reasonable to assume that platforms which allow us to play are also ideally suited to helping us learn.

There is already a great deal of evidence, both anecdotal and scientific, that people learn from video games. Extensive testing by the US government has resulted in the use of simulators for everything from language training to hostage negotiation (Morris, 2004), while recent research has demonstrated the link between working memory and certain types of games (Gordon, 2004). The widespread popularity of 'brain-training' games, as well as scare stories that violent games promote violent behaviour in players, attests to the general belief that we can learn from computer games, for good or ill.

It is in this fusion of gaming experience and learning opportunities that video gaming will come to be a general pastime, widely accepted across society. Video games offer a visceral and exciting environment to the player/learner, a promise of new experiences that will become even more vivid as gaming technology improves. They also offer the possibility of creating what Shales et al. describe as 'original social worlds' (2004, p.3). In these new worlds we can incorporate valid experiences that will allow people to learn new skills 'invisibly' while they are enjoying the game. For instance, people playing Massively Multiplayer Online Role-playing Games such as World of Warcraft or Lineage can learn valuable social skills which are necessary to cooperate successfully in the games, as well as transferable soft skills which employers value, such as teamwork, strategic planning and handling money. These learning experiences are currently a side effect of games which were designed mainly for entertainment, but it is not too much of a leap to imagine that we could deliberately design these learning experiences into games. People who tended to resist playing video games in the past due to the negative stereotype of gaming as 'childish' may be persuaded to try a game if it is marketed as a learning tool. Shales et al. give as an example a game designed so that the player would learn a language as they engage in the simulation of running an international business. The 'playful target' of the game would be the success or failure of the business, whilst the language package would be learned almost as a side note.

With increasing sophistication of video-game technologies, the range of skills which could be packaged into immersive, and above all exciting, game environments is vast.

As a love of play is part of human nature, so satisfaction at learning new things is also part of what it means to be human. The two things combined will lead to a revolution in the acceptance of gaming.

References

Abbot, P. (2009). Economic prospects in the gaming industry. *Futurology, 3*(1), 104–107.

Dahl, C. (1994). Trends in research on learning. *Educational Issues, 16*(2), 242–271.

Gordon, M. (2004). Games and learning. In Johanssen, A. (Ed.), *Research on gaming technology* (pp.428–435). New York: Velocity Inc.

Johanssen, A. (2010). *The Gaming Revolution*. New York: Velocity Inc.

Morris, T. (2004, January 16). US Government gets wired. *Plugged In, 48*. Retrieved from http://www. pluggedin/features/

Shales, P., Snook, P., Martinez, M.T., & Bell, J. (2004). Video games, learning, and mass appeal. *Future Prospects, 7*(9), 713–729.

a Remind yourself of the essay title for this unit task (p.72). Read these two texts. Write notes about the argument and supporting evidence in the box below each text.

Text A – The paradox of tourism

Table 1: Tourist arrivals (millions) by year and region

Region / Year	2000	2005	2008	2009
South Asia	100.5	142.6	173.1	170.4
Oceania	9.6	11.0	11.1	10.9
Central America	4.3	6.3	8.2	7.6
South America	15.9	19.1	21.8	21.3
North Africa	10.2	13.9	17.1	17.6
Subsaharan Africa	16.3	21.5	27.4	28.4

Source: *World Tourism Organization*

Tourism is a valuable source of income for third-world countries. The World Bank, World Trade Organization and United Nations all encourage countries in the developing world to exploit their environmental, historical and cultural resources in order to attract foreign tourists (Gregory, 2003). This includes the exploitation of smaller ethnic groups, whose vibrant and exotic cultures can be a powerful draw for so-called 'ethno-tourists'. As such, the important role that ethno-tourism plays in supporting the national economy of many third-world and developing nations should not be underestimated. In this paper, ethno-tourism will be taken to mean tourism with isolated but recently contacted tribal groups, or any tourism offering the possibility of first contact with supposedly uncontacted peoples who live in ignorance of the outside world.

Ethno-tourism should, by rights, benefit both the visitors as well as the contacted tribal communities. However, many recent studies strongly assert the negative impact of ethno-tourism on the subject communities. In this paper we take the position that claims of this sort exaggerate the negative consequences of contact with tourists and the tourism industry. Ethno-tourism can be an enormously positive force if it is implemented in the right way.

Critics of ethno-tourism oppose the use of recently contacted or 'uncontacted' tribal communities for commercial purposes. Two arguments in particular are characteristic of the anti-ethno-tourism stance. Firstly, that tribal communities do not enjoy material or economic benefits from contact with tourists. Most travel companies and governments promoting ethno-tourism emphasize that it brings opportunities for the contacted tribal communities to take jobs in the local area and to enjoy an improvement in their standard of living as a result. However, studies by Malloy and Fennell (1998) and Ahmed et al. (1994) suggest that the jobs on offer are for menial work, with low salaries, and do not really contribute to the economic well-being of the tribes. Secondly, native tribes are also sold short by governments which promise that the tribal groups will have access to benefits such as education and modern healthcare, but which usually fail to deliver.

A further complaint aimed at ethno-tourism is its effect on the cohesion of the contacted communities. This includes stratification in the society, where some members of the community take jobs dealing with tourists and making more money, comparatively, than others of their tribe, which can have the effect of creating wealth divisions in a society where none existed before (Hitchcock, 1997, p.119). Hitchcock also makes the accusation that when members of a community are drawn to work in the tourist industry, they are no longer able to contribute to important community work such as gathering or harvesting food or taking care of livestock (1997, p.95). This is said to contribute to social breakdown.

While we do not dispute claims that some instances exist where tribal communities have not received all that was promised them, or suffered social breakdown as a result of exposure to the tourist industry, we see this more as a problem of implementation rather than with the concept of ethno-tourism itself. The benefits of well-managed ethno-tourism ventures outweigh objections to it based on isolated examples of negative outcomes.

Ethno-tourism offers economic benefits both to the contacted tribal communities and the nation located geographically on the land in which they reside. The establishment of ethno-tourist resort hotels in places such as Kenya and Costa Rica (Vidal, 2009) have provided jobs for local tribes people, who can then use the money to support the material wealth of their communities. This windfall opportunity extends also to the country at large, as others are needed as guides, interpreters and hospitality and construction workers to support the resorts. Ultimately this flows to the coffers of the national governments, who are able to use the money to invest in useful social welfare projects such as schools and housing.

Economic benefits alone lack the moral power to convince us that ethno-tourism is on the whole good for both visitors and contacted tribal communities. Far more important, from a human rights viewpoint, is the fact that ethno-tourism can help to generate a heightened sensitivity towards the importance of these people's cultures. Ethno-tourism, despite arguments that it helps to destroy the cultures exposed to outside tourists, is frequently one of the strongest forces for their preservation. Tribal communities themselves are encouraged by the incentive of tourist money to maintain their own distinctive traditions, knowing that if they allow themselves to lose these unique attributes, the tourists will move elsewhere. A clear example of this is seen in the tribal communities worldwide which have chosen to manage their own ethno-tourist lodges, giving access to tourists on their own terms, and using the money to further promote their own cultures (Tourism Concern, 2009). These communities have recognized that tourism can serve their interests and use it to help maintain their society and the continuity of their traditions.

Tourists who have experienced contact with isolated tribespeople return from these holidays with a greater awareness of the need to protect these communities. Thus ethno-tourism can serve as a vehicle for native-rights movements.

Visiting isolated communities helps returning tourists to identify emotionally with the people they have visited and be more inclined to support them afterwards. Such identification between visitors from the outside world and the tribal communities is one of the strongest defences they have against ill-treatment at the hands of unscrupulous companies or governments.

None of this is to deny that there are many examples of the negative consequences resulting from contact between developed-world tourists and isolated tribal communities. Nevertheless, the examples given here suggest that these are the result of poor management of the tour business rather than a problem with ethno-tourism itself. A well-managed ethno-tourist business can be a rich source of benefit for all.

References

Ahmed, Z.U., Krohn, F.B., & Heller, V. (1994). International Tourism Ethics as a way to World Understanding. *Journal of Tourism Studies, 5*(2), 36–44.

Gregory, S. (2003). Men in Paradise: Sex Tourism and the Political Economy of Masculinity. In D.S. Moore, J. Kosek, & A. Pandian (Eds.), *Race, Nature and the Politics of Difference* (pp.323–355). London: DUP.

Hitchcock, R. (1997). Cultural, Economic and Environmental Impacts of Tourism among Kalahari Bushmen. In E. Chambers (Ed.), *Culture and Tourism: an applied perspective* (pp.93–128). New York: New York University Press.

Malloy, D.C. & Fennell, D.A. (1998). Eco-tourism and ethics: moral development and organizational cultures. *Journal of Travel Research, 36*(4): 47–56.

Tourism Concern & Pattullo, P. (2009). *The Ethical Travel Guide*. London: Earthscan.

Vidal, J. (2009, July 25). Are we here just for your amusement? *Guardian*. Retrieved from http://www.guardian.co.uk/travel/2009/jul/25/tribal-adventure-ethical-tourism-jarawa

Clarke, D. (2012). The Paradox of Tourism. *Tour and Travel Journal, 7*(13), 202–203.

Text B – Tourism and disease

Decline of Great Andamanese population after contact

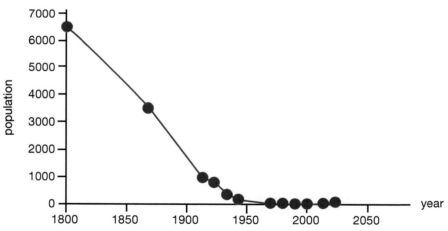

Source: Survival International (2007)

Disease presents the most direct of threats to isolated tribal communities contacted by outsiders. It is claimed that such societies routinely see 30–50% of their number die from introduced diseases shortly after contact (Hurtado et al., 2001, p.427). Numerous commentators have identified negative effects on tribal societies from ethno-tourist encounters, including social degradation, economic impoverishment and sexual exploitation. However, disease is arguably the most damaging result of this type of contact, resulting not only in high death rates but also acting as the cause for the other problems which follow from it: mental anguish at the loss of the greater part of one's community, culture shock, substance abuse (addiction to alcohol or narcotics) and social breakdown. A number of tourist agencies now offer high-stakes tours in which the aim is to make first contact with remote tribes, or which have established resorts on land near recently contacted groups which nevertheless currently remain largely separate from the resort communities. Either way, the inevitable consequence of such contact will be to introduce these people to diseases against which they have no natural protection. Other writers have already made a forceful case against such ethno-tourist ventures, but I will argue here that the risk of death from disease is such that we have a moral responsibility to leave these people in peace.

Diseases which are considered superficial or easily treatable in most modern societies present a particular danger to remote tribal communities. The common cold, influenza and measles are all relatively insignificant in terms of mortality in the developed world and large parts of the developing world. Citizens in these societies have developed strong natural immunity to these and a range of other illnesses, which may cause only temporary discomfort if properly treated. However, such diseases are unknown among most isolated tribal communities which have had extremely limited contact with the outside world. Consequently, they tend to have no immunity to them, which has had devastating results for a number of societies. In the 1980s, for instance, 50% of the Nahua tribe in Peru died of disease shortly after contact was made (Survival International, 2007). This figure is matched or exceeded in a number of cases, such as the Murunahua in the mid-1990s, with a 50% death rate after contact with loggers (Survival International, 2009), the Nukak Maku in Colombia suffered a disease-induced death rate as high as 65%. Further back in history we have significantly higher death tolls, such as the Great Andamanese in the Indian Ocean, whose numbers were reduced from 5000 to around 40 within a few years of contact (UNHCR, 2008). Despite the best intentions of outside visitors, there is almost nothing that can be done to guarantee the safety of isolated societies during contact. An absence of contact, it seems, is the only manner in which their survival may be assured.

The consequences for tribal communities which suffer such shocking death rates are predictable. Alcoholism, poverty and depression become commonplace. As community numbers decline, the social fabric becomes strained and has frequently resulted in the complete breakdown of some communities.

Some supporters of responsible ethno-tourism argue that well-managed tourism programmes can avoid the effects of social breakdown and keep outside visitors at a 'safe' distance, thus preventing, or at least reducing the risk of, contagion. This seems like a reasonable position to take but it is one-sided. The members of recently contacted tribes, after they get over their initial wariness, are often just as curious about the visitors as the tourists are about them. In the case of the Andamanese Jarawa, reports of Jarawa youths venturing into tourist areas are becoming more common. Tempted by the opportunity of meeting outsiders, they are exposing themselves to the danger of diseases which they know nothing about. We cannot expect them to be aware of such an existential threat and therefore it falls to those of us who are aware, the outside world, to ensure their safety by keeping our distance from them.

References

Hurtado, M., Hill, K., Kaplan, H., & Lancaster, J. (2001). The Epidemiology of Infectious Diseases among South American Indians: a call for guidelines for ethical research. Current Anthropology, 42(3), 425–432.

Survival International (2007). Amazon leader – uncontacted tribes suffer worst experience in 500 years. Retrieved from http://www.survivalinternational.org/news/2586

Survival International (2009). Aerial photos reveal loggers inside uncontacted Indians' territory. Retrieved from http://www.survivalinternational.org/news/4847

UNHCR – Minority Rights Group International (2008). World Directory of Minorities and Indigenous Peoples – India: Andaman Islanders. Retrieved from http://www.unhcr.org/refworld/docid/49749d133c.html

Efimov, T. (2012). Tourism and Disease. Tour and Travel Journal, 7(11), 119.

Notes on *Tourism and disease*

---

b What is the writer's main argument for each text? Work in pairs and discuss these questions about the two texts.

1 How strong is the argument?

2 How do the opinions of these writers compare with the opinions of the lecturers in Part A?

3 What assumptions are these writers' arguments based on?

4 How, if at all, has your position on the topic been affected by reading the texts?

 Go to the checklist on p.199–200. Look again at the tips relating to Unit 2 Part A and tick (✓) those you have used in your studies. Read the tips relating to Unit 2 Part B on p.200.

Investigating

By the end of Part C you will be able to:

- develop your own stance on a topic
- use logic and reasoning
- evaluate and select sources.

1 Developing your own stance on a topic

> Background research will often provide you with alternative stances and your own temporary conclusions on a topic. However, in an essay you will need to develop your own stance on which to base your argument.

1a Review your stance on the topic of video games in Part B. Work in small groups and discuss your opinions about this assignment question. Then write your own preliminary conclusion in the table.

To what extent can video games be used to enhance learning in school and higher education?

Preliminary conclusion (after your initial discussion)
Temporary conclusion 1 (after first reading on the topic)
Temporary conclusion 2 (after second reading)
Final conclusion (Your stance after considering all of the information you have discovered)

1b Read the two articles about video games (Texts 1 and 2) on p.89–90 and consider whether the information they contain changes your preliminary opinion on the subject. Complete the table above with your temporary conclusions for each text.

Text 1

The number of students graduating each year from universities with degrees in the hard sciences and applied subjects like engineering is dwarfed by comparison with the number of enthusiastic players of modern online video games such as Lineage or Civilization. While these games have entertainment as their explicit purpose, there is evidence that games with a deliberate instructive aim are also highly popular. Food Force, for instance, a game produced by the UN to teach players about food aid distribution, has several million players. A growing body of scholarly work suggests that the future of education lies in gaming. Gaming offers a singularly effective way to improve the student learning experience.

Firstly, it is important to realize that gaming-as-educational-tool is not some possibility which lies only in the distant future; a number of popular educational games designed for students in the sciences and engineering already exist. Initial studies investigating the effectiveness of these games show a clear improvement in assessment marks from students who were taught using the games compared with others who received courses by attending conventional lectures. One study recorded an average increase of over 40% on test scores in the groups learning through interactive games.

However, not all results have been as positive as this – depending on how well the games are designed. A poorly designed game can still clearly inhibit learning in the way that a dull series of lectures can. Learning benefits appear to have resulted from games that incorporated effective learning practices and situations.

Possible reasons for the apparent superiority of games when compared to learning from a series of lectures are various. Information in a lecture is delivered in an almost entirely aural mode, while in a game the players/students receive input both through listening to speech or sounds in the game environment, as well as visually. An increase in the modes by which information is received has long been acknowledged to have clear learning benefits. There is more input and feedback available in a game than a lecture. Something new happens almost every time a player presses a button during a game, giving the player feedback and new information about their environment, while students in lectures have perhaps only one or two opportunities to interact with the information by asking questions. Literacy professor Paul Gee, a strong proponent of learning through videogaming, also points out that the challenges or tasks in many games need players to develop skills in thinking logically – the formation of hypotheses, experimentation, and reflecting on their performance if they fail at first. Games, far from being superficial or childish entertainment, are loaded with a variety of learning experiences.

Text 2

There is by now a strong body of evidence that video games can afford valuable learning opportunities to students, and this has led to serious discussion about the deliberate design of school and higher education courses designed to be taught through a games medium. While this potential clearly exists, we need to consider whether it will ever actually translate into educational practice. The answer to this is probably that games will never be a widespread learning and teaching tool, for a number of reasons.

Firstly, there is the issue of the quality of the product. There is currently an enormous gap in the experience and quality of so-called 'entertainment' games and deliberately 'educational' ones. Commercial entertainment-focused games boast visually stunning graphics and exciting, often violent, scenarios, alongside pulse-raising soundtracks, often created by tie-ins with the movie and record industries. It is to this that they owe their enduring popularity and market success. Contrast this with the range of 'educational' games currently available. The majority of these are developed as free-to-download software, with basic 2D graphics and none of the visual sophistication of their commercial counterparts. Unfortunately, the relatively low sensory quality of educational games like this means they are unlikely to hold the attention of serious gamers for very long, with the result that their educational value will be limited. In terms of the educational quality of the games, the picture is also rather gloomy. No standard test exists which can be applied to measure the educational effectiveness of games and, without funding, it is unlikely that such tests will ever be developed. Without guarantees of the quality of the games, how will educators ever be convinced to begin using them with their students?

Staying on the subject of funding, we can see here too that the future of games in education is not bright. Entertainment games released for commercial profit are backed by enormous, financially powerful software development companies which are willing to invest in future games that they know will turn profits. Educational games, on the other hand, are generally produced and distributed by interested researchers relying on higher education research funding. This funding does not stretch to covering distribution, packaging and marketing costs, which is part of the reason that these games are often distributed for free online.

There is no dispute that games have a great potential to assist human learning but, in short, this will never come to pass because it will be impossible to sustain a business attempting to sell educational games.

1c Compare the contents of your table with the rest of your group.

1d Now complete the table with your final conclusions on the subject.

2 Using logic and reasoning

The three sentences below form a famous syllogism – a kind of logical puzzle.

All men are mortal.

Socrates is a man.

Therefore, Socrates is mortal.

The first two sentences of the syllogism are the premises. If the premises are true, then the conclusion in the final sentence must, logically, be true:

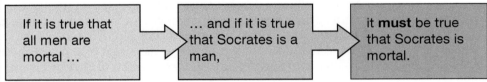

If it is true that all men are mortal … → … and if it is true that Socrates is a man, → it **must** be true that Socrates is mortal.

The kind of information about the world that you encounter in your studies is, however, likely to be a lot more complicated than this, and require careful thought to decide if the premises of an idea give logical support to the conclusion.

2a Read the argument below. Identify the premises and conclusion. Then answer these questions:

1 Does the conclusion follow from the premises?

2 Can you think of any other conclusions which the writer hasn't considered?

Nanorobots, incredibly small robots which can be programmed to perform a variety of tasks, are nearly a reality. Scientists predict that functioning, safe nanorobots will be commonplace within five years. One important potential use for these machines is in medicine, for example, with nanorobots programmed to attack cancer cells being injected into a human body. Within five to ten years we can expect to see a remarkable decrease in cancer rates as a result of this technological advance.

2b Repeat 2a with these two arguments.

> **1** Scientists believe that there may be substantial reserves of gas and oil under the Arctic Ocean seabed. Some predictions put the potential oil reserve as high as 20% of the world total, which is similar to the reserve in Saudi Arabia. The ice cover over the North Pole, which has prevented exploitation of this resource, is melting rapidly and is expected to have disappeared by mid-century. Because of this, from 2050 onwards, oil and gas prices will fall dramatically as this new supply becomes available.

> **2** Internet accessibility is expanding rapidly around the globe. It is now commonplace for students to have their own Internet-accessible laptops, used for research as well as writing assignments. At the same time, higher education institutions and academic publishers are increasingly making digital versions of their texts available online. As a result, higher education libraries, the actual buildings where hard copies of books and journals are stored, will see fewer and fewer visitors walking through their doors and will eventually become obsolete.

2c In the space below, write a paragraph with your own response to this question. Then work in pairs and analyze each other's paragraphs to decide if the conclusions follow logically from the premises.

The video-games industry is expanding rapidly and its popularity appears to be expanding to all sectors of society. How will the increasing popularity of video games affect social relationships in the future?

3 Evaluating and selecting sources

3a Imagine that you are writing an essay on this subject. Which source from p.92 (1–6) would be most suitable to use for your essay?

To what extent can video games be used to enhance learning in school and higher education?

Source 1
Written in 1907. The author, a teacher at a technical school, claims that students can learn best by a series of 'learning games'. This is based on his experiences as a classroom teacher, and his reasoning that play is a 'natural talent' for all humans.

Source 2
Written in 2008. The author claims that video games are a superior method of teaching to lectures. This argument is based on the premise that students often find lectures boring, but that video games enjoy widespread popularity and must therefore be exciting.

Source 3
Written in 2010. The author presents the results of a study looking at how marketing strategies can be used to improve sales of a new video-games console. The study found that sales increased when the console was sold with a bundle of free games, even if the overall cost was slightly higher than when the console was sold by itself.

Source 4
Written in 2004. The author presents research on a study investigating the effect of video games on maths scores in undergraduate students. Three students were given a maths test, then spent half an hour playing a car-racing game, before repeating the test. The study found that the students' scores in the test improved by 80%.

Source 5
Written in 2009. The authors present the results of a three-year project using an online game environment to teach undergraduate students about marketing. The authors found that average scores on end-of-term tests were about 30% higher than average for students who participated in the study.

Source 6
Written in 2001. The author makes the claim that video games teach players to be violent, aggressively competitive, and sexist. This is based on the results of research investigating emotional responses to gaming in teenagers.

3b Work in pairs. Read this list of factors which might cause you to decide not to use a particular source. Can you find any of these shortcomings in the texts in 3a?

- The claims made by the source are logically flawed.
- The source is irrelevant to the topic.
- The source is only passingly relevant, i.e. it deals with a similar topic but is not focused on the same issue.
- The source presents the results of a study in which the methodology is flawed.
- The source is extremely old.

a Remind yourself of the essay title for this unit task (p.72). The speakers that you listened to in Part A and the authors whose work you read in Part B clearly belong to two different schools of thought on this topic. In the spaces below, make a note of the common characteristics and beliefs of the two schools of thought represented by the speakers in Part A and the authors in Part B.

The pro-ethno-tourism school

The anti-ethno-tourism school

b Look at the graph below and position yourself on the graph depending on your stance towards ethno-tourism. Then work in pairs. Discuss your reasons with a partner.

Anti-ethno-tourism   Pro-ethno-tourism

c Before the next lesson, search for material about ethno-tourism which will help you develop your knowledge on the topic and refine your stance. When you find possible sources, follow these steps.

- Read each source critically, considering the author's argument, strength of reasoning and evidence and underlying assumptions.
- Decide how close the authors are to either of the schools of thought.
- Evaluate your own position on the topic after reading the sources. Write the source references.

Source reference	Position on the topic

 Go to the checklist on p.199–200. Look again at the tips relating to Unit 2 Parts A–B and tick (✓) those you have used in your studies. Read the tips relating to Unit 2 Part C on p.200.

Reporting in speech

By the end of Part D you will be able to:
- incorporate graphics into a presentation
- improve the quality of your graphics
- acknowledge sources in a presentation.

1 Incorporating graphics into a presentation

> The key aims when designing presentation visual aids are simplicity and clarity. However, a presentation must still include enough evidence to support the conclusion that you propose. A convenient and effective way of doing this is to use graphics to present numerical data.

1a Look at this example slide. It has a lot of information, but too much text. On a separate piece of paper, draw a graph to represent the information.

Learning benefits of video games

A number of different experimental video games have been used with college students, testing whether the games could improve maths scores. Students were separated into two groups:

1st group – received their maths tuition through traditional lectures
2nd group – received their maths tuition through the use of certain maths games
After the tuition, all students took a standardized maths test.

Solver game – average test scores for the 2nd group were 15% above the 1st group
NU Metrix game – average test scores for the 2nd group were 7% higher than the 1st group
Math Evo game – average test scores for the 2nd group were 40% higher than the 1st group

1b Compare your graphs in small groups. Explain the graph form (e.g. pie chart, bar graph) that you chose.

> Graphics are an efficient way of representing information, but their effectiveness can be greatly reduced if they are not designed properly.

1c Work in pairs and discuss what is wrong with the graphs on p.96–97. Make notes about the problem(s) under each graph.

1

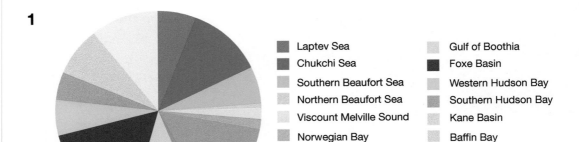

Figure 1: Approximate polar bear population by region

Problem(s):

2

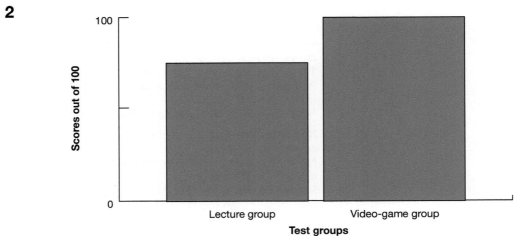

Figure 2: Maths test scores

Problem(s):

3

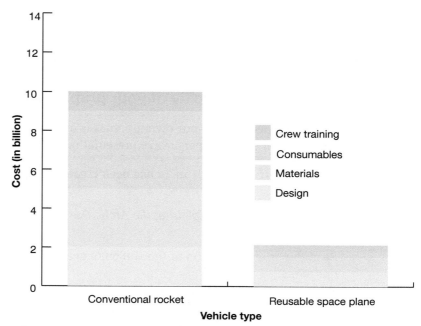

Figure 3: Estimated development costs for major components of different space vehicles

Problem(s):

4

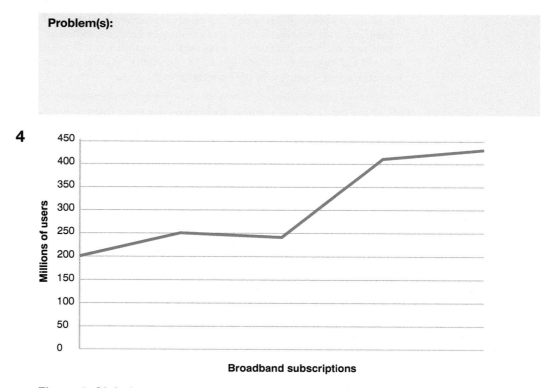

Figure 4: Global increase in broadband subscriptions

Problem(s):

2.6

1d Listen to a professional public speaker talking about mistakes to avoid when designing graphs. Make a note of the mistakes that the speaker mentions.

1e In pairs, check your answers. Discuss how you could improve the graphs in 1c.

2 Improving the quality of your graphics

Critical reflection on your own graphics is an important part of the process of creating an effective, persuasive presentation.

2a The pie chart in Figure 1 in 1c has been created to support a presentation with this title:

Examine the case for exploiting the Arctic Ocean for fishing, transport and oil production.

Read the brief description of the student's presentation below and answer the questions.

1 What is the relationship between this graphic and the student's main idea? How well does it support it?

2 Which of the presenter's points is this graphic supposed to support? How well does it do this?

The student begins by giving some background information about the Arctic and its history. He then explains what the potential benefits are from melting Arctic ice, including fishing, transport and oil production. He notes that there are some negative consequences of exploiting the Arctic, including ice-melt and damage to the eco-system. He concludes by claiming that the potential economic benefits are great enough to justify exploitation of the Arctic.

2b This checklist is a useful guide to ensure your graphics are as accurate, relevant and persuasive as possible. Read the list and add at least three questions of your own.

1 Is the graphic form you have chosen the most suitable one for the information you want to represent?

2 Is the information in the graphic you are using directly relevant to your topic?

3 Does the information clearly support your conclusions?

4 Is the graphic the right size for your audience to view all of the key information?

5 If you are using colour to represent separate pieces of information, are the colours sufficiently different that your audience can tell them apart?

6 Does the graphic have any unnecessary elements such as decorative pictures or three dimensions?

7 Is there a suitable amount of information on the graphic, or too much for your audience to take in?

8 If you are using a graph, is there a 'zero' baseline?

9
10
11

2c Review what you have learned in Part D and see if you can add any other ideas to the checklist.

3   Acknowledging sources in a presentation

Just as in a piece of academic writing, it is important to acknowledge your sources properly in a presentation, using citations and a reference list.

Here are some basic rules for acknowledging sources in a presentation:

1   Any information from another source, whether in the text or a graphic, needs a citation.

2   In a PowerPoint presentation, the final slide should list your references.

3   In a science poster, the references should be included in a space at the bottom of the poster.

4   Every citation which appears in the main body of the presentation must have a corresponding reference in the final list.

3a These four slides come from a presentation about mining in the Arctic and contain a number of mistakes in the way the sources have been acknowledged. Use the rules above to help you identify the problems.

Slides	Problem

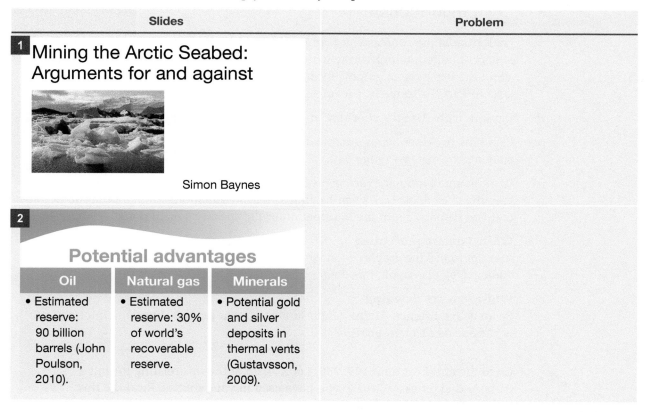

Slides	Problem

3

Drawbacks

- Over 80% of recoverable oil and gas is offshore
  Douglass Syme (1999) *Exploiting the Wilderness.*
  London: Mulberry.

- Negative environment impacts of human activity
  1. Contribution to ice-melt
  2. Death of Arctic wildlife
  3. Risk of accidents

4

References

- Gustavsson, D. (2009). Chasing shadows? The Difficulty of Accessing Mineral deposits in the Arctic.

- Douglass Syme (1999) *Exploiting the Wilderness* London: Mulberry.

3b Compare your answers with a partner.

> **UNIT TASK** **Ethno-tourism**

a Look back at the sources you read in the unit task for Part B. They contain a lot of data about ethno-tourism which could be presented in graphic form. Think about the best type of graphic format to use in order to present the data in the texts in Part B effectively. Create a graphic.

b Work in pairs. Use the checklist in 2b to evaluate each other's graphic.

c Plan how to present your graphic. Consider what you are trying to prove to your audience by displaying the data.

d Work in small groups. Practise presenting the information, including your graphic, to each other. As you listen to other presentations, think of questions that you can ask about the information or the speaker's main point.

While you are presenting
Attempt to use the graphic to make a point. What are you trying to prove to your audience by displaying this data?

While you are listening
Be an active listener – think of questions that you can ask about the information or the speaker's main point.

Go to the checklist on p.199–200. Look again at the tips relating to Unit 2 Parts A–C and tick (✓) those you have used in your studies. Read the tips relating to Unit 2 Part D on p.200.

Reporting
in writing

By the end of Part E you will be able to:

- structure an argument-based essay
- structure an essay to incorporate counterarguments
- support your argument effectively.

1 Structuring an argument-based essay

Many academic essays ask you to discuss or evaluate a topic. There are two basic types of response to essay questions like this:

- taking a relatively neutral stance on the topic
- taking a strong stance on the topic.

In the first case, the writer may present both supporting and opposing points in the main body of the essay, but not introduce their own opinion until a summary discussion at the end.

The second type is one in which the writer clearly presents a stance on the topic in the introduction, and then spends the essay trying to prove that this stance is correct or justified.

1a Read the essay below. Decide if it is opposing or supporting the use of in-vitro meat ('artificial' meat grown in an industrial tank). Then read the essay again. Underline any clear expressions of the author's stance on the topic.

Discuss the benefits and drawbacks of using in-vitro meat for human consumption

In-vitro cultured meat could soon be an everyday reality for millions of consumers. In-vitro meat is grown in a tank by culturing muscle cells from a living animal and enhancing them with artificial proteins. This is essentially the same technique as is already used for the production of yoghurt cultures. The ability to produce artificial meat in this way offers benefits to human health, the environment, and the welfare of animals currently bred for slaughter. However, it is a technology in its infancy, and though such meat has been successfully created in a number of experiments, no in-vitro meat is currently approved for human consumption. Important questions remain to be answered before it becomes a commonly accepted human food resource. This essay will consider arguments supporting the production of in-vitro meat, as well as those that maintain that such a method of meat production should not be pursued. The essay will conclude with this author's own view on the topic.

Experiments in the culturing of artificial meat have been continuing since the early 1990s, originally derived from NASA interest in a source of artificial protein for long-term space flights. In-vitro cultured meat offers a number of benefits: it is claimed that it is healthier than animal-grown meat, as food developers can control the nutritional content, in particular the fat content. A recent experiment (Olson, 2010, pp.43–44) showed that tank-grown in-vitro chicken was 80% leaner than its animal equivalent. Also, in-vitro meat is arguably kinder to animals. Scientists researching the possibilities of growing artificial meat find themselves in the rather odd position of being supported by vegetarian and vegan groups, as well as animal rights campaigners who normally focus on arguing against meat consumption. In a statement to the UK Food and Biotechnology Council, a leading in-vitro researcher noted that current methods of intensive farming of live animals for meat production clearly caused pain and distress for the animals involved. It was further noted that the culturing of completely artificial meat would be an effective answer to this, as the meat is grown without a nervous system, and therefore manufacturers are not faced with the ethical problem of causing pain (Chavez, 2009, p.108).

Some questions remain, however, about the wisdom of pursuing research into in-vitro meat for human consumption. At a recent cross-disciplinary conference addressing issues raised by cultured meat production, leading experts in food anthropology, bioethics and tissue engineering argued that there are problems with public acceptance of this source of food (Lawton, 2009, p.21). Many people are likely to be 'extremely hostile to the idea of "lab-grown" meat' (Lawton, 2009, p.24) and it is likely that it would take a very long time for the food to gain widespread acceptance. This would mirror the situation with Genetically Modified (GM) vegetables, which remain deeply unpopular in many nations. Sheer disgust at the idea, however, is not the only problem affecting public acceptance. In order for public adoption of the new meat resource, developers must first create a meat which is not only essentially the same as animal meat on a molecular level, but looks, feels and, above all, tastes like the 'real thing' (Chavez, 2009, p.113). Without that it is unlikely that in-vitro meat would ever overcome public prejudice against it, no matter how healthy, safe or ethically kind it was.

Despite the problem with consumer acceptance, researchers are confident that cultured meat will appear on supermarket shelves at some point in the near future. According to Monk (2000), this is due to external factors forcing the public to accept it, even perhaps in spite of themselves. Studies focusing on human population (indeed, overpopulation) and resource consumption have demonstrated that the adoption of artificial food technologies including cultured meat and GM crops will increasingly be seen as effective solutions to problems of world hunger and food security. One of the strongest claims in favour of pursuing the development of artificial meat is that it is better for the environment (Monk, 2000; Burwell, 2004a, 2004b; Wang, 2006). Cultured meat does not have any of the negative impacts associated with rearing cattle for slaughter, such as pollution from slurry and waste nitrates, as well as methane produced by the animals themselves. It also requires less water and makes land normally given over to rearing animals available for growing crops.

These claims of the positive benefits of cultured in-vitro meat have been challenged by economists, however. According to Keirle (2000, p.120), any environmental benefits from this method will be outweighed by the fact that it is economically uncompetitive when compared to traditional animal rearing. Farms are geared towards animal rearing, and the creation of enough of the right facilities to develop cultured meat would not only be enormously expensive in itself, but would mean the end of animal farming and consequent mass unemployment in that sector, with knock-on effects in the economy at large. Added to this is the problem of funding the further research needed to bring in-vitro meat to the point where it will be ready for commercial sale. Studies by Keirle (2000) as well as Monk (2000) estimate the investment of three to four billion dollars a year over the next decade in order to finish research and begin production of even a modest in-vitro meat operation.

The view that cultured meat will be economically unviable is echoed by Aagard (2007, p.98), who believes that the consequences to the economy of the failure of the existing farming and associated industries will make cultured meat production entirely unviable, at least in the medium term.

It is clear from the discussion outlined above that there are both potential benefits as well as philosophical and practical impediments to the production of in-vitro meat for human consumption. Benefits include healthier food achievable without inflicting cruelty on animals, as well as fewer negative impacts on the environment. Opposing arguments point out the huge amount of research work that needs to be done before in-vitro meat is deemed fit for human consumption, as well as the enormous problem of public revulsion at so-called 'Frankenfoods'. Potential benefits may be more than offset by the economic difficulties inherent in implementing such a system of meat production.

Taking all these arguments into consideration, it seems certain that in-vitro meat can be an effective solution to the problems of world hunger, human nutritional health and animal welfare. While it is certainly true that there is public opposition to the introduction of such a clearly 'unnatural' food source, world events may force its adoption despite initial reluctance. With more people around the world concerned with the ethical issues involved in food production, in-vitro meat may quickly come to be seen as an entirely positive development in the consumption history of our species.

References

Aagard, D. (2007). A brief introduction to the future of your food. *Journal of Tissue Science,* 2(2), 91–98.

Burwell, B. (2004a). In-vitro meat – a radical food innovation? *Food Chemistry Quarterly,* 7(2), 45–62.

Burwell, B. (2004b). *Public responses to new foods.* London: Guild Publishing.

Chavez, T. (2009). The acceptance problem. In P. Clarke & T. Haise (Eds.), *Food in the New Millennium* (p.107–119). New York: College Press.

Keirle, F. (2000). Culture, philosophy and IT. *Tissue Technologist, 16*(3), 111–130.

Lawton, P. (2009). Culture, bioethics and in-vitro meat. In P. Clarke & T. Haise (Eds.), *Food in the New Millennium* (19–29). New York: College Press.

Monk, Z. (2000). Perspectives on food production and the environment. *The Food Resource Journal, 6*(2), 1507–1516.

Olson, K. (2010). Controlling nutritional values in cultured proteins. *Journal of Enhanced Food Production, 9*(3), 40–51.

Wang, A. (2006). The environment and the development of 'artificial' meats. *Food Chemistry Quarterly, 9*(4), 97–109.

In the essay above, the writer has presented different views on the topic in a fairly neutral way. The essay contains the author's viewpoint in the concluding paragraphs, but not in the main body. As a result, the essay gives a neutral overview of the topic but does not present the author's own stance very strongly.

1b Work in pairs. Think of other ways to structure the essay above, which would allow the author to present a stronger argument, either in favour of or opposed to in-vitro meat.

1c Work with another pair of students. Compare your ideas.

2 Structuring an essay to incorporate counterarguments

A good argument should provide clear reasons and supporting evidence for your stance.

However, an argument which is based only on evidence that supports your point of view is likely to be relatively weak; there are almost always opposing views, or counterarguments, on any topic. A really strong argument might therefore include not only supporting points, but also counterarguments and refutation (evidence or comments which you include to prove that the counterargument is incorrect).

A possible basic plan for an argumentative essay is as follows:

Introduction: State viewpoint
- Situation or background
- Definitions of key words in your argument
- Central argument

Body: Support your viewpoint
- Reconfirm the central argument: usually the first argument presented
  - supporting argument 1
  - supporting argument 2
  - supporting arguments 3, 4, 5 … (depending on how long your essay is)
- Counterargument (any argument your opponent may present)
  - supporting counterargument 1
  - supporting counterargument 2
  - supporting counterarguments 3, 4, 5 …
- Refutation: any reasons which prove the counterargument is wrong
  - refutation of counterargument 1
  - refutation of counterargument 2
  - refutation of counterarguments 3, 4, 5 …

Conclusion: Restate viewpoint
- Restating the main argument and major supporting evidence
- Suggestions and recommendations

2a Think about the unit task topic on ethno-tourism. Work in small groups. Use the example structure above to brainstorm supporting arguments in favour of ethno-tourism, as well as counterarguments and refutations.

The plan above is only one way to include counterarguments and refutation in an essay. There are, of course, many possible ways to shape an academic argument in order to effectively express your stance on the topic.

A stronger argument normally includes a clear expression of the writer's stance in the introduction and then uses the main body to attempt to prove that the stance is correct through counterargument and refutation.

2b Work in groups. Look at these ways of organizing an argument-based academic text.

- Tell each other which of these structure plans you have used before and what the main arguments/counterarguments were.
- Discuss which of the structure plans might be a) simpler for the writer, b) easier for a reader to follow.

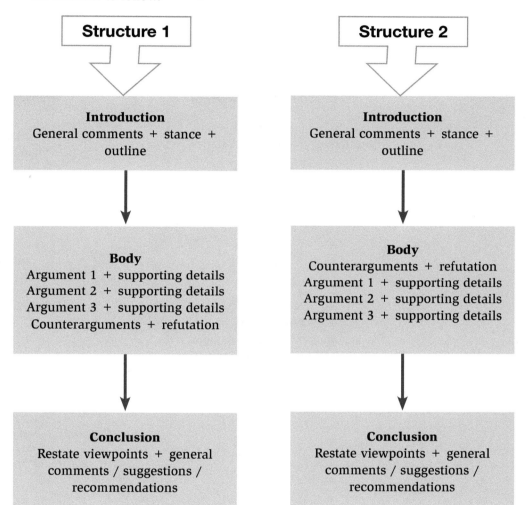

Structure 1	Structure 2
Introduction General comments + stance + outline	**Introduction** General comments + stance + outline
Body Argument 1 + supporting details Argument 2 + supporting details Argument 3 + supporting details Counterarguments + refutation	**Body** Counterarguments + refutation Argument 1 + supporting details Argument 2 + supporting details Argument 3 + supporting details
Conclusion Restate viewpoints + general comments / suggestions / recommendations	**Conclusion** Restate viewpoints + general comments / suggestions / recommendations

Structure 3

Introduction
General comments + stance + outline

↓

Body
Counterargument 1 + refutation + argument 1
Counterargument 2 + refutation + argument 2
Counterargument 3 + refutation + argument 3

↓

Conclusion
Restate viewpoints + general comments / suggestions / recommendations

Structure 4

Introduction
Definition + background (e.g. why this discussion is meaningful) + thesis statement

↓

Argument 1
State argument 1
Supporting source
Personal explanation / comments

↓

Argument 2
State argument 2
Supporting source
Personal explanation / comments

↓

Counterargument 1
State counterargument 1
Supporting source
Personal explanation / comments
Refutation

↓

Counterargument 2
State counterargument 2
Supporting source
Personal explanation / comments
Refutation

↓

Conclusion
Summary of the arguments + counterarguments
Restating the thesis/stance

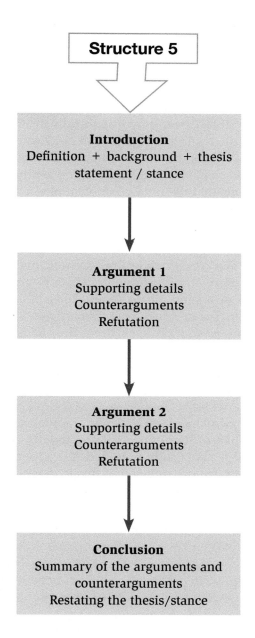

Structure 5

Introduction
Definition + background + thesis
statement / stance

Argument 1
Supporting details
Counterarguments
Refutation

Argument 2
Supporting details
Counterarguments
Refutation

Conclusion
Summary of the arguments and
counterarguments
Restating the thesis/stance

2c Work in pairs. Discuss your opinions about this essay question, based on what you have read in 1a. Then read the essay on p.108. Identify the writer's main idea and supporting claims.

To what extent is in-vitro meat a suitable substitute for reared animal meat?

To what extent is in-vitro meat a suitable substitute for reared animal meat?

1 A recent conference in Sweden optimistically concluded that in-vitro meat, a cultured meat grown artificially in a biotank, would be a viable commercial product within a decade (Van Der Zwan, 2009). The technology for developing this type of meat is sufficiently advanced that some test samples have already been created (though they are currently unfit for human consumption), and it seems that the prediction of commercial-grade in-vitro meat (hereafter IVM) within a decade is realistic. However, it is highly unlikely that this type of food will ever be a sufficient substitute for animal-reared meat, because of problems with nutritional content and public acceptance.

2 The current aim of researchers involved in the development of IVM is to produce an artificial meat which is 'equal in protein and calorific content to animal-reared meats' (Naes, 2008, p.317). However, this ignores the fact that animal-reared meat is a much richer source of dietary nutrition than simple calories and protein. According to Sands (2007), all IVM samples so far created lack the range of nutrients which natural meats can provide, including irreplaceable vitamins and minerals.

3 The true test of IVM's suitability as a commercial meat substitute is whether it sells well. Commercial IVM is unlikely to be readily adopted by consumers for two key reasons. Firstly, among the public at large there is a widespread dislike of highly artificial foodstuffs. This is evident in the suspicion with which genetically modified (GM) foodstuffs such as vegetables are treated. Sands (ibid.) argues that this is more likely to be the case with animal flesh, as the thought of creating artificial flesh strikes many people as particularly revolting.

4 Furthermore, public acceptance of IVM is likely to be low because of the difficulty of producing a product which tastes sufficiently like meat. While IVM test samples have demonstrated that the muscle tissue can be grown, there is, to put it simply, more to the taste of meat than the tissue itself. For instance, many world cuisines rely on the use of animal bone marrow to enhance the flavour of the food. A related issue is the texture of the meat, which relies on muscular development through active movement of a healthy animal. It is unlikely that a tank-grown artificial meat would have a texture that many consumers would find satisfying due to the simple fact that the muscle was never stimulated by exercise.

5 In summary, IVM is a clear example of a product which, despite being technically possible, is extremely unlikely to enjoy commercial success. This is due to the fact that in-vitro meats are not a satisfactory nutritional substitute for existing natural meats. There seems to be a strong emotional attachment to the idea of natural meat, which any artificial substitute will struggle to overcome.

2d Read the above essay again. Identify the purpose of each paragraph.

2e The essay could be made stronger by adding in some of these paragraphs. Work in pairs. Decide what the purpose of each paragraph is (e.g. argument, counterargument, refutation) and where you would insert it into the essay.

Paragraph A

In contrast to this, Keogh (2008) has responded to claims that consumers would reject IVM on grounds of taste and texture with the observation that most IVM, at least initially, will be offered as mince. Mince has an advantage over chunks of meat in this sense because it is relatively easy to add artificial flavourings to it which would make up for the absence of bone marrow, and it is likely to be used in highly flavoured dishes rather than eaten alone, as a steak would be. Keogh claims that consumers are less likely to notice a difference between IVM in mince form and the 'real' thing.

Paragraph B

Though vegetarian and animal rights groups are undoubtedly correct in saying that IVM is an ethical alternative to reared animal meats, Bell's assertion that this will be enough to overcome widespread consumer suspicion about IVM seems doubtful. Many people around the world (perhaps the majority) still refuse to eat GM food, despite the fact that it is routinely eaten by millions of Americans and there is no evidence, either scientific or anecdotal, to show that GM food is unhealthy. In light of this, I would argue that humans have a deep-seated horror at the idea of manipulating food, and this horror is unlikely to be shifted by ethical arguments or scientific evidence.

Paragraph C

However, whilst it may be true that mince is more acceptable on grounds of taste and texture than any other form of IVM, this is not the same thing as saying that it will be readily accepted at all. A number of blind taste studies investigating consumers' abilities to taste the difference between free range and battery meats suggested that most people were sensitive to the difference. It seems likely that this would also be the case with animal-reared meat versus IVM.

Paragraph D

Nevertheless, for those in favour of IVM, Bell (2008) notes that a number of vegetarian and animal rights groups actively support its development, on the grounds that it allows for a rich source of protein that does not involve pain, cruelty or the death of an animal. According to Bell, this sentiment is likely to become more common as people recognize the quality of IVM, and will help people to overcome their initial caution about consuming this new food.

3 Supporting your argument effectively

> Although organizing your argument appropriately and including opposing views can help strengthen your argument, you also need to carefully select and integrate any supporting sources into your writing.

3a There are several problems with the type and citation of evidence in this excerpt from a student essay. Read the essay carefully and underline any evidence that the author has provided.

Outline potential improvements in video-game technology in the next ten years and discuss their likely social impact

Video gaming is rapidly attaining the status of a revolutionary new social phenomenon. Since the introduction of the first primitive video games in the 1970s, and for the next twenty years, it remained either an amusing distraction or a niche hobby for computer enthusiasts. By 2010, however, over 35 million people worldwide are registered as members of online game communities, and the industry for buy-to-play video games in formats such as PC, handheld devices and home consoles is worth over £3 billion annually. This trend looks set to continue over the coming decade as video-games technology improves, perhaps prompting a far-reaching and permanent change in the way people spend their time, as gaming platforms come to be used for learning, communicating online in a synergistic combination of virtual worlds and messaging, or simply escaping from the real world for the pleasures of a high-fidelity futuristic universe.

Future technological improvements can be divided into three categories: graphical realism, online applications, and player interaction. According to Michael Jones (1999, p.203), 'Looking ahead we can see the much anticipated release of Zombie Dungeon 3 with improved AI and an awesome soundtrack from goth-metal band Organgrinder, then in December we have the release of SunCorporation's mouth-watering Gamebox, which boasts a mighty 2.5 gig processor.'

As a famous futurologist at MIT has said, games evolution will not stop at processing speeds. It will also include advances in online applications. Most people now have broadband Internet access and enjoy gaming for a hobby. Developments in online gaming will include streaming of high-quality games direct to the user's PC or game console, so that no initial purchase of a disk is required. This will allow for higher processing speeds, better graphics and less memory used on the player's home platform.

The gaming experience is likely to become even more vivid. The player currently interacts with the game through the medium of a glass screen, which reduces the sensation of realism. Proposed developments which could address this issue include a pair of goggles which the player can wear and on which the game is displayed, both giving a more direct experience of the game world as well as blocking out distractions (Norris, 2009). A further development in this concept has been proposed by Pantech, a high-tech systems integration company which is designing contact lenses that can display digital information to the wearer.

3b Work in pairs. Discuss what is wrong with the evidence.

3c Work in small groups. Discuss how the quality of the evidence could be improved in each case.

> **UNIT TASK** **Ethno-tourism**

Use all the work you have completed in Unit 2 on ethno-tourism to write an essay with this title: *Should ethno-tourism be encouraged?*
Your teacher will tell you how long the essay should be. The essay should express your own stance on the topic but also evaluate counterarguments.

a Complete the table with your essay plan.

Title		
Your main idea:		
Your supporting ideas:	**Evidence or citations:**	
	For	**Against**
1		
2		
3		
4		

b Write your answer to the essay title.

Remember:

- Use information from other sources to support your ideas.
- Use citations and a reference for each source you use.

 Go to the checklist on p.199–200. Look again at the tips relating to Unit 2 Parts A–D and tick (✓) those you have used in your studies. Read the tips relating to Unit 2 Part E on p.200.

Unit 3 The individual in society

Unit overview

Part	This part will help you to ...	By improving your ability to ...
A	Understand and identify the strength of speakers' claims	• evaluate the strength of a speaker's claim • recognize speculative claims and why people use them • judge speculations as you listen • investigate claims through questions
B	Evaluate the logic of written texts	• identify logical flaws in the relationship of ideas • understand necessary and sufficient conditions • understand correlation and causation
C	Organize information from notes	• take notes which are relevant to an assignment • synthesize information from your notes • reference sources correctly in synthesized notes • reflect on notes to help clarify your ideas
D	Plan for an effective presentation	• identify your purpose in giving a presentation • present an oral summary of research • include alternative points of view in a presentation
E	Use information from other sources in your writing	• synthesize sources in writing • incorporate quotations into writing • incorporate paraphrase into writing • understand plagiarism and patchwriting • use hedging

Understanding spoken information

By the end of Part A you will be able to:
- evaluate the strength of a speaker's claim
- recognize speculative claims and why people use them
- judge speculations as you listen
- investigate claims through questions.

1 Evaluating the strength of a speaker's claim

A claim is a statement made by a speaker or author, in which they state their position on a topic. A claim can appear as the speaker's main idea, or thesis, or it may be a supporting claim that contributes to the main idea. A claim is a component of an argument.

1a Read this short excerpt from a speech and identify the claim that the speaker has made.

'Humans are essentially like other living creatures: we are made of cells, we have a similar chemical composition, we have a system of organs inside our bodies, and we reproduce. We also carry basic genetic information inside our bodies. But one of the things that makes us distinct from other creatures is that each one of us has a clear sense of our own, individual identity.'

1b In pairs, review the information in Unit 2 Part B about evaluating arguments (p.77), then decide which of these factors can make a claim more valid. Finally, decide how valid the claim made in the excerpt in 1a is.

1 The speaker strongly believes that the claim is true.

2 It is based on reasonable premises.

3 Many other writers agree with the claim.

4 There are no illogical leaps in the argument.

5 The claim is supported by evidence.

6 The claim is common knowledge.

7 The claim is not based on mistaken assumptions.

1c You are going to listen to part of a lecture about human identity. Before you listen, work in groups and discuss these questions.

1 Which of these are parts of your identity?

the ideas you have   the way you behave   your language   the colour of your skin

your DNA   your fingerprints   your body weight   your gait

the colour of your eyes   the colour and style of your hair   your religion

your culture   your education   your nationality   your gender

the shape of your face   the clothes you wear   your political beliefs

your emotions   your posture

2 How would you define 'individual identity'?

3 Do you have the same identity all the time, or does it change depending on the situation you are in?

4 How do you feel about the police or government keeping records of your identity? What information do you think it is necessary for them to keep?

3.1

1d Listen to the lecture. Make a note of any claims that the speaker makes.

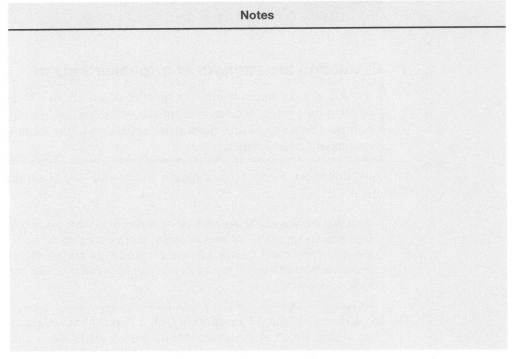

Notes

1e Compare your notes with your partner. Then work together to answer these questions and decide how strong the claim was.

1 What premises did the speaker base her claims on?

2 Is the speaker's idea about this logical?

3 What evidence did the speaker provide for the claim?

2 Recognizing speculative claims and why people use them

> *Strong claims* are based on reasonable premises and supported by suitable arguments and evidence.
>
> *Speculation*, on the other hand, is really just a reasoned guess about what might be true. Speculation is not usually supported by evidence, and the premises on which it is based may be faulty.

2a Look at the two sentences below. Which is an example of a strong claim, and which is speculation?

1 Fingerprints are probably the most practical and effective way of identifying criminals.

2 Because of technical and ethical problems with the building of DNA databases (Thorpe, 2008; Dunn & Hurst, 2010), fingerprints are, at present, probably the most practical and effective way of identifying criminals.

> Why speculate? As we have seen above, speculation is not based on strong premises, argument or evidence. This raises the question of why people speculate in academic situations.

2b In pairs, read these possible explanations for speculation. Decide why the speaker might be speculating. Is the speculation acceptable to an academic audience or not?

1 The speaker is making a claim in order to deliberately persuade listeners to agree. However, the speaker knows that they have no evidence to support it.

2 The speaker believes the claim so strongly that they overlooked the need for supporting evidence.

3 The speaker is guessing about events in the past for which no evidence is available.

4 The speaker is proposing possible future developments.

5 The speaker is trying to encourage discussion or inspire new thinking on a topic.

3 Judging speculations as you listen

3a Work in pairs. Review your notes on individual identity from 1d. What is your stance on this topic now?

3b Work in pairs. You are going to listen to the rest of the lecture about individual identity. In this section of the lecture, the speaker adopts the stance that the idea of 'identity' will become more flexible in the future. Before you listen, discuss your response to the speaker's stance, using these questions to help you.

1 To what extent do you agree with the speaker?

2 If you disagree, what problems can you see with the stance?

3 What evidence or support would the speaker need to provide to help you agree fully?

3.2

3c Listen to the excerpt from the lecture. Write notes on these topics.

- physical identity in the future
- online behaviour
- privacy in the future

3d Work in pairs. Use your notes to help you discuss these questions.

1 What point did the speaker make about DNA testing?

2 What evidence did the speaker provide to support this?

3 Can you think of any arguments against this?

4 Was the speaker's point a valid claim, or speculation?

4   Investigating claims through questions

> Identifying speculation can give a good opportunity for questions and discussion on a topic.

4a   Read and underline the speculations in Audioscript 3.2 in **Appendix 5**. Then compare your ideas with a partner. Try to agree on what you both consider to be speculation.

4b   For each of the speculations you identified in 4a, try to create a suitable type of question based on premises 1–4 below. (You may wish to review Unit 2 Part A3, about types of questions.)

1   The speaker has speculated that people will radically change their physical identity several times in their lives. You think that this is very unlikely. Try to form a question in order to dispute this.

2   The speaker has speculated that people will be more comfortable with the idea of dramatically changing their physical identity through surgery. You think that this is very unlikely. Try to form a question in order to dispute this.

3   The speaker has speculated that DNA testing for identity will become routine. You are not sure if you think that this is likely and would like the speaker to give some evidence or a better explanation. Ask a question which will help you decide whether you think the speculation is reasonable.

4   You think that the speaker's speculation about the effects of greater openness on individual identity is interesting. However, you would like to know more about the speaker's ideas about the consequences of this. Ask a question to enquire about the consequences of this speculation being true.

➤ UNIT TASK   Biometrics

The Unit 3 task is about biometrics – the way that physical characteristics can be used to identify people. At the end of each part, you will be asked to complete a stage of the task as follows:

Part A: Listen to an introduction to the topic.

Part B: Read two texts about it.

Part C: Work in groups to research the topic.

Part D: Prepare and deliver a group presentation on the topic.

Part E: Write an essay on one of these titles:

1   *Give an overview of art projects or installations that have been created relating to biometrics. Suggest an art project or installation that could be created using biometrics to explore ideas of identity and privacy.*

2   *A single mother who relies on benefit payments from the government was asked to join a biometric database to enable her to be fingerprint-scanned when she collected her payments each week. The woman refused on religious grounds and the government office cancelled her benefit payments as a result. To what extent was the government justified in doing this?*

3 *You wish to create a biometric scanning system to control access to a secure workplace. Two possible methods for this are Iris Recognition and AFIS (Automated Fingerprint Identification System). Use existing literature to evaluate the effectiveness of the two methods and make a recommendation about which method is preferable. Use the findings from your evaluation as a justification.*

4 *Use of biometrics for security in commercial organizations such as banks is becoming more widespread. However, members of the public are still wary of the use of biometric systems. Assess the benefits that different biometric systems offer compared to conventional security measures such as passwords and written signatures. Consider reliability, price and public acceptance.*

a You are about to listen to a general introduction to biometrics. Work in groups. Discuss these questions.

1 How much do you know about the uses of biometrics?

2 How do you feel about the use of biometric systems (like iris scans or the use of your DNA) for checking your identity?

b On a separate piece of paper, prepare a Cornell-style layout to take your notes.

3.3

c Listen to the lecture. Make general notes on the topic.

d Spend some time reflecting on your notes. Add comments and questions to the notes.

e Work in small groups with classmates who are interested in writing the same assignment title as you. Share the ideas from your notes and discuss the topic with your group.

Go to the checklist on p.201 and read the tips relating to Unit 3 Part A.

Understanding written information

By the end of Part B you will be able to:

- identify logical flaws in the relationship of ideas
- understand necessary and sufficient conditions
- understand correlation and causation.

1 Identifying logical flaws in the relationship of ideas

1a Read this text. What is the writer's main idea?

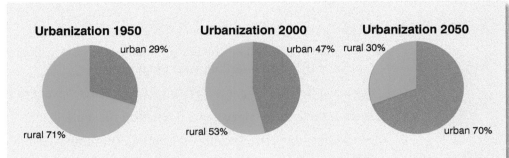

Figure 1: Urbanization since 1950

The human race is very rapidly turning into an urban species. In the past 50 years there has been a massive increase in the number of people living in cities around the world. In the mid-1950s about 850 million people, approximately 30% of the world's total population, lived in cities. By the year 2005 that number had climbed to a little over three billion, or about 48% of the world's population (BBC, 2006). In the developed nations that represents about 70–80% of the population. Analysts predict that by the middle of the 21st century the global population will also be about 80% urban. An interesting parallel can be seen in the rise of stress-related mental illnesses. An in-depth World Health Watch report (WHW, 2008) which surveyed respondents in 112 countries found that people who considered themselves to be suffering from stress had risen 38% in the ten years since the previous study. Symptoms included headaches, feelings of fatigue, sleeplessness and irritability, as well as secondary health problems like gain or loss of weight and a lowered immunity to infection.

Cities, with their crowds, 24-hour culture and busy lifestyles, are stressful places to live. As the evidence above clearly demonstrates, the increase in urbanization worldwide is causing a huge increase in the number of people suffering from stress. As the urban population is predicted to continue growing throughout the 21st century, it is of vital importance that more funding be given to mental health programmes in order to help combat the negative effects of this shift in lifestyles.

1b In the text in 1a there is something wrong with the writer's argument. Read through the text again and discuss what the problem might be with a partner.

> The text above has a *logical flaw*, meaning that there is some mistake in the logic of what the author has claimed; either the reasoning isn't correct, or it doesn't support the conclusion. You can develop your skill as a critical thinker by questioning whether logical flaws exist in the work that you are reading.

1c Look again at the text in 1a. Work in pairs. Try to imagine why this flaw has appeared in the author's work. Think of as many possible explanations as you can.

1d Read through the ideas from the two people below. What are the differences in their explanations for the flaw

> I think that whoever wrote this made a basic mistake with their thinking. Sure it may be true that urbanization is increasing and also true that stress is on the rise worldwide, but that doesn't mean that the two of them are related. Stress could be rising for all sorts of reasons besides the fact that more people are living in cities. And even if there is a connection, is it the only reason? The author's mistake here is to be too simplistic and jump to the conclusion that because stress is rising, it must be caused by urbanization and that urbanization is the only cause.

> This is rather suspicious. The fact that urbanization and stress are both on the rise doesn't automatically mean that they are related, or that one of them is causing the other one. I think the writer is insisting that there is a connection between them without considering other possible explanations. But I'm not sure it's just a mistake. The bit at the end where it talks about the need for more funding … is the person who wrote this a doctor? It looks to me like a deliberate attempt to get more funding by claiming that there's a link between stress and urbanization.

Logical flaws can appear in a piece of work for a number of reasons. They could be the result of a genuine mistake by the writer. However, it may also be that the writer is deliberately trying to persuade the reader to accept an idea which is false.

There are different types of logical flaws, many of which will be explored further throughout the book. This unit will look at flaws in the relationship between ideas or parts of an argument.

---

2 Necessary and sufficient conditions

2a Work in small groups. Make a list of things which are necessary for something to be called a university.

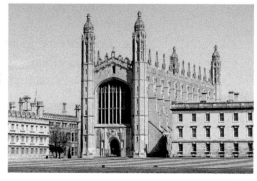

All universities …
have a library.

2b Share your ideas with your classmates. Do you agree?

> The things you have chosen may be called the *necessary conditions* for being a university. In other words, for something to be called a university it is necessary that it has these things. For example, if something does not have students, then it cannot be a university. Therefore, having students is a necessary condition of being a university.
>
> It is relatively easy to decide what the necessary conditions for some things are. However, it is usually more difficult to determine the necessary conditions for claims in many academic subjects.

2c Read this text. Identify the writer's main claim.

> A love of music is one of the greatest gifts that we can give our children. Psychological studies show that adults who listen to music regularly are more relaxed and report being happier overall than those who do not enjoy listening to music. This effect is even more pronounced with adults who actually play musical instruments. It seems that being involved in making music stimulates areas of the brain that are important for academic achievement, relaxation, emotional understanding, a sense of happiness and empathy with others. A 2004 study by Carlsson, in which groups of top performers in the fields of music, art, science, business and education were surveyed for psychological well-being, found that the group of music professionals were significantly calmer and had a greater sense of well-being than their counterparts in other professions. Moreover, in a test of empathy for others, they scored higher on average than any other group. It seems clear, therefore, that involvement in music at a high level can provide a number of psychological benefits. From this we may conclude that providing extra musical education to children is critical in order for them to become happy and psychologically mature adults.

2d Use your own knowledge of the world to help you decide your answers to these questions.

    1 Is it possible to become a happy adult without having extra musical education?

    2 Do you know any adults who play musical instruments but who are not especially happy?

2e Work in small groups. Compare your answers. Then decide if having extra musical education is a necessary condition for being a happy adult.

2f Look at the list of possible conditions for a child to grow up to be a talented musician in adult life. Which of them are necessary to become a talented musician?

1 Receiving a lot of extra music education in childhood

2 Being interested in music

3 Coming from a musical family

4 Knowing how to play a musical instrument

5 Owning a musical instrument

6 Being able to read music

2g Work in small groups. Can you think of any other necessary conditions?

> It is important to distinguish between necessary conditions and sufficient conditions. Most people would probably agree that Point 2 in 2f is one of the necessary conditions for being a talented musician. However, is Point 2 by itself *sufficient* to be a talented musician? In other words, do you think that this statement is true or false?
>
> *If you are interested in music, then you will become a talented musician in adult life.*

2h Complete this rule about necessary and sufficient conditions by choosing the best underlined word.

We can only say that a claim has met the sufficient conditions for being true if *some/all* of the necessary conditions have been met.

2i Read this text about children who behave violently or aggressively. Identify the writer's main claim.

The link between violent video games and childhood aggression

A case study by researchers at the National Institute for Health investigated the case of 'Billy', an 11-year-old American male who routinely exhibited particularly violent behaviour. This included vicious attacks on his family members, resulting in broken bones on more than one occasion and three instances in which the police were called in response to violent outbursts. Billy was also responsible for a series of violent incidents directed at passersby outside his house. Over the course of the study (three years) Billy was expelled from a total of four schools, in each case because of violence directed at pupils or staff, and at the time of writing had been out of the education system for six months.

Besides recording physical expressions of violence, researchers also conducted a number of interviews with Billy aimed at investigating the triggers for his violent behaviour. It emerged from these interviews that Billy feels empowered by engaging in violence and that he lacks empathy with his victims to a significant extent.

Academically, Billy is an underachiever. He is socially marginalized because of his behaviour and has few friends. His sole interest is playing violent video games, for an average of seven hours a day. Though the research evidence is inconclusive, it seems reasonable to conclude that these games are the cause and inspiration of Billy's violent behaviour.

2j Work in pairs to discuss these questions.

1 Is the writer's claim sufficient to explain why Billy is a violent child?

2 Do you think that playing violent video games is one of the necessary conditions for becoming a violent child?

3 Correlation and causation

3a This text describes two phenomena: the popularity of certain celebrities, and the popularity of certain baby names. Read the text, then complete the table below.

> Studies show a clear link between the popularity of certain celebrities and choices of new baby names, with more babies being given the same name as top celebrities in the years when those celebrities are at the peak of their popularity. In the year 1984, for instance, the singer Mike Jackman was listed as the most popular entertainer in the country by Modern Times magazine. This was based on a national popularity survey as well as sales of albums and concert tickets and the value of associated merchandise. In the following year, the name Mike had jumped in the rankings of most popular boys' names from 8th place to 1st. By 1997, singer Alyssa Dickens was top of the charts, and placed 3rd in Modern Times' rankings. The name Alyssa jumped into the top 10 baby girls' names for the first time ever in the following year. By 2006, the actor and singer Jacob Stringer was voted most popular entertainer, as well as being voted world's sexiest man and being selected as a UN cultural ambassador. In the year 2007, the most popular name for baby boys was Jacob, which had risen from 9th place two years previously.

Year	Popular celebrity	Popular baby name
1985		
1998		
2007		

3b Work in pairs. Decide what we can conclude about the relationship between the names of celebrities and babies from the information in the text.

> We can say that there is a relationship of *correlation* between two phenomena if knowing the value or quality of one allows us to predict the value or quality of the other.
>
> We can say that there is a relationship of *causation* between two phenomena if a change in the value or quality of one is followed by a change in the value or quality of the other.
>
> *Example*
> The correlation between the number of books in a child's home and their adult salary does not mean that if you artificially introduce a large number of books then you'll increase their eventual salary. It instead suggests that families who value books are also likely to be families who emphasize the importance of learning. It is the emphasis on the value of school that causes the increase in the likelihood of academic success, which in turn leads to higher salary.
>
>
>
> Emphasis on importance of study
>
> ↓
>
> Number of books in home + Likelihood of academic success
>
> ↓
>
> Higher salary
>
>

3c Work in pairs. Answer these questions.

1 In the case above, which of these statements is probably true?

   a When certain baby names become popular, this causes celebrities with the same name to become more popular.

   b When certain celebrities become very popular, this causes other people to name their babies after the celebrity.

   c The popularity of certain celebrities and the number of babies with the same name are coincidental; they are caused by different things.

2 Are celebrity and baby names correlated?

3 Is there a relationship of causation between celebrity and baby names?

> In the case of celebrity popularity and baby names, the two things are correlated (when one changes, either rising or falling, the other is also seen to change) and it is likely that one of them causes the other one as well. However, things can be correlated without being causally related.

3d Read the two paragraphs, which describe different phenomena, and the three possible explanations which follow them. Which one do you think is the most likely explanation?

A

Many people believe that road traffic accidents tend to be at their highest in winter when it is cold and dark and roads can be slippery with ice or snow. However, according to a recent Canadian road safety report, this view, while understandable, is incorrect. The report states that the number of serious road accidents reaches its yearly peak in August, with 80% of accidents happening in clear driving weather on roads which are dry.

B

Rainbows are the optical phenomenon in which the spectrum of visible light appears in an arc in the sky. In order for a rainbow to occur, there must be a combination of bright sunshine and localized rain, so that from the viewer's perspective, sunlight is shining through the water droplets in the sky. Rainbows tend to occur more frequently in the summer months than in winter.

1 Drivers are distracted by rainbows, therefore when more rainbows appear in the sky, there are more road accidents.

2 Both the increase in road traffic accidents and the incidence of rainbows are caused by summer conditions – the weather is more suitable for rainbows at that time of year and there are more cars on the road during the summer holidays.

3 The fact that both car accidents and the number of rainbows increase at the same time is purely coincidental.

> In this case, the two phenomena are correlated (when one changes, the other also changes), but most people would agree that neither one causes the other. Instead, some other factor explains why they both rise at the same time.

3e Read the two texts. Identify the phenomena that are being described.

Neighbourhood residents fear rise in gang crime

The children of this inner-city district have become accustomed to gang violence – CCTV cameras are now a routine fixture in schools, and reports of gang-related crimes occur two or three times a week. According to one local police officer, there is a rise in the number of gang crimes involving young teenagers, as well as an increased tendency to use weapons. Everyone agrees that the gang culture is spreading. Approximately 78 people were injured in gang attacks last month, up by 20% for the same month in the previous year. Official police statistics for this district show that, despite an overall decrease in the amount of crime, the number of gang crimes is on the rise.

According to a local youth worker, young people in this area feel desperate and excluded from the mainstream culture. They feel that they have no opportunities and nowhere to go and are trapped in a cycle of poverty. Joining a gang gives them a sense of identity, new friends, and relationships which are meaningful to them. It has become the norm for children as young as 13 and 14 to join local gangs and an increasing number of them are involved in more serious violence.

Children, branding and adult fashions

A wealth of recent evidence indicates that high-end clothing brands are increasingly targeting their products at younger consumers. A number of well-known brands, which were previously seen as luxury items that only adults could afford, now target products at the 11 to 14 age group. Of particular interest in this study is the rise in popularity of clothing items and accessories that are associated with the 'gangster rap' image.

Robins and Hill (2007) have noted the rising incidence of major brands producing children's or even infant versions of typically 'adult' items, ranging from logo-branded wallets, purses and jewellery to underwear items. Robins and Hill discovered that over 200 companies which had previously produced adult-only fashions had introduced children's versions of their products between the years 2004 and 2006. What is notable about this is that the items were not, strictly speaking, children's clothing, but were simply smaller-sized copies (or imitations) of products available in their adult ranges. A similar finding exists in statistics published by the National Retailers Association (2008). According to that report, sales of branded goods for children by luxury retailers had risen 18% on the previous year. Lerner et al. (2009) have characterized this as marking a shift in the notion of childhood, from wearing typically childish or youthful clothing to that which mimics clothing worn by adults. Lerner et al. argue that this encourages children to identify with the symbolically adult message of the brands.

This study will focus on the increasing popularity of brands which are associated with gang and street styles among children and teenagers, and the increasing promotion of child-sized versions of clothing and accessories which carry a gang-like symbolic theme. This trend is evident both in sales figures and in recent product lines aimed directly at children. For instance, the apparel company MDK, which produces clothing, footwear and accessories that are self-consciously styled on gang motifs (MDK marketing report, 2007), released a range of jeans and sweats in 2005 which were sized for children in the 8 to 14 age group. Sales of the jeans have shown steady growth since then, encouraging the company to plan a larger range of children's goods.

3f Work in pairs. Answer these questions about the texts.

1 Are the two phenomena related?

2 Does one of the phenomena cause the other one?

3 Is there some other cause which may explain the phenomenon in the first text?

3g Read the text on p.125 and identify the writer's claim about the relationship between two phenomena.

Musical ability as a predictor of academic success?

An issue of particular interest to teachers involved with secondary and further education is the relationship between music education and academic achievement. A number of studies suggest that there is a positive link between them, with students who receive music education typically outperforming their peers on tests in other academic subjects. Gardener (1995), for instance, reports in a study of approximately 20,000 UK sixth-form students that those participating in music received better grades in languages, science and maths than those students who did not. Similar results have been reported by Cardarelli (2003) and Trent (1996).

Cardarelli's study measured the impact of a special course of music instruction on academic test outcomes in US third-grade students compared to a control group who did not receive such classes. Cardarelli found a statistically significant difference in the grades achieved by the students who received the specialized music programme, and concluded that the music education had a positive effect on academic grades overall.

Trent (1996) investigated the effects of enrolment in a specialized music programme among US students, tracking their grades from the sixth to twelfth grades. Trent found a significant difference in the language and maths scores of students who had received the extra music classes compared to peers who had not received particular music instruction. Similarly to Cardarelli, Trent has concluded that the study of music helps students to achieve higher academic grades overall.

3h Compare your answer with a partner, then discuss whether you think the claim is effective or not.

➤ UNIT TASK **Biometrics**

In this unit task, you will research information for the essay title you chose in Part A.

a Take Cornell-style notes on a separate piece of paper while reading the two texts below.

While you are reading, bear in mind these points:

- Think about how the information you are reading relates to the assignment title you have chosen.
- Pay attention to the logic of the author's claims. Underline any parts of the text where you think there is a logical flaw.

b After you finish reading, critically review your notes.

Text 1

Commercial factors in the growth of biometrics

Sales of biometric recognition systems are booming. Since the first stage of their widespread adoption in the mid 1990s, we have witnessed the introduction of a 'flood' of technologies (Crompton, 2002, p.4), with a corresponding increase in sales. This growth has been propelled by interest both from the commercial sector and consumers, as well as government involvement, though the motives for adoption are varied.

For businesses involved in financial transactions, biometric technology offers a fully secure means of authentication. More traditional authentication methods such as PIN numbers and signatures, while offering a measure of certainty, are by no means foolproof. A trained forger can replicate most signatures with ease, while PINs, if written down, can be lost or stolen. Even if the valid user of a PIN number has not been foolish enough to write the information down, the number can still be acquired through coercion such as the threat of violence. The expansion of interest in commercial applications of biometric authentication comes at the same time as a general increase in the number of digital transactions; increasingly sophisticated online fraud has accompanied this growth as neither PIN numbers nor signatures offer enough security in an electronic marketplace. It is now more important than ever to have strong methods of ID authentication which can be transmitted digitally, hence the rising use of biometrics, which offer a high level of certainty about the user's ID and are difficult – if not impossible – to forge or steal.

Besides offering a higher level of security, commercial biometric alternatives to PINs, signatures and passwords have quickly become popular with users. In a non-biometric world, each of us is forced to remember several different PINs, carry a number of identity cards, perhaps, and remember an impossible number of passwords. The results are predictable: PINs are written down for the sake of convenience, while users resort to simple passwords that are easy to guess, or make the mistake of using the same password to secure a number of different systems. Biometric identity systems, by contrast, offer the pleasing convenience of a single identifier, such as a fingerprint or face scan. It does not need to be remembered, you carry it with you all the time (how could you not?) and it is impossible to lose. Public acceptance due to the convenience that biometrics offer, therefore, has greatly helped in the diffusion of such technologies. The spread of commercial biometrics in the last ten years has also been assisted by a general decrease in the price of such units. Hand and iris scanners remain expensive, but fingerprint scanners are relatively cheap, and facial recognition need be no more expensive than a camera and some software. A number of biometric companies, with large budgets for development and marketing, have emerged in the last decade and aggressively promote the growth of their industry.

With an eye to the future, we can predict that technological improvements will continue to propel growth in this area, despite claims from some critics that biometric systems are not reliable enough. The reliability of biometrics is in fact already very high, though it remains true that any current biometric system will incorrectly recognize a proportion of unauthorized users (or reject legitimate ones). This is due to environmental and physical factors. For instance, with face-recognition technology, light or darkness can impact the quality of the reading, as can the angle at which the individual stands in response to the reader. Scans of the iris or retina currently require the subject individual to position themselves precisely in relation to the scanner and can also be confounded by people wearing dark glasses or contact lenses. Even fingerprint scans are not currently foolproof. However, as technology improves we can expect to see biometric systems having consistently better recognition rates, which will encourage consumer and business confidence in using the technology to secure financial transactions. It is likely that, as we move towards a cashless economy in which all goods and services are bought and paid for electronically, biometrics will come to replace PINs, passwords and signatures entirely.

References

Crompton, M. (2002). *Biometrics and Privacy: The End of the World as We Know It or The White Knight Of Privacy?* Paper presented at the Biometrics Security and Authentication Biometrics Institute Conference in Sydney, 20 March 2002.

Source: Willis, A. (2009). Commercial Factors in the growth of biometrics. *Security Systems, 31*(3), 103–129.

Text 2

Biometrics: current growth and future trends

Brigitte Wirtz, writing more than a decade ago, observed that biometric technologies had 'left their childhood behind' (Wirtz, 2000, p.12). A recent report by the industrial market research group Acuity supports this claim, noting that the biometrics market has enjoyed strong growth in the first years of the 21st century and predicting sustained growth of the market at least to the year 2020 (Acuity Market Intelligence, 2009). The boom in biometrics has been fuelled by a combination of market enthusiasm for a secure identification system, as well as government interest and investment in its development. This paper will briefly outline some of the drivers behind the growth in biometrics and also look forward somewhat to likely trends in the years ahead.

Commercial drivers of growth

It has been noted elsewhere that the current healthy status of the biometrics market owes itself to enthusiasm in the business community for security devices which offer genuine protection against fraud and identity theft. Conventional authentication devices such as signatures, PINs and passwords have obvious security weaknesses to which biometrics offer a tempting solution. This offers obvious benefits for companies and consumers involved in electronic financial transactions in which trust is paramount. However, biometrics have also proved themselves useful in providing physical security for high value consumer items: we are seeing an increasing number of laptops, mobile phones and cars which are securely locked by biometric fingerprint scans and which present no opportunity to even the most enterprising of thieves. This has helped to raise public confidence about consumer biometrics and, alongside the perhaps 'sexy' image that this technology enjoys ("Biometric Statistics in Focus", 2006, p.8), has contributed to a great deal of enthusiastic acceptance of its introduction.

Government drivers of growth

Government agencies can also claim credit for helping to popularize biometric technologies. Identity theft is a serious threat for official government services, everything from tax returns to applications for driving licences and passports, resulting in the need for strong ID authentication measures to guard against the serious risk of criminal misuse of such sensitive data. A large (and steadily increasing) number of government departments have started inviting citizens to enrol biometric data such as fingerprints or DNA to help make official work more efficient (identification becomes faster) but also more secure against the risk of fraud.

Despite its clear usefulness for situations where it is necessary to authenticate that an individual is actually who they claim to be, biometrics has also proved its worth for government and law enforcement in situations requiring identification of anonymous individuals in a crowd. Biometrics enjoyed a boom in sales worldwide after the September 11th terror attacks in New York, and government funding for law or national security linked biometric systems has shown no signs of drying up in the years since. The deployment of biometric identification systems by police is becoming commonplace. Recent examples of this, of which there are many, include the use of biometric iris scanners in an effort to identify individuals on 'wanted' lists ("Biometric Statistics in Focus", 2006, p.8) as well as the proliferation of face-recognition systems on public cameras in the UK (Nieto et al., 2005).

A view of the future

If Acuity's forecasts are correct, we can expect to see continued strong growth of the biometric market over the coming decade, as well as the appearance of greater numbers of biometric ID systems in all aspects of daily life.

At the time of writing, the most common biometric systems are AFIS type (Automated Fingerprint Identification System), which are relatively cheap and enjoy the benefit of familiarity among the public. However, AFIS scans are less reliable than, say, iris or retinal scans. These latter systems are still far from perfect as they require the user to position themselves in relation to a machine in order for the scan to take place. Nevertheless, it seems reasonable to suggest that with continued research investment, these problems will be overcome within a few years and iris and retinal scans will become more commonplace. Even stronger authentication is possible using vein pattern recognition or even body odour. However, such systems are still either experimental or have had very limited application so far. In the long term, however, it is probable that the greater security these offer will mean that they are widely introduced.

The drawback of most current systems (with the exception of face recognition technology) is that they require the person being identified to actually have contact with a scanner of some sort – pressing their finger or hand to a glass pad, or allowing a laser scan of the rear of the eye. These are seen as being invasive, unhygienic and infringing on privacy rights in some cases. Overall, there will be a trend in the coming years towards remote scanning systems which allow the user to be scanned without having to make contact with the scanner, or even possibly without their knowledge. It is certain that whatever technology is introduced, fraudsters and professional criminals will attempt to find ways around it with increasingly sophisticated forgeries and so we will probably witness the introduction of integrated biometric systems which increase the reliability of identification matches. Integrated systems, for instance, will link an iris scan with a check of the subject's heart rate, sweat level and so on at the moment of the scan for the possibility of telltale signs of dishonesty.

Further into the future we must consider the likelihood of 'function creep'. As integrated biometric scans become more commonplace, and better able to reveal the most intimate details of your physical condition, it may be that a single scan for ID purposes might also be used to give a simultaneous health check, revealing information which could affect an individual's ability to get health insurance, lead to problems with the boss if it emerges that they've been drinking too much or taking illegal drugs, or be sold on to marketing companies who could use it to target advertising at the subject of the scan.

Some of these claims may rightly be dismissed as speculation, but what is undeniable is that biometrics is here to stay, and that its use is only likely to become more widespread. It will increasingly impact our lives in the years to come.

References

Acuity Market Intelligence. (2009). *The Future of Biometrics* (Revised Edition). Louisville CO: Acuity Market Intelligence. Retrieved from http://www.acuitymi.com/Future_of_Biometrics.html

Biometric Statistics in Focus. (2006, February). *Biometric Technology Today, 14*(2), 7–9.

Nieto, M., Johnston-Dodds, K., & Simmons, C. (2002). *Public and Private Applications of Video Surveillance and Biometric Technologies*. Sacramento: Californian Research Bureau.

Wirtz, B. (2000, Autumn). Biometric Systems 101 and Beyond. *Secure: The Silicon Trust Quarterly Report, 1*, 12–21.

Source: Siebold, P. (2011). Biometrics: current growth and future trends. *Surveillance Technology Quarterly, 2*(3), 433–436.

Go to the checklist on p.201. Look again at the tips relating to Unit 3 Part A and tick (✓) those you have used in your studies. Read the tips relating to Unit 3 Part B.

Investigating

By the end of Part C you will be able to:

- take notes which are relevant to an assignment
- synthesize information from your notes
- reference sources correctly in synthesized notes
- reflect on your notes to help clarify your ideas.

1   Taking notes which are relevant to an assignment

> You may be expected to read a large amount of material by yourself in preparation for writing essays or reports. It is tempting to assume that all of the material you have been given must be relevant to the topic simply because the teacher has assigned it to you. However, the most successful notes are selective, containing only information which is directly relevant to the assignment title that you have been given.

1a   Work in small groups. Discuss how you feel about fashion and clothes. Is the way your clothes look an important part of your own identity?

1b   Work in pairs. Read the assignment title below. Discuss what the assignment is asking you to do.

To what extent do items of clothing and jewellery reflect the true identity of the wearer?

1c   Three different students have taken notes on the topic. Work in pairs. Look at the notes (A–C). Decide which one is most relevant to the assignment title.

A

Svendsen, L. (2006). Fashion : a philosophy.
London : Reaktion.

Fashion origin   =   Late medieval period
       ↓   e.g. renaissance.
                              (little change in clothing
"decisive event   before that.) P. 21
in world history"
P. 23

1770's – 80's–   first fashion mags. (P. 23)

Important aspects of fashion
     =   Beauty + originality (P. 27)

Fashion =   art / Modern art (P. 28)

Boris Groys   =   fashion is anti–authoritarian (P. 34)

"Fashion has conquered most areas, but lost
itself in the process." (P. 34)

Common people excluded from fashion
       until C19 –> Too expensive (P. 38)
but mass production   =   cheaper fashion (ibid)

B

Svendsen, L. (2006). Fashion : a philosophy.
London : Reaktion.

		Page.
So innovation is a way to show own identity?	Fashion + Modern art driven by 'urge to innovate'.	28
Check	N.B. Simmel -> "philosophy of fashion" - claims link fashion + identity.	19
∴ becomes more important to express ident?	Postmodern - Making one's own identity + more important.	75
	Consumption of fashion purpose = "to create an identity".	p.113
Clear statement !	"'Identity' is one of the seminal concepts for describing the function of fashion."	p.137
	As 'self-realisation' becomes more important, so does expressing identity through f.	

C

Davis, F. (1994). Fashion, Culture, and Identity.
Chicago : University of Chicago Press.

	Page
"That the clothes we wear make a statement is itself a statement that in this age of heightened self-consciousness it has virtually become a cliche."	p.3
Phenomenon of fashion intrigues cultural scientists -> it illustrates basic feat. of modern society including mass-produced tastes. -	p.4
Fashion is a way to communicate symbols = So fashion symbolizes our identity?	p.4
Clothing is "code" -> it gives clues about what we want to communicate	p.5

1d Review Unit 1, Part A, about methods for critically evaluating notes. Work in pairs. Annotate the notes above with questions or comments. When you finish, swap your notes with another pair to see if you have the same ideas about their content.

2   Synthesizing information from your notes

> Having taken basic notes from a range of sources, the next step is to put the information together. This is known as synthesizing the information and is an important step in developing a full understanding of the topic, as well as helping you to generate new ideas. Synthesizing the information that you have collected from two or more sources makes it easier to compare ideas, highlight similarities and identify differences between them.

2a Look at this assignment title. Work in pairs. Briefly discuss your thoughts about it.

The use of Closed Circuit Television Cameras (CCTV) in public places is growing rapidly. Assess the extent to which CCTV provides effective community security and evaluate claims that the growth in CCTV in public places threatens individual privacy.

2b Work in pairs. Brainstorm a list of possible topic areas that could be relevant to this assignment in the space below.

Possible topic areas
Background info about CCTV
Other forms of security
Privacy

2c Work with another pair. Use this space to write questions that this topic raises.

Possible questions relating to this topic
What other forms of public security are there?
Which countries use the most CCTV? Which the least? Differences between them?
How effective is CCTV compared with other forms of security?

2d Read two pages of notes made by a student working on this assignment. The notes relate to two different sources. Analyze these notes for information that relates closely to the topics and questions you thought of in 2b and 2c.

Armitage, R. (2002). To CCTV or not to CCTV? A review of current research into the effectiveness of CCTV systems in reducing crime. London: NACRO

A "belief" that CCTV works (Note, not proof!) (p. 1)

Funding for CCTV ↑
1996 - 1998 = 75% of Home Office crime spending.
Annual cost may be £12,000 per camera (p. 1)
↓
Initial investment + running costs + maintenance

CCTV coverage ↑
1990 - 3 towns + 100 cameras / 1997 towns = 167 cams = 5,238 / 2002 systems = 500 cams = 40,000 (p. 1)

CCTV Aims (p. 1)
1. Deter crime
2. Improve police efficiency
3. Guard public areas
4. Detect crime + prosecute

Possible effects

Car park crime ↓
Burglary ↓ (p. 2)

Personal crime
e.g. mugging + violence etc
= no real effect
(p. 2)

Problems

1. Evaluation of effectiveness is not sufficient — needs more study (p. 3)
Many studies are "methodologically weak" (p. 4)

2. Street lighting may be more effective than CCTV.
(one study = 20% crime ↓ from lighting !!) (p. 5)

3. May be a "life-cycle" - i.e. CCTV is effective at first but people soon ignore it. (p. 3)

4. Invades privacy? - May conflict with 1998 Human Rights Act if it is not managed properly (p. 3)

Welsh, B., and Farrington, D. (2007). Closed-circuit Television Surveillance. In Welsh, B. and Farrington, D. (Eds.), Preventing Crime: What works for children, offenders, victims and places (pp. 193-208). NY: Springer Science + Business Media

Alternative measures ⟶ security paint
Lighting

How cost-effective
is CCTV ⟶ cutting back foliage
by comparison? (p.206) police patrols

Aim of CCTV ⟶ To prevent
1) personal crime p.193
"Tremendous growth" 2) property crime p.193
of CCTV in UK. (p.194) 3) Aid crime detection p.194
1999-2001 £ 170 mill. 4) Increase public   p.194
in UK.   confidence

Problems

"Much debate" about effectiveness of CCTV. (p.195)
Many studies of benefit are not conclusive.
Evaluates findings from 22 studies.
1) city centre + public housing → "mixed results"
     (p.198)
2) public transport "conflicting evidence" (p.202)
3) car parks - most positive effects
Overall vehicle crime ↓ 28% !
     violent crime ↓ 3%

Effect is "small but significant" (p.203)
However, positive effects may not continue long after
     first installation (p.206)
public support + privacy

UK - public support for CCTV is high (p.205)
USA - low public support - fear 'Big Brother'
     and invasion of privacy   (p.205)

2e Synthesize the two sets of notes using these headings or the sub-topics and questions you thought of in 2b and 2c.

Background information about CCTV:

Other forms of security:

Privacy:

2f Now consider the original assignment title while you review your synthesized notes. Is there any part where you need more information?

2g On a spare piece of paper, practise synthesizing information from the notes you have taken so far for the Unit 3 unit task.

3 Referencing sources correctly in synthesized notes

3a Use this extract from some synthesized notes to write a short paragraph giving background information about CCTV in the space below.

CCTV Background Info.

Coverage

1990	–	3 systems + 100 cameras
1997	–	167 Towns + 5000+ cameras
2002	–	500 systems + 40,000+ cams.

(Armitage, 2002: 1)

'Tremendous growth' of UK CCTV
(Welsh + Farrington, 2007: 194)

Costs etc.

Funding for CCTV is rising – 1996–98 =
75% of Home Office crime spending.
Approx £12,000 per camera ⟨— Initial invest.
(Armitage, 2002: 1)   Running costs.
1999–2001 £170 million   Maintenance.
(Welsh + Farrington, 2007: 194)

Aims

1.	To prevent personal crime	(Welsh + Farrington, 2007: 193)
2.	" " property "	(Armitage, 2002: 1)
3.	Aid crime detection	(both sources agree)
4.	Guard public areas	(Armitage, 2002: 1)
5.	Improve police efficiency	(Armitage, 2002: 1)
6.	Increase public confidence	(Welsh + Farrington, 2007: 193)

3b Work in pairs. Look at the synthesised notes below on the same topic and discuss how useful these notes would be in these situations:

1 You are trying to develop your own stance on the topic.

2 You are doing background research.

3 You are trying to write an essay.

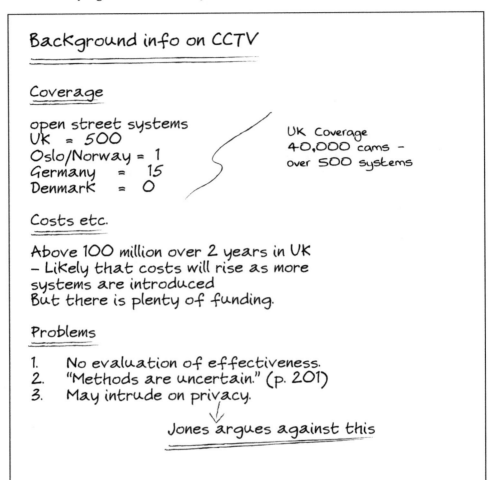

3c Review the synthesized notes you made for the CCTV assignment title in 2e. Check that you have included all citations and source details.

4 Reflecting on notes to help clarify your ideas

Look back at the synthesized notes you created in 2e. In pairs, use the questions below to help you analyze them.

1 To what extent do the two sources agree on the growth of CCTV?

2 How similar is the stance that the two sources take on the effectiveness of CCTV?

3 Based on what you have read in the two sources, what locations are most effective for CCTV in reducing crime?

4 What similar problems do they identify?

5 Welsh and Farrington claim that public support for CCTV is high. To what extent do you think that Armitage would agree with this claim? What reasons do you have for your answer?

Later in this unit you will give a presentation and then write a short essay on your chosen biometrics assignment title. By now you have already started synthesizing information about the topic from the notes you took in the listening (Unit Task Part A), as well as the two readings (Unit Task Part B). However, these are rather general introductions to the topic and you will need to find other sources of information which are more relevant to the assignment title you have chosen.

a Look closely at your assignment title again. Then think of topic areas which are relevant to this subject, or other questions that it raises. Make a note of them in the spaces below.

Possible topic areas

Possible questions relating to this topic

b Before the next lesson, search for material about biometrics which is specifically relevant to your assignment title. When you find possible sources, read them critically and take notes (including a reference and page number).

c Synthesize your notes together with the other information you have. Use the topic areas or related questions that you thought of above to help you organize the synthesized information.

Go to the checklist on p.201. Look again at the tips relating to Unit 3 Parts A–B and tick (✓) those you have used in your studies. Read the tips relating to Unit 3 Part C.

Reporting in speech

By the end of Part D you will be able to:

- identify your purpose in giving a presentation
- present an oral summary of research
- include alternative points of view in a presentation.

1 Identifying your purpose in giving a presentation

1a In the groups that you will work with to give a presentation for the unit task, look at the assignment titles on p.116–117 again. Choose the statement that best expresses what you are trying to communicate to your audience.

- To instruct your audience or explain something to them.
- To present an argument in support of an idea or to argue against it.
- To describe observations or an experiment.
- To present a summary of your own research.
- To persuade your audience to accept your point of view, or change their existing point of view.

1b Consider each section of the presentation (i.e. introduction, overview, first part of main body and so on). Do all the sections have the same purpose? If not, work in your group to decide the purpose of each section.

2 Presenting an oral summary of research

> In some presentations you may include the results of your own research. This might happen in one of two ways:
>
> **1** The main focus of the whole presentation is your research work. This may be more common for senior undergraduates or postgraduate students.
>
> **2** A piece of research you have done may form part of the evidence that you are using to support a claim in an argumentative presentation.

2a Work in pairs. Look at these stages of a piece of research work. Decide which should be included in any presentation of your own research. In which order would they normally be presented?

Results	References	Method
Background on the topic	Discussion of the results	Conclusion
A description of the aims	A review of related literature	Limitations of the research
Introduction	Recommendations	Description of equipment used

The emphasis that you put on each section might depend on how long you have for the presentation and also the reason why you are including your own research in the presentation. For instance, if the main focus of the whole presentation is your research work, you would probably have time to cover most of these points. However, if you were presenting information about your research as just one part of the evidence for an argument, the focus would probably be different.

2b Look at the two scenarios below. Work in pairs. Decide which parts of your research you would focus on, and how much time you would give to them.

1 You have completed a piece of primary research as part of an assessment for your course. You have 30 minutes to give your supervisors an overview of your research.

2 You are giving a presentation on the topic:

To what extent can violent video games be said to explain violent behaviour in teenagers?

You must present your own argument on the topic, as well as any information that you have discovered from secondary sources as support for your argument. However, in the past you have also carried out some primary research about teenage violence which is relevant to the topic and could be included to support your ideas.

2c Compare your answers with another pair when you finish.

Vivas tend to occur at postgraduate doctoral level. A viva (/vaɪvə/) is a combination of a presentation and an interview, in which the student researcher is expected to present details of the dissertation research which they have completed independently and then answer detailed questions from a panel of experts (normally including their academic supervisor) in order to defend their research aims, methods, findings and conclusions.

The method by which vivas are delivered differ between academic institutions and departments, but generally it is possible to prepare for them by planning a brief presentation of each of the sections of your dissertation. This would include the following:

- Introduction
- Research aims
- Literature review
- Methods used to collect data
- Analysis of findings
- Discussion
- Conclusions
- Recommendations
- References/Bibliography

In some cases the use of PowerPoint slides or visual aids is accepted in order to help explain the dissertation.

Besides having written and edited your dissertation to the best of your ability, it is sensible to prepare for a viva by anticipating the questions that the panel might ask. Rehearsing the viva with a group of friends who are prepared to ask detailed and challenging questions can help you to ensure that the real viva is a success.

3 Including alternative points of view in a presentation

A persuasive presentation shares similarities with an essay in that the content of both must be structured to show clear reasoning for your arguments and provide evidence for support. If the purpose of your presentation is to present an argument, then including counterarguments and alternative points of view can help in strengthening your claim, just as it would in an essay.

3a Review Unit 2 Part E, which contains example structures for essays that incorporate counterarguments. This can be equally relevant to presentations.

3b You are about to listen to a short presentation on the topic of teenage violence and video games which addresses the question:

To what extent can violent video games be said to explain violent behaviour in teenagers?

Before you listen, briefly discuss your opinions on the topic with a partner.

3.4

3c Now listen to the presentation. What is the speaker's main argument?

3d Listen again and make a note of the speaker's supporting points in this space.

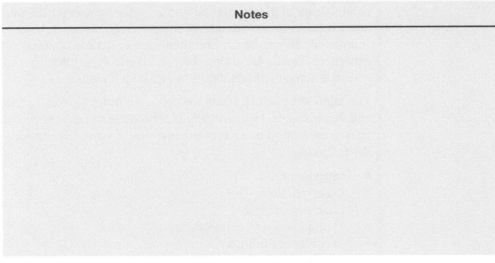

Notes

3e Work in pairs. Use your notes to help you outline the structure of the speaker's talk. Identify and label these parts in your notes (note that not all of these were included in the lecture):
- argument
- conclusion
- counterarguments
- introduction
- refutation
- supporting points

3f Compare your notes with another pair. Discuss where you might include the missing parts.

3g Imagine that you have been asked to make a presentation on the same topic, and that you think there is a link between violent video games and teenage violence. You wish to convince your audience to agree that this is true.

However, an eminent neuroscientist named Susan Greenwold has written a book on the subject, as well as a number of academic papers. She is considered one of the world's leading authorities on the topic and, unfortunately for you, she argues against the idea of a link between violent video games and teenage behaviour. It is unlikely that your audience will be persuaded to accept your argument if you do not attempt to refute her claims.

Work in pairs. Decide how you would structure a fifteen-minute presentation to incorporate both your own argument as well as counterarguments and refutations.

Presentation structure

3h Compare your ideas with another pair. Explain your reasons for the structure that you chose.

3i Work with the other members of your group. Review the unit task. By now you should all have started doing extra research to get information on the topic. Discuss these questions.

1 What is the main argument that your group will adopt?

2 What counterarguments have you discovered in your reading?

3 How will you deal with counterarguments in your presentation?

Biometrics

In this unit task, you will prepare and deliver a group presentation on the biometrics assignment title that you have chosen.

a Discuss these questions to help you plan your presentation.

- What is your purpose in this presentation?
- What is the main idea of your presentation?
- What kind of evidence will you present to support your ideas?
- How will you structure the content of the presentation for best effect?
- Will you include visual or graphic data of any sort?
- What roles will each member of the group take?

b Plan the main body of your presentation. Bear in mind these points.

- Check with your teacher how long the presentation should be.
- Each member of the group should take turns presenting.
- You should use visual aids to support your presentation.
- You should include counterarguments in your presentation if you have discovered them while researching the topic.

c When you have prepared the main body of your presentation, review Unit 2 Part A3, about asking questions. Work as a group. Try to anticipate the questions that you might be asked by the audience or your teachers.

d Practise asking each other and responding to the questions.

Go to the checklist on p.201–202. Look again at the tips relating to Unit 3 Parts A–C and tick (✓) those you have used in your studies. Read the tips relating to Unit 3 Part D.

Reporting in writing

By the end of Part E you will be able to:

- synthesize sources in writing
- incorporate quotations into writing
- incorporate paraphrase into writing
- understand plagiarism and patchwriting
- use hedging.

1   Synthesizing sources in writing

> Your writing should be original work created by you alone. However, it should also include supporting *ideas* and *information* from other authors, though you should try to explain these in your own words. Many students find it difficult to create a balance between expressing their own ideas and the support included from other sources. By understanding how to synthesize ideas in your writing you can find this balance more easily.

1a   Read the two texts below giving background information about CCTV. These are based on the synthesized notes in Part C. Identify the main ideas in each paragraph.

1   CCTV use is expanding rapidly in the UK. According to Armitage (2002, p.1), the number of camera systems in operation in public spaces rose from 100 in 1990 to 500 in 2002. It seems likely that the trend will continue because of a 'belief' that CCTV works (ibid.). Armitage writes that the aims of CCTV systems are to deter crime, improve police efficiency, guard public areas and help to prosecute criminals caught on camera (ibid.).

2   There has been 'tremendous growth' in CCTV in the UK and around £170 million was spent on CCTV between 1999 and 2001 (Welsh & Farrington, 2007, p.194). They argue that the main aims of CCTV are to prevent personal and property crime, to help with crime detection and to increase public confidence.

3   According to Welsh and Farrington (2007, p.194), there has been 'tremendous growth' in CCTV in the UK, with approximately £170 million spent on such systems between 1999 and 2001. A similar observation is made by Armitage (2002, p.1), who notes an increase of nearly 350 CCTV systems between 1997 and 2002. This suggests that there is both official enthusiasm and ample funding for such systems.

4   Both Armitage (2002, p.1) and Welsh and Farrington (2007, pp.193–194) note that the main aim of CCTV is deterrence, as well as helping with detection and prosecution of those crimes which do occur. Welsh and Farrington, however, also note that such systems are partly designed to raise public confidence (ibid.). This would suggest that, at least in part, the benefits of CCTV are not limited to crime reduction figures.

1b   Use these questions to help you decide which text in 1a synthesizes the information from the notes more successfully.

1   How similar is the information about funding given by the two sources?

2   To what extent do the two sources agree about the aims of CCTV systems?

3   Are there any differences between the claims made by the sources, Armitage (2002) and Welsh and Farrington (2007)?

1c Look again at the notes on CCTV that you synthesized in Part C, 2e. In the space below, write a paragraph (or more) explaining the issues with personal privacy surrounding CCTV.

1d Swap your work with a partner. Check that the ideas have been synthesized in your own words.

2 Incorporating quotations into writing

2a Look at this excerpt from a student essay, which contains a quotation. What problems can you identify with the way this quotation has been used?

CCTV in the UK has spread so rapidly in little more than a decade that it is now nearly ubiquitous across the country. The sheer number of CCTV cameras in public space, as well as their technical sophistication, has led to a number of claims that such technology invades individual privacy. However, it can be used to safeguard privacy as well. 'A new technology being developed by video surveillance company CBG Hamburg will use facial-recognition technology to blur the images of anyone whose image is captured on the camera, but whose details do not appear on a list of known criminals. This will allow CCTV operators and police to scan crowds of people for wanted criminals more quickly, while at the same time allowing innocent members of the public to pass by with their identities concealed. A spokesman for CBG Hamburg has claimed that the technology has performed well in tests and is able to handle rush hour crowds in busy city centres without difficulty, with a false recognition rate of only 0.00008%. The technology presents, for the first time, an opportunity to identify criminals quickly and securely, while reassuring the public that their right to privacy is not being compromised' (Ellis, 2009, p.221).

CCTV offers many benefits to society at large. It allows public areas to be monitored to increase public safety, aids in the capture of known criminals, and allows resources to be freed up for ...

It is important to incorporate quotations clearly and effectively into your wrting. Here is a list of common mistakes to avoid:

1 <u>Using overly long quotes.</u> As far as possible, you should express your own ideas in your own words. However, sometimes a quote from another author may be suitable as support. In this case, think about how it supports your idea and only quote as much as you need to achieve this.

2 <u>Failing to use quotation marks (" ") or ('').</u> Many students quote directly from another writer's work and include a correct citation to show where it came from. However, without adding quotation marks, you would be guilty of poor scholarship or, in the worst case, accused of plagiarism. Either way, forgetting to include quotation marks will probably impact on your grade.

3 <u>Adding quotations without explaining how they are relevant; without giving a commentary about the quote's meaning; or without a clearly expressed link to the rest of your essay content.</u> Your writing should be an expression of your ideas, using quotes for support. You are not writing your own work if you simply present a collection of quotations from other people.

2b Read the three extracts from student essays (A–C), all of which include quotations. Complete these activities while you read to help you decide how well the students have used the quotations.

1 Identify any phrases that the student has used to introduce the quote. Can you think of any similar phrases?

2 Underline comments about the quote that the student has written in their own words and that appear to be the student's own ideas.

3 How many of the quotes are complete sentences? Discuss with your partner why the students have quoted only partial sentences.

A

The continued growth of CCTV in public areas of the UK has led to concern about the extent to which it impacts personal privacy. Supporters of the technology point to its benefits for reducing crime and increasing public safety. However, according to Ward et al., there are 'very few studies which support the claim that CCTV is effective in reducing crime' (Ward et al., 2009, p.27). This view is supported by claims in a number of other studies and poses a question about how CCTV came to be deployed so broadly in the absence of proof that it helps to reduce crime.

B

As the use of CCTV in public spaces becomes more commonly accepted, so the technology on which the systems are based improves. Recent developments have included integrated citywide CCTV systems which link the cameras on public transport, shopping centres, university campuses and city-centre streets to a single control centre, as well as facial-recognition technology and privacy-enhancing software that blurs the faces of innocent passersby. The technical difficulty of scanning large numbers of people has prevented these technologies from being deployed until only very recently. However, at least one company now claims to have completed trials on a system that is able to 'handle rush hour crowds in busy city centres without difficulty' (Ellis, 2009, p.221). This development would suggest that, at least for the immediate future, the number and uses of CCTV camera systems on UK streets will continue to grow.

According to an influential 1997 study by the Ministry of Justice, 'CCTV cameras are a fundamental part of the police armoury in the fight against street crime' (MOJ, 1997, p.415). However, this contrasts with claims that CCTV has 'significantly less impact on crime levels than increasing the number of police officers on the streets, or even simply improving street lighting' (Doi, 2006, p.11). Doi's claim, however, is based on only one study dating back to 1998, when the system was in its infancy, and may no longer be an accurate description of the reality.

2c Use the guidelines about common mistakes in 2a to help you decide how well the students have incorporated the quotes into their own work.

2d Check your answers with a partner. Explain how well you think the students have used the quotations.

2e Imagine that you are writing an essay about CCTV, claiming that CCTV has helped to reduce crime in urban areas. A prominent expert on the subject has written this text with similar ideas. You think that including a quote from the expert would help to support your claim. Read the text, then complete the essay excerpt below by adding an appropriate quotation and comments from the expert that will support your claim.

The installation of cameras in a city centre is closely followed by a clear fall in a number of different crimes. Burglary and other types of property crime such as car theft show the most significant decrease, while there are also encouraging reductions in physical attacks. Anti-CCTV campaigners claim that such camera systems simply push crime to other areas of the city, but there is in fact no evidence of this happening.

(Boyes, M. (2003). *Crime and crime prevention*. London: SA Publishing, p.23.)

CCTV has become a commonplace feature of city centres across the country since its widespread introduction a little over a decade ago. The obvious intent of CCTV is to deter crime, the public belief in which has clearly helped the number of cameras to grow so rapidly. Nevertheless, a large number of commentators have claimed that CCTV is ineffective in reducing crime rates. While this argument has become popular among crime researchers in the last few years, the fact is that ...

_____

_____

_____

_____

_____

_____

3 Incorporating paraphrase into writing

The common mistakes that student writers make when paraphrasing are in fact largely the same as the problems with quotations.

1 The paraphrased section is too long.
2 No comment on the relevance of the paraphrase is added.
3 The writer does not clearly link the paraphrase to the rest of the text.
4 The writer does not include a citation to the original source.

The reason why these are mistakes relates again to the need to produce original work. Presenting a series of paraphrased passages from other writers, even if it is written entirely in your own words and is properly cited, is not your own work.

3a Read this text below from an academic article about privacy. Identify the writer's main idea.

Social trends and the growth of CCTV

CCTV technology is being used in an ever-widening number of public spaces. Despite claims by civil rights campaigners that this represents a serious and deliberate attack on privacy rights by authoritarian governments, it seems in fact to be a natural response by law enforcement agencies to the problem of anonymity in massive, globalized, urban communities. Rising populations, a trend towards urbanization, and greater mobility of the civilian population, both within and between countries, make it more difficult for police to identify criminals or terrorists in the mass of unidentified individuals living and working in, or moving through, our modern cities. Police forces, like any other organization, strive to be efficient, and CCTV cameras are a technological measure which helps to improve the efficiency with which the police operate.

Clarkson, P. (2009). Understanding the rise in CCTV in the UK. *Surveillance Issues Bulletin*, 6(3), **p.37.**

3b Read an excerpt from a student essay on the same topic. Underline the section that has been paraphrased from the article in 3a. Work in pairs. Identify the problems with the paraphrase. Discuss ways that the student could improve it.

CCTV is becoming a common feature of public life. However, many people are suspicious of the idea that the police or security guards can monitor everything we do 24 hours a day. However, there are several arguments in favour of CCTV, which I will consider below.

Firstly, even though civil rights campaigners say that CCTV is a major and intentional attack on the right to privacy by governments which want to control their populations, in fact the use of CCTV technology is simply a natural thing for the police to do because of the fact that globalization and urbanization make it more difficult for the police to recognize people. Because the population is rising, urbanization is increasing, and more people are moving around in their own countries as well as internationally, police have a hard time finding criminals and terrorists in the anonymous population of people in modern cities. Just like any organization, the police must operate effectively using the resources that they have and CCTV technology helps the police to be more effective (Clarkson, 2009, p.37).

Secondly, some studies have strongly indicated that CCTV has a positive effect on reducing crime rates …

3c Read extracts A and B written by two students. Both texts include examples of good paraphrasing. Complete these tasks (1–4) to help you analyze why the paraphrasing is suitable.

1 Highlight sections of the student's writing that appear to have been paraphrased from Clarkson's text about privacy in 3a.

2 Identify any phrases that the student has used to introduce the paraphrases. Can you think of any similar phrases?

3 Underline comments about the paraphrased section that appear to be the student's own ideas.

4 Identify which type of paraphrase is most common:

   a complete sentences or passages

   b partial phrases.

A

There are arguments both for and against the widespread use of CCTV in public places. Suspicions about the purpose of constant observation of the public are balanced by arguments that CCTV plays an important part in reducing crime. Another justification offered by Clarkson (2009, p.37) is the argument that CCTV represents an attempt by the police to improve their operational efficiency. Clarkson claims that globalization has caused modern cities to become more anonymous places, thus making it difficult for law enforcement agencies to identify undesirable individuals such as criminals or terrorists, and that CCTV can help to address this problem. While Clarkson's argument seems plausible, it does not explain why CCTV has been introduced so widely in the cities of some developed countries but not in others.

B

It has been suggested that the boom in CCTV is a natural result of the trend towards increasing anonymity in highly globalized modern cities (Clarkson, 2009, p.37). This claim has some merits, particularly because it gives a common-sense explanation that CCTV is simply used to improve efficiency rather than for some sinister Orwellian social control.

3d Use this space to write a short paragraph, giving your opinion about CCTV and privacy. Explain your ideas in your own words. You may include paraphrases from any of the sources you've read, or the notes in Part C2, to support your opinions, or help you build your paragraph.

4 Plagiarism and patchwriting

4a Read these extracts (A–C) from two different reports about the use of CCTV around Europe. Compare them with the extracts from student essays (1 and 2) which follow. How well have the sources been incorporated into the students' writing?

A

As we have shown, CCTV has become an essential part of urban life across Europe. Surveillance cameras monitor banks, petrol stations, chain stores, transportation centres, public and private office buildings, shopping malls, universities, schools, hospitals, museums, sports arenas, residential areas, etc. ... However, the extent of CCTV differs from country to country. Our findings suggest that its diffusion ... in semi-public space is most advanced in Britain, where we found 40% of the studied publicly accessible locations under surveillance. The extent of CCTV is least developed in Austria, where in 18% of these locations cameras were in operation.

Source: Urbaneye. (2004). *On the Threshold to Urban Panopticon? Analysing the Employment of CCTV in European Cities and Assessing its Social and Political Impacts – Final Report to the European Union*, p.60. Technical University of Berlin.

B

For Britain it is estimated that around 40,000 cameras monitor public areas in more than 500 cities. In France around 300 towns are reported to operate more or less extensive CCTV networks monitoring public areas, and in the Netherlands one fifth of the municipalities run a system. In contrast, open-street CCTV is only in operation in around 20 German cities, and in Denmark no such system exists.

Source: Urbaneye. (2004). *On the Threshold to Urban Panopticon? Analysing the Employment of CCTV in European Cities and Assessing its Social and Political Impacts – Final Report to the European Union*, p.61. Technical University of Berlin.

C

In Sheffield, for example, the Sheffield Wide Image Switching System, or SWISS, which was launched in 2003, has a control room staffed 24 hours a day and can now control around 150 publicly funded cameras covering the city centre streets. However, SWISS has also integrated other public and privately owned camera systems, including those of an out-of-town shopping mall, tram system and university.

Source: Norris, C., McCahill, M., & Wood, D. (2004). Editorial: the growth of CCTV: a global perspective on the international diffusion of video surveillance in publicly accessible space. *Surveillance and Society, 2*(2/3), p.120.

1 CCTV, or Closed Circuit Television, is a security system using cameras to monitor public space. Reports indicate that CCTV has become an essential part of urban life across Europe. Surveillance cameras monitor banks, petrol stations, chain stores, transportation centres, public and private office buildings, shopping malls, universities, schools, hospitals, museums, sports arenas, residential areas, etc. However, the extent of CCTV differs from country to country. Our findings suggest that its diffusion ... in semi-public space is most advanced in Britain, where we found 40% of the studied publicly accessible locations under surveillance. The extent of CCTV is less developed in Austria, where in 18% of these locations cameras were in operation. This suggests a remarkable growth of CCTV in Britain in particular compared to other European countries. For Britain it is estimated that around 40,000 cameras monitor public areas in more than 500 cities. In France around 300 towns are reported to operate more or less extensive CCTV networks monitoring public areas, and in the Netherlands one fifth of the municipalities run a system. In contrast, open-street CCTV is only in operation in around 20 German cities, and in Denmark no such system exists. Moreover, British CCTV is often more technically sophisticated than in other countries, as it allows CCTV networks to be integrated and monitored from one control centre. An example of this is the city of Sheffield, where the Sheffield Wide Image Switching System, or SWISS, which was launched in 2003, has a control room staffed 24 hours a day and can now control around 150 publicly funded cameras covering the city centre streets. However, SWISS has also integrated other public and privately-owned camera systems, including those of an out-of-town shopping mall, tram system and university (Norris et al., 2004, p.120).

2 CCTV monitoring is becoming an essential part of urban life in many countries in Europe. These days it is common to see cameras in many areas open to the public, such as an out-of-town shopping mall, tram system or university. However, there are differences in the way CCTV is employed in different countries. The extent of CCTV is most developed in Britain, where it is estimated that approximately 40,000 cameras watch public areas in more than 500 cities (Urbaneye, 2004, p.61). Britain operates more or less extensive CCTV networks monitoring its public areas, which have control rooms staffed 24 hours a day controlling publicly funded cameras covering city centre streets. Though this may seem normal to the people of Britain, they might be surprised to learn that in other countries, no such system exists.

4b Work in pairs. Read the student essays again. Underline any sections which are the same as the original text in extracts A–C. Then decide whether or not these student essays match your definition of plagiarism.

Most people would agree that the first essay is clearly an example of plagiarism. However, the second essay is an example of *patchwriting* – stitching together pieces of other people's work, while altering some words, grammar or expressions. This can be common with new student writers, or those attempting academic writing in another language for the first time. Patchwriting is a grey area – some academic institutions consider it plagiarism, while others would view it as 'poor scholarship'. In either case, patchwriting suggests to your teachers that you have not really understood what you are writing about and it is likely to affect grades for written work. Patchwriting, like outright plagiarism, should be avoided.

4c Read another excerpt from a student essay on the same topic. As you read, identify the parts which are the same as the original text in 4a, then discuss with your partner which of these best describes the work:

1 plagiarized

2 patchwritten

3 written properly, with appropriate paraphrasing and quotations.

> Closed Circuit Television (CCTV) is becoming ever more common in the world's cities. However, the extent to which CCTV is deployed differs from country to country. In a report prepared for the European Commission, the Urbaneye project indicated that around 300 CCTV systems were monitoring public space in France, compared to just 30 systems in Germany and none in Denmark (Urbaneye, 2004, p.61). However, the Urbaneye study observed that by far the largest number of CCTV systems were to be found in the UK, with about 40,000 cameras 'in more than 500 cities' (ibid.).
>
> Not only is CCTV monitoring more common in the UK, but it tends to be more technically sophisticated. Many organizations use separate CCTV systems, but the tendency in the UK is to integrate these under the control of a single organization, which can monitor them all simultaneously. For instance, in the city of Sheffield a system known as SWISS (or Sheffield Wide Image Switching System) operates, which has 'integrated other public and privately owned camera systems, including those of an out-of-town shopping mall, tram system and university' (Norris et al., 2004, p.120). The integrated feeds from the cameras are all monitored by a single control room, which arguably has efficiency benefits compared to each organization running its own system. It seems likely, therefore, that SWISS is a model of future CCTV systems in other British cities.

4d Work in pairs. Discuss which of the following suggestions is the best way to 'fix' the patchwritten essay in 4a.

1 Fix the patchwritten sections by paraphrasing them completely into your own words.

2 Add more citations after each patchwritten section.

3 Start again and write an original essay.

5 Using hedging

> When writing your own claims, or commenting on another writer's work that you are synthesizing into your own writing, it is necessary to express your comments with caution (i.e. in a way that is not too definite). This is usually known as *hedging*.

5a Compare the two texts below. Underline the expressions in the second text that 'hedge' the writer's claims.

1

> A recent study of attitudes towards CCTV found that, of 200 people questioned, over 80% of them had positive feelings towards camera systems in public places (Morris & Howell, 2006, p.27). Therefore it is clear that CCTV is supported by the public. At present, no thorough studies have found conclusive proof that CCTV reduces crime rates. However, the absence of research evidence does not mean that CCTV is ineffectual. The reason for public support of CCTV is that it reduces crime and provides a feeling of security in the areas where it operates. As a result of these benefits, the number of CCTV systems in operation around the UK will continue to grow in the coming years.

2   A recent study of attitudes towards CCTV found that, of 200 people questioned, over 80% of them had positive feelings towards camera systems in public places (Morris & Howell, 2006, p.27). This suggests, therefore, that CCTV is supported by large numbers of the public. At present, no thorough studies have found conclusive proof that CCTV reduces crime rates. However, the absence of research evidence does not necessarily mean that CCTV is ineffectual. Possible reasons which might explain public support for CCTV are that it reduces crime and may provide a feeling of security in the areas where it operates. As a result of these perceived benefits, it seems likely that the number of CCTV systems in operation around the UK will continue to grow in the coming years.

5b Work in groups. Brainstorm other examples of hedging expressions.

> Here are some of the advantages of using hedging expressions:
>
> **1** The people whose ideas you are commenting on may have a great deal more experience and knowledge on a topic than you, so it is important to respect this.
>
> **2** No matter how strongly you believe any original claims that you make, you must acknowledge that you may be wrong.
>
> **3** If you claim something strongly without any hedging, it becomes very easy to attack your argument.

5c Read the claim at the beginning of this diagram and decide whether you agree or disagree with it. Then answer the questions which follow.

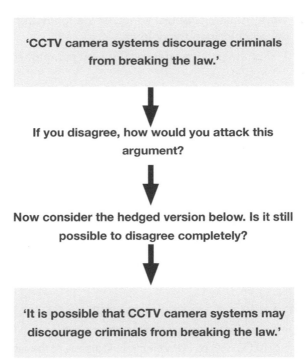

'CCTV camera systems discourage criminals from breaking the law.'

If you disagree, how would you attack this argument?

Now consider the hedged version below. Is it still possible to disagree completely?

'It is possible that CCTV camera systems may discourage criminals from breaking the law.'

5d Read the short excerpt from a student essay on p.153. The student has not included any hedging expressions, so it is likely to be seen as too direct. Edit the text so that it contains more suitable hedging expressions.

Many writers claim that CCTV is an important crime-reduction tool. In fact, this claim explains why it has been introduced in so many cities. This is a common-sense notion; we expect that cameras must discourage criminals from breaking the law. However, the claim is incorrect. Firstly, not enough studies have been done which systematically evaluate CCTV. Secondly, the studies which have been done showed that the effect of CCTV on crime is not reliable. For instance Nieto et al. point out that few studies have been done in the US and provide 'limited evidence' of CCTV benefits (2002, p.13). Winge and Knutsson (2003) found the same thing in a study of CCTV in Norway. A former CCTV manager in Glasgow claimed that CCTV development was due to the availability of funding rather than any real crime-fighting benefit (MacKay, 2002). These examples clearly demonstrate the fact that CCTV does not actually reduce crime.

➤ UNIT TASK   Biometrics

Draw together all the work you have been doing in this unit on biometrics to write an essay on your chosen title.

a   Complete this table to help you plan.

Title:		
Your main idea:		
Background information:		
Your supporting ideas:	**Evidence or citations:**	
	For	**Against**

b   Write your answer to the essay title.

Remember:
- Use information from other sources to support your ideas.
- Use citations and a reference for each source you use.

Go to the checklist on p.201–202. Look again at the tips relating to Unit 3 Parts A–D and tick (✓) those you have used in your studies. Read the tips relating to Unit 3 Part E on p.202.

Unit 4 Choices

Unit overview

Part	This part will help you to ...	By improving your ability to ...
A	**Listen critically**	• listen for logical flaws • listen for logical conclusions • review your active listening skills
B	**Critically evaluate logic in texts**	• identify arguments 'against the person' • identify 'you too' arguments • identify circular arguments • identify weak analogies • identify the use of limited options
C	**Develop as an independent learner**	• understand more about independent learning • analyze your own independence as a learner
D	**Conclude a presentation**	• draw suitable conclusions in a presentation • speculate on findings • make recommendations • prepare and rehearse for a presentation
E	**Conclude, review and edit an essay**	• write a suitable conclusion • proofread written work • review written work for logical flaws • edit written work for logical flaws • reflect on completed work

Understanding spoken information

By the end of Part A you will be able to:

- listen for logical flaws
- listen for logical conclusions
- review your active listening skills.

1 Listening for logical flaws

> Active listening skills include considering the logic of what you are listening to. In the following section you will practise listening to some speeches to decide if they contain logical flaws in the relationship of information. (You may find it helpful to review the information on logical flaws in Unit 3 Part B before continuing.)

1a You are going to listen to a lecture about factors that can affect the way people make choices. Work in pairs. Before you listen, discuss these questions about decision-making.

1 How decisive are you?

2 Do you find it easy to make satisfactory choices quickly?

3 Have you ever experienced difficulty choosing an item from a range of options when shopping? What caused your hesitation?

4 Have you ever been unable to make a decision when you needed to? What prevented you from making the decision?

4.1

1b Listen to the lecture. Write notes on the speaker's claims about the causes and effects of the difficulty that people face when making decisions.

Difficulty in making decisions
Causes:
Effects:

1c Compare your notes with a partner.

1d Use these questions to help you assess the claims that the speaker made.

1 What evidence did the speaker give to support the claim that people like to have more choice?

2 What evidence did the speaker give to support the claim that having too many options makes it difficult to make any choice at all?

3 What claim does the speaker make about levels of depression in affluent societies?

4 Can you think of any other explanations which the speaker does not offer?

5 What evidence does the speaker offer for the claim that too much choice causes accidents?

6 Can you think of any other possible causes of accidents which the speaker has not considered?

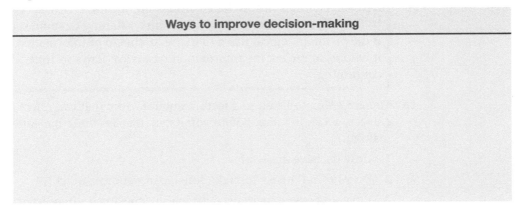

1e Listen to the speaker make some suggestions about how decision-making can be improved. Make notes in the space provided.

Ways to improve decision-making

1f Work in pairs. Use your notes to answer these questions.

1 What is the speaker's main argument?

2 What premises is the argument based on? How reasonable are they?

3 Does the speaker present any evidence to support their argument?

4 In order to improve decision-making, do you think it is necessary to follow the speaker's key recommendation?

5 Do you think that the speaker's key recommendation is sufficient to improve decision-making?

2 Listening for logical conclusions

> Part of the skill of listening critically is deciding whether the speaker's reasoning is consistent. In other words, the speaker's initial claims must be supported by logical reasons throughout the main body of the speech. The reasoning must also extend to the speaker's conclusions.
>
> Here, the *conclusion* refers not only to the final section of a formal presentation. It can also mean the speaker's interpretation of the evidence that they have collected on a particular topic.

2a Listen to a short speech presenting more research about how multiple choices can affect decision-making. Use the space on p.157 to make a note of the speaker's research aim.

The effects of multiple choices on decision-making
Main argument:
Claim:
Evidence:

2b Work in pairs. Predict what conclusions about decision-making are logical, based on the evidence given by the speaker.

2c Listen to the speaker. Make a note of her conclusions.

4.4

2d Work in pairs. Discuss whether the conclusion is logically supported by the evidence and reasoning or is not logically supported.

2e Imagine that you have attended this lecture. Work in pairs. Decide some questions that you could ask the speaker at the end of the talk.

3 Reviewing your active listening skills

Active listening skills can help you listen attentively even when there are distractions or if your motivation is low. For example, during your time in higher education, there may sometimes be a high level of background noise during a lecture; you may sometimes be tired or ill; or perhaps there will be times when you're simply not very interested in the topic.

3a Work in pairs. Imagine that you have to attend a lecture on a topic that you are not familiar with, or which you know you will find difficult. Complete these activities.

1 Make a list of the things you could do **before** listening to help you get more from the lecture.

> *Pre-read if possible.*

2 Make a list of the things you could do **during** the lecture to keep you active and focused on the content.

> *Listen for flaws of logic or method.*

3 Make a list of the things you could do **after** the lecture to help you consolidate what you have learned and get the most out of it.

> *Decide to what extent you agree with the speaker's stance.*

3b Share your ideas with another pair of students.

3c You are going to listen to a speech about factors affecting the choice of whether to go on to higher education or not. Use some of your ideas about what to do before a lecture to help you prepare to listen to it. Choose a specific point to listen for (for instance, listening for logical sequence of ideas, for flaws, etc.).

3d Listen to the lecture. Write notes on the point you identified in 3c.

3e Work in pairs. Discuss what you have heard. To what extent do you agree with the speaker's stance?

3f Use this checklist to help you review and strengthen your active listening skills.

Skill	Check this section for more advice
Identify whether the speaker is trying to inform or persuade you	• SS3 Unit 1 Part A2 • SS3 Unit 2 Part A2
Try to recognize the speaker's stance on the topic	• SS3 Unit 2 Parts A1–A2
Think of questions you can ask about what you are hearing	• SS3 Unit 2 Part A3 • SS3 Unit 3 Part A4
Take organized notes which you can review and annotate with your own ideas	• SS3 Unit 1 Parts A3–A4
Consider the logic of what the speaker is saying	• SS3 Unit 2 Part C2 • SS3 Unit 3 Parts B1–B3 • SS3 Unit 4 Parts A1–A2
Evaluate the strength of any claims that you hear	• SS3 Unit 3 Parts A1–A3

> **UNIT TASK** **Decision-making**

The Unit 4 task is about decision-making. At the end of each part, you will be asked to complete a stage of the task as follows:

Part A: Listen to an introduction to the topic.

Part B: Read one text about it for background information.

Part C: Work in groups to research the topic.

Part D: Prepare and deliver a group presentation on the topic.

Part E: Write an essay on one of these titles:

1 *Examine the factors that can affect consumer purchasing decisions. Evaluate the implications of this for the ways companies market their goods.*

2   The 'tyranny (or paradox) of choice' has been used to explain why people have difficulty making complex choices and also as an explanation for high levels of stress in modern societies. Suggest an art project or installation that can help people to explore themes of individual choice.

3   What factors do designers and programmers need to take into account in order to make web pages as user-friendly as possible? Examine ways that web-page designers can ease decision-making by end users.

4   A telecoms company is intending to place a new mobile phone base station in a residential area, approximately 15 metres from a row of houses. Residents are strongly opposed, believing that mobile phone towers emit Radio Frequency (RF) energy which is dangerous for health. You have been asked to assess the risk posed by the base station. Evaluate the available information about the potential health risks posed by RF energy from mobile phone base stations and decide whether it should be moved or not.

a   You are about to listen to a general introduction to the factors involved in successful decision-making. Work in pairs. Predict as many factors involved in successful decision-making as possible. Besides the so-called 'tyranny of choice' problem, what other factors can make decision-making difficult?

b   On a separate piece of paper, prepare a Cornell-style layout to take your notes.

c   Listen to the lecture. Write notes. Pay attention to the logic of the speaker's claims.

4.6

d   Spend some time reflecting on your notes. Think about how this information connects to the title you have chosen. Add comments and questions to the notes.

e   Discuss your ideas with a partner who has chosen the same topic as you.

Go to the checklist on p.202 and read the tips relating to Unit 4 Part A.

Understanding written information

By the end of Part B you will be able to:

- identify arguments 'against the person'
- identify 'you too' arguments
- identify circular arguments
- identify weak analogies
- identify the use of limited options.

1 Identifying arguments 'against the person'

1a Work in pairs. Discuss this question on the problem of climate change. Justify your ideas, using evidence or reasoned argument.

Whatever its cause, how great a risk do you think climate change poses to our societies and way of life?

1b Read this text on the topic of climate change risks and decide if you agree with the author or not.

> It is now patently clear that climate change – or global warming, call it what you will – is a myth. Moreover, it is a dangerous myth which will wreck our economies in the pursuit of a dream of 'green energy'. There is absolutely no evidence whatsoever that global warming is taking place. In fact, if you consider all of the evidence fairly, as I and a few others like me have done, the evidence shows clearly that the Earth is not warming. However, if you accept the argument that we should stop using oil because of the risk that climate change might be true, what you are actually doing is ruining the economy. The risk of climate change actually being true is tiny and, even if it turns out that some warming will happen in the future, our societies will be able to handle it through technological measures. People who say climate change is real are exaggerating the risks.
>
> Marston, C. (2009, August). Climate Change myths we can all stop believing in. *Informed Scepticism, 4*, 12–18.

1c Now read this *refutation* of the argument by another author. In pairs, discuss how effective you think the refutation is.

> People like Carl Marston would have us believe that climate change is not happening. What evidence do they have for this? Nothing, really, except claims about research that they have done by themselves. But how much faith can we put in Marston's ideas? Well, remember that this is the man who notoriously claimed that poor people do not deserve medical treatment.
>
> Worsley, S. (2009, October). The ugly pedigree of climate change denial. *Sentinel, 36*, 107–108.

> In the example above, Worsley has clearly shown that he disputes Marston's claim and is trying to persuade his readers not to accept it either. However, he does not provide any arguments against Marston's climate change argument itself, but instead asks us to reject the argument with an attack on Marston for something unrelated to the topic. This is a logical flaw known as an *ad hominem* ('against the man') argument.

1d Read this argument and two responses from other writers, and decide whether they contain examples of *ad hominem* attacks.

> The problem with climate change is that it is a long-term risk and humans are just not very good at assessing long-term risks very accurately. Experimental studies in human behaviour by Brashears (1978), Foster (1996), Zinni (2008) and many others indicate clearly that people tend to underestimate the seriousness of risks when they are remote in time. This has a serious impact on the public's ability to accurately understand the risks of climate change, which IPCC reports say will only become very apparent after a lapse of decades.
>
> Zinni, P. (2009). Climate change, risk, and human behaviour.
> *International Journal of Decision Analysis*, *20*(4), 1371–1382.

Response 1

> Zinni (2009) claims that ordinary citizens are unable to estimate climate change risks accurately, which he presumably feels is justification for stronger Government action on climate change. This is characteristic of Zinni's attraction to alarmist positions, which is unsurprising in light of his association with the eco-terrorist Earth Now! movement in the 1960s.

Response 2

> Contrary to Zinni (2009), who claims that members of the public are unable to make accurate long-term assessments of risk, we would argue that people are capable of accurately assessing long-term risk and its impacts if they are *well-informed*. This view is supported by findings in a number of different studies (notably Parkin, 2003; Parkin & Lowell, 2003; Jackson, 2004; and Timmermans, 2007).

1e Look back at the responses in 1d. To what extent do you agree with them? If you disagree, try to think of valid ways to refute these claims.

2 Identifying 'you too' arguments

2a Read this text, in which one author criticizes another's work. What are the grounds for the criticism?

> Barlow (2009) seriously exaggerates the risks of climate change, choosing only the most extreme evidence to support his views and enthusiastically agreeing with the predictions of climate models which most other climate scientists believe to be unlikely.
>
> Hollis, G. (2009). Why the climate debate is too serious for hysteria. *Climate Letters*, *14*(4), 848.

2b Now read Barlow's response. How does the author defend himself against Hollis's claim?

> Hollis (2009, p.848) attacks my argument for confirming climate change trends on the grounds that I have adopted 'extreme' evidence and 'unlikely' climate change models to support my views. However, Hollis himself frequently uses only the most extremely optimistic risk models to support his own views.
>
> Barlow, N. (2010). Comments: In answer to Graeme Hollis. *Climate Letters*, *15*(1), 1119.

2c Work in pairs. Discuss how valid the defence offered by Barlow against Hollis is.

> *Tu quoque*, or 'you too' arguments, are sometimes given as a defence against a criticism. The writer rejects criticism of their actions from another person by claiming that they are also guilty of doing the same thing.

2d Work in pairs. Discuss why you think 'you too' arguments are considered to be logical flaws.

2e Read these short arguments. Each one is a defence of the writer's position against claims by another author. Work in pairs. Decide which ones are 'you too' arguments. Make a note in the right-hand column of any problems that you find with the argument.

Those nations which criticize our policy of oil exploration on the grounds that it heightens the risk of climate change would do well to remember that we are only doing what is in the interest of our economic development. Many of those nations which criticize us have themselves achieved their wealth through the same means and it is hypocritical to place responsibility for climate-change risks on us now.	
Parsons (2008, pp.97–99) objects to my claim that engineers often make unduly optimistic risk assessments, presenting evidence from his own risk-assessment studies in the oil industry. However, while I do not dispute that some engineers are capable of making accurate risk assessments, I would nevertheless argue that the tendency is toward optimism.	
The Council for European Energy (2009) criticizes the government's decision to recommence the construction of three nuclear power plants, arguing that proper risk assessments for the surrounding environment have not been completed. However, this criticism seems unreasonable, as the risk assessments performed at each of the three sites met quality guidelines set by the IAEA in 2003.	
Taylor (1999) attacks my suggestion that people engaging in risky sports should pay higher premiums for their insurance. According to Taylor, this would be an unfair burden on a legitimate lifestyle choice (1999, p.203). However, Taylor himself has made claims of a similar sort in the past (see, for instance, Taylor 1991a; 1991b; 1994).	

3 Identifying circular arguments

3a Read this text. Identify the author's claim. What reasoning does the author offer to support the claim?

> Studies by Brashaw (2006; 2009b) and others have shown that the quality of decisions made by participants in stressful or risky situations declines as the perceived stress or risk increases. This effect was noted in a variety of perceptually risky circumstances and was constant across all occupational types or situations. This is a significant issue for emergency-service personnel for whom timely and accurate decision-making is critical. As such, emergency responders such as ambulance crews would benefit from receiving training in decision-making in high-stress environments. Such training would clearly be beneficial because it would improve their ability to choose the best course of action in stressful situations.

3b Work in pairs. Decide how well the reasoning supports the claim that emergency crews should receive training in decision-making skills.

> The example above is a circular argument. The author has supported the claim that emergency crews should receive decision-making training by saying that it would help them to improve the way they make choices in stressful situations. The supporting reasoning is the same as the overall argument, but expressed in different terms. It does not explain why or how they would benefit, so it is impossible for the reader to decide if the claim is reasonable or not.

3c Read texts A, B and C. Decide which include examples of circular argument.

Text A

> Omer and Alon (1994) have claimed that the idea that people tend to panic during emergency situations is false. Citing their own experience working on emergency teams, they assert that most people in fact remain calm and are capable of making rational decisions for their own safety, and that thoughtless panic is rare. However, this seems unlikely. It is, unfortunately, a matter of common sense that people panic in disasters, precisely because they are extreme situations which threaten severe danger, or even death, to people experiencing them. In situations of this sort, panic is a natural response.

Text B

> Studies show that people tend to judge risks as low when they are associated with an activity which the individual has positive feelings about. Thus, for instance, people who have positive feelings about smoking tend to judge the risks from smoking as being low. According to Epstein (1994) and others, this results from the fact that people automatically make intuitive risk judgements based on 'gut feeling' before considering risks more logically. Similar behaviour has been observed in individuals working in a variety of fields where accurate risk assessments are vital, such as financial analysts (Ganzach, 2001).

Text C

> There are two different methods by which people make judgements about risk. The first is based on fast, intuitive 'gut feeling' reactions about whether a situation is good or bad. The second is 'rational' and, as might be expected, this describes slow, deliberate risk analysis by weighing up all the pros and cons of a situation. People, it seems, base most of their judgements of risk on their gut feelings, because this is a faster method. However, rational risk decisions are arguably better because they are based on logic.

3d Compare your ideas with a partner.

4 Identifying weak analogies

4a Read these texts, which offer descriptions of the human mind. In each case, identify what the writer compares the human mind to.

Text A

In emergency situations people must often make life-or-death decisions very rapidly. Risk analysis is the process by which a person calculates possible risks, then compares them with so-called mitigating factors – those factors in a situation which can reduce the danger involved. In normal situations this is simple enough: the human mind is well-adapted to making such calculations. However, as the situation becomes more complex, or more dangerous, and a quick decision becomes necessary, the human mind, like the CPU on a computer, can be overloaded by tasks and fail to reach a timely decision about what to do.

Text B

Making decisions in a crisis is something like driving a car. The driver must handle a large amount of information about the world around them while simultaneously operating a number of controls to guide the car to where they want to go.

The comparison between the human mind and a computer or the controls of a car are analogies which attempt to illustrate the characteristics of human decision-making by comparison with the way a computer or car operates. Analogies can be useful when the two things compared are similar in respect of the characteristic which is being highlighted. For example, in A above, a CPU is used to illustrate the way in which the processing power of the brain can be overloaded. In this respect, a computer is similar to the human brain. A common mistake is to draw an analogy between two things which are superficially similar but which do not share the most relevant characteristic. For example, in B above both decision-making in a crisis and driving a car are complex activities. But by focusing on the physical operation of the car's controls the analogy becomes weaker, as this characteristic is not shared by both activities.

4b Work in pairs. Look again at the two analogies in 4a. Discuss which analogy is better. Compare your answers with another pair of students. Decide if you agree about which analogy is stronger.

4c Identify the analogy in this text and decide how strong it is.

It seems that the defining problem of our age will be climate change – the threat from a planet that is growing ever warmer. The great danger here is that we will fail to act on this until it is too late, because of the fact that the most serious possible consequences of climate change are decades or even centuries away and are difficult to imagine now. Most climate change models predict devastating consequences by the end of the twenty-first century, a point in time when few of the readers of this article will still be alive and, as a result, it is very difficult to persuade people to make choices about solving a problem that they cannot really see clear evidence of yet. Many climate scientists argue that the hard decisions about how to tackle this problem must be made now, even before it is clear to everyone that climate change is a real threat. This is known as the precautionary principle – the idea that we may be wrong, but it is better to change our habits and be wrong than to wait too long until climate change becomes obvious and then discover that it's too late to do anything about it. The risks of being wrong about that are too great to ignore. Those who argue that we should not take precautions now, and merely gather more evidence, are like gamblers placing all of their chips on one bet. Taking sensible action now, even if we are unsure whether the threat is real, seems like a wise precaution.

4d Work in pairs. Discuss your answers.

5 Identifying the use of limited options

5a Read the text below and identify the author's claim. Then answer these questions.

1 What options does the writer present?

2 Which one does the writer support?

3 To what extent do you agree with the writer's claim?

> Despite the introduction of smoking bans in public places, the litter of cigarette butts on the streets of our cities shows that there is little change in the popularity of smoking. Some studies suggest that the number of teenagers who take up smoking each year has hardly declined at all (Peterson, 2009). Years of anti-smoking education seem to fail to educate teenagers to appreciate the risks of smoking. Under these circumstances, the case for a complete ban on all sales of cigarettes is strong: only in this way will we be able to prevent teenagers and children from making the dangerous decision to begin smoking in the first place.

5b Can you think of any alternatives that the writer hasn't mentioned?

> A common logical flaw is to frame an argument with only two options – one of which the author supports and another which is clearly negative. In this way the reader may be persuaded to agree with the author's argument, though in fact there may be more options available which the writer deliberately has not presented. Doing this may make the writer's point appear more persuasive, but by not presenting other alternatives the writer may, in fact, make their claims or argument weaker logically.

5c Read these texts. Can you think of any options which the writer has not presented?

Text A

> Climate change presents an almost unimaginable challenge to the prosperity, comfort, health and even survival of our societies. It is now perfectly clear that this is a threat unlike any our species has ever faced before, bringing the risk of nations disappearing under the seas, mass dislocation of refugees, food shortages and the destruction of our precious ecosystem. The evidence shows conclusively that if we do not wish to see a world changed beyond all recognition and one in which humankind will undergo huge suffering, then we must all act now. The choices we make today, such as immediately replacing dirty carbon fuels (for example, oil and coal) with nuclear energy and the development of non-carbon transport systems, are essential if we are not to suffer a similar fate to that of the dinosaurs who became extinct millions of years ago.

Text B

> A number of studies (for example, Iyengar and Lepper, 2000; Schwartz, 2000; 2004) have demonstrated clearly that an excess of options can prevent people from making timely decisions. This presents a particular danger for operators of industrial machinery, as well as the pilots or drivers of vehicles on our public transport network, who must handle a multitude of options presented by their increasingly sophisticated control equipment. In order to reduce the number of accidents each year caused by this so-called 'choice overload', control systems should almost certainly be intentionally designed in order to have less flexibility in the way their operators use them. By reducing the control choices available in this way, we also reduce the risk of serious accidents.

In this unit task, you will research information for the essay title you chose in Part A.

a Take Cornell-style notes on a separate piece of paper while reading the text below.

b After reading, answer these questions.

1 Try to identify the writer's main idea. How strong is the reasoning and how suitable is the evidence?

2 How strong is the logic in the argument? Are there any flaws?

3 How well does the information in this text relate to the assignment title that you have chosen?

Is individual decision-making rational or irrational?

The rise in popularity of scientific theories of management has led to many theoretical models which attempt to explain, and predict, the way that decisions are made in large organizations. By using insights about the decision-making process, managers are believed to be able to improve the strategic and everyday business decisions within their organizations, making them more systematic and rational. There is a widely held assumption that individual decision-making, too, is a rational, logical process, in which the individual collects, processes and analyzes information in order to help them make the most rational decision. According to Stewart (1994, p.63), one popular view of individual decisions is that they are 'the result of a logical analysis of available information'. However, it may be an oversimplification to view the choices that individuals make in this way.

Many models of how individuals make choices assume a rational basis for their decision. However, psychological evidence indicates that individuals tend not to make their decisions in this way. The following paper will outline some of the typical assumptions about how individuals make decisions (so-called rational models), then offer contrasting research evidence from psychology which suggests that in reality individuals do not routinely appear to make decisions in a rational way (so-called descriptive models).

Rational models of decision-making

Attempts to outline rational models of decision-making are not new. Hansson (2005) identifies the eighteenth-century philosopher Nicolas de Condorcet as the author of the first model of a rational decision process. However, it was throughout the twentieth century that more formalized models, which identified logical sequences in the decision-making process, became common. One example of a rational–sequential model of decision-making is that produced by Herbert Simon (1960). Simon's model separated rational decision-making into three phases: finding an occasion for a decision; finding possible courses of action; and, finally, choosing a course of action. This three-step model has largely become accepted as the simplest explanation of the rational decision process. In the first step, a problem is identified, in the second step, options are evaluated and, finally, a decision is made.

A more sophisticated variation on this model was the seminal work by Mintzberg et al. (1976), which effectively retained the three steps outlined by Simon, but renamed them Identification, Development and Selection. In the first stage, a need or problem is identified; in the second step, a search is made for solutions to the problem; and, finally, in the Selection stage, the available solutions are evaluated and a final choice is made. While this bears outward similarities to Simon's earlier model, it improved upon it by recognizing that decisions did not need to progress through the three stages in strict order. This model allowed for the possibility of individual differences in the way people make choices, as well as the fact that decisions do not always proceed smoothly and that sometimes problems are encountered that force the decision-maker to repeat steps or abandon options.

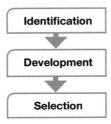

Figure 1: Mintzberg Decision-Making model

Assumptions under rational decision models

Rational models of decision-making rely on a number of assumptions about how individuals arrive at decisions. Most importantly, there is an assumption that the decision-maker's evaluation and choice is logical, as is made clear in the definition of decision-making offered by Stewart (ibid.). The rational–sequential model is arguably a logical method for making good choices, but it requires that the decision-maker is indeed acting logically. (Whether this is the case or not will be considered below.) Another assumption is that the decision-maker is aware that there is a problem of some sort at all. In some cases, such as extreme toothache, the decision-maker is clearly aware that there is a problem and presumably feels a need to seek a solution for it (visiting the dentist). However, this is not the case with all decision situations. To take one example, the problem may be that an individual lives in a house which is in serious need of repair, but does not perceive this to be the case. Here the person's perception of the situation means that they are not aware of a problem at all, so no decision about fixing it can be made. This is not as problematic with simple choices, like deciding which socks to buy, for instance, but can be serious when the problem is one of risk rather than consumer choice. There is also a tendency to assume that the decision-maker evaluates all of the factors involved in the decision accurately. The question is whether such rationality is actually central to the decision-making process in real life. Descriptive accounts of decision-making based on evidence of how people do make choices in reality tend to point to greater irrationality in the way individuals make their decisions and that many of the assumptions above are unfounded.

Descriptive accounts of decision-making

Most rationalistic views of decision-making place emphasis on the third stage of Mintzberg et al.'s model (the so-called 'selection' phase). It is at this stage that the individual is assumed to make rational, logical choices which will help them to make the best choice from the options available. However, psychological research evidence suggests that the reliability of the decision can be undermined by problems at the first stage (identification). One of the assumptions that rational models are based on is that the decision-maker is aware of the problem facing them, but in fact this is not often the case. Individuals interpret events differently and it is common for one person to see in a situation a problem that requires a decision, while another person perceives no problem at all and hence no need for a decision. An interesting example of this is the so-called 'normalcy bias', which can affect people in risky situations. (People tend automatically to try to reduce their own feelings of anxiety in dangerous situations and so underestimate the amount of risk facing them, thinking 'everything is OK', even though the evidence of their senses is different. Examples of the normalcy bias include people in nightclub fires continuing to dance or order drinks even when it is very apparent that their lives are in danger, or when people warned to stay away from the sea during a violent hurricane nevertheless choose to stand on the beach to watch the waves.) Thus each individual's perception of risk is different and we cannot assume that every decision-maker interprets situations as other people do.

Differences in identification of problems may also depend on the individual's so-called decision-making style. Arroba (1977) identified different types of decision-making styles which individuals may adopt, including no thought (those who make decisions without any particular consideration), logical (those carefully following a rational sequence of thought and investigating all options in detail), emotional (those who base their decisions on whether they 'like' or 'dislike' possible outcomes), and intuitive (those who make a decision based on their instincts – what they 'feel' to be right). With the obvious exception of the logical-type decision-maker, the other styles are hardly rational and Arroba's study found a large percentage of people whose decision styles fell into these irrational categories. Similarly to Arroba's identification of an intuitive style, Slovic et al., in a study of decision-making in situations of risk, claim that 'intuitive feelings [rather than rational methods] are … the predominant method by which humans evaluate risk' (Slovic et al., 2004, p.311).

During the evaluative 'selection' phase of Mintzberg et al.'s decision model (when it is most often assumed that the decision-maker will be acting logically to evaluate choices), other factors can interfere with the choice. Rational models assume that the decision-maker can evaluate all options to reach a 'best' decision. However, as noted above, perceptions tend to differ widely between individuals, and this is equally the case with interpretations of 'best' outcomes. As Stewart (1994, p.64) points out, there is frequently no agreement between individuals about what a 'best' choice might be. External factors also impact the individual's ability to make a rational 'best' choice. External factors include choice overload (Iyengar & Lepper, 2000) – when the decision-maker is presented with too many options to be able to make any sort of choice at all – and time pressure. Time pressure can combine with psychological factors to make choice overload even worse. As time pressure increases, so the individual has to attempt to handle more information in a shorter amount of time, which increases the complexity of the decision, thereby making the individual even more uncertain about the best choice (Jennings & Wattam, 1994, p.25). In circumstances such as these, apparently irrational decisions become much more likely. However, it is important to note that 'irrational' here does not mean incorrect: an individual may still make a good decision even if their method for making the decision was irrational. As an example, a would-be tourist attempting to choose a holiday destination from a vast range of different options may opt for the apparently irrational decision strategy of choosing a destination based on 'gut feeling'. This is an irrational method compared to the strict sequence of rational models, but experience tells us that this can often be a perfectly satisfactory way of making some decisions.

Conclusion

Rational models assume that logical rules govern decision-making behaviour and that such rules can be used to predict how future decisions should be made. They offer the possibility of controlling, or at least guiding, the decision-making process through a logical sequence in which problems are identified, options are found and evaluated, and a choice is finally made. Though such models may be useful tools for making long-term strategic decisions within organizations, descriptive evidence shows that individuals do not often make decisions in this way, preferring instead to use simplified and apparently 'irrational' bases for their choices. Nevertheless, there may be some truth in the argument that individuals might benefit from adopting strict rational models, as this would help to improve the quality of their decision-making.

References

Arroba, T. (1977). Styles of decision making and their use: an empirical study. *British Journal of Guidance and Counselling 5*(2), 149–158.

Hansson, S. O. (2005). *Decision Theory: A brief Introduction.* Stockholm: Royal Institute of Technology (KTH).

Iyengar, S. & Lepper, M.R. (2000). When choice is demotivating: can one desire too much of a good thing? *Journal of Personality and Social Psychology 79*(6), 995–1006.

Jennings, D. & Wattam, S. (1994). *Decision Making: An Integrated Approach* (2nd Edition). London: Financial Times Management.

Mintzberg, H., Raisinghani, D. & Théorêt, A. (1976). The Structure of 'unstructured' decision processes. *Administrative Science Quarterly 21*, 246–275.

Slovic, P., Finucane, M.L., Peters, E., & MacGregor, D.G. (2004). Risk as analysis and risk as feelings: Some thoughts about affect, reason, risk, and rationality. *Risk Analysis, 24*, 311–322.

Stewart, J. (1994). The psychology of decision making. In D. Jennings & S. Wattam (Eds.), *Decision Making: An Integrated Approach* (2nd Edition) (pp.56–82). London: Financial Times Management.

Source: Hersh, W. (2010). Is individual decision-making rational or irrational? *Journal of Decision and Risk Management 12*(3), 109–112

Go to the checklist on p.202. Look again at the tips relating to Unit 4 Part A and tick (✓) those you have used in your studies. Read the tips relating to Unit 4 Part B.

Investigating

By the end of Part C you will be able to:

- understand more about independent learning
- analyze your own independence as a learner.

1   Independent learning

At school and in some education systems, learning tends to focus on acquiring and remembering factual knowledge, while in higher education the focus shifts to independent evaluation and analysis by the student. As a result, success in independent study requires personal responsibility and motivation. There is a sliding scale between dependence and independence and it's always possible to move along it and become more effective in the way you study. In this section, you will evaluate your ability to learn independently and identify some ways that you can develop this skill.

1a Work in pairs. Discuss your answers to these questions.

1   How confident do you feel about handling study tasks by yourself?

2   What methods do you use to motivate yourself?

3   How would you rate your own resourcefulness?

1b 'Self-starter' is a relatively recent buzzword which describes one characteristic of successful students, employees and entrepreneurs. Look at the excerpts from recent job adverts below. Work in pairs. Decide what characterizes a 'self-starter'. Write your ideas in the box on p.171.

An exciting opportunity exists to develop a new sales team. We are seeking a dynamic individual to develop and expand a base of clients. The successful applicant will be a self-starter with a proven track record in developing sales.

We are looking for an energetic self-starter to join our busy events team. You will work independently to prepare, carry out and follow up a large events programme in the central London area.

A self-starter who will design, write and test security applications. Must have experience with Unix, C+ +, Java. Working from home.

Characteristics of a 'self-starter'

1c Compare your ideas with another pair of students. Then read this definition to check your answers.

> Self-starters are people who are able to motivate themselves to get on with a project without waiting for very much instruction from anyone else. An employer or academic supervisor trusts that a self-starter can successfully handle a project from the outset largely by themselves.

Students in higher education are normally expected to be self-starters. This includes *resourcefulness* – the ability to find information by yourself and to take responsibility for your own improvement. Less resourceful students tend to wait to be told where to get information from a single person (quite often their teacher). They rely on the help of other people in order to be successful, rather than relying on themselves.

1d Work in pairs. Several problems are listed below. For each one, decide whether you would feel confident to deal with it by yourself, or would need to seek help or advice from someone else. Justify your answers to each other.

1 You have been told that your lectures will be in a different building next week, but you have no idea where the building is.

2 You don't know how to search for information on the library computers.

3 You are having trouble understanding some of the ideas in one of your courses.

4 Your lecturer has asked you to use a software package to analyze statistics, but you have never used it before and don't have a copy of the software.

5 You have to do an individual research project but have never done one before.

6 One of your lecturers speaks too fast, gives confusing instructions about assignments and is generally unhelpful towards you and the other students.

7 Your lecturer has told you that you 'need to improve your writing'.

8 Your accommodation is noisy and distracting. It's very difficult to study well there.

9 You don't know how to operate a printer in the library.

10 You are trying to find information on a topic for an essay but you don't know where to start.

> One of the most basic resourceful attributes that a student can have is being skilled at finding information sources.

1e Imagine that you have been asked to research the topic of the 'normalcy bias' in decision-making. (The normalcy bias is a state of mind which can affect how well individuals make decisions in risky or dangerous situations.) You have found only one book in your library, which is about decision-making in general, and an online search didn't turn up anything very useful.

The book about general decision-making gives you some very basic information about the normalcy bias, but not enough to understand it properly. Look at the reference page from the book about decision-making below. Answer these questions.

1 Which of the sources on the reference list could you try reading next in order to increase your knowledge about the normalcy bias?

2 Which journals appear in the list?

3 Judging from the reference list, which of these journals might contain more articles on the topic?

References

Addison, T. (2000). Aid in conflict. In Finn, R. (Ed.). *Foreign Aid and Development: Lessons Learnt and Direction for the Future*. London: Routledge.

Aguirre, B.E. (2004). Can sustainable development sustain us? *International Journal of Mass Emergencies and Disasters, 20*(2), 111–126.

Christopolis, I., Mitchell, J., & Liljelund, A. (2001). Re-framing risk: The changing context of disaster mitigation and preparedness. *Disasters, 25*(3), 185–198.

Clarke, L. (1989). *Acceptable Risk: Making Decisions in a Toxic Environment*. Berkeley, CA: University of California Press.

Cohen, J. (1977). *Statistical Power Analysis for the Behavioural Sciences* (Revised Edition). New York: Academic Press.

Duany, A. & Talen, E. (2002). Transect Planning. *Journal of the American Planning Association, 68*(3), 245–266.

Dynes, R.R. (2004). Expanding the horizons of disaster research. *Natural Hazards Observer, 27*, 1–3.

Eagly, A.H. & Chaiken, S. (1993). *The Psychology of Attitudes.* Fort Worth: Harcourt, Brace, Jovanovich.

Hackman, J.R. & Wageman, R. (2005). A theory of team coaching. *Academy of Management Review, 30*, 269–287.

Jackson, E.L. (1981). Response to earthquake hazard: The West Coast of North America. *Environment and Behaviour, 13*, 387–416.

Lindell, M.K. & Brandt, C.J. (2000). Climate quality and climate consensus as mediators of the relationship between organizational antecedents and outcomes. *Journal of Applied Psychology, 85*, 331–348.

Lindell, M.K. & Prater, C.S. (2003). Assessing community impacts of natural disasters. *Hazards Review, 15*, 439–447.

Litynski, D., Grabowski, M., & Wallace, W. (1997). The relationship between three-dimensional imaging and group decision making: An exploratory study. *IEEE Transactions on Systems, Man and Cybernetics, 27*(4), 401–411.

The most successful independent learners do not rely only on information given to them by their teachers. Instead, they hunt for information which can improve their understanding on a subject. There are many websites which offer useful information and practice activities for academic skills, and it is likely that your library also stores a range of books on the subject.

1f Do some independent research to find out what academic skills resources are available to you. Use the space below to keep notes on useful resources that you could consult in the future.

Information	Notes on sources
Advice about academic writing	**Books in your library**
	Websites
Study skills handbooks	**Books in your library**
	Websites
Advice about doing research	**Books in your library**
	Websites
Information about critical thinking	**Books in your library**
	Websites

2 Analyzing your own independence as a learner

2a Use this questionnaire to help you identify your strengths as an independent learner, as well as areas that you could continue to improve. For each statement, give yourself a score from 1 to 5, where 1 is entirely untrue for you and 5 is entirely true. (The list continues on p.175.)

Statement	Score
I understand my own long-term goals for studying.	
I am able to tell the difference between things I can do on my own and things that I need help with.	
I have the self-discipline to follow my own study schedule, even if I am tempted by distractions.	
I read more than is required to try to understand the subject as fully as possible.	
I make sure that I understand all the rules and requirements for my course so that I do not accidentally affect my own grades.	
I try to match my study style to the expectations of my teachers and college.	
I am able to change my methods after someone gives me advice.	
After making a mistake once, I don't repeat it.	
I do not give up easily when I meet problems with my study.	
I have confidence in my own independence.	
I reflect on my work and think of ways to improve by myself.	
I understand that problems may occur which I cannot control (for instance, difficult courses, confusing teachers, language problems) and think of strategies that I can use to deal with them.	
I am able to balance my work and study time for effective results.	
I can prioritize study tasks effectively.	

I plan ahead.			
I am able to find resources by myself.			
I don't just want to pass my courses, I want to pass as well as possible.			
Total			

2b Compare your answers with a partner. Explain your reasons and think of things you could do to improve. Then add up your total score and compare it with this guide. Do you agree with this assessment?

Total = 17–33: You urgently need to take steps to become more independent.

Total = 34–50: Plenty of room for more independence in your approach.

Total = 51–68: You seem to be well on the way to being an independent learner.

Total = 69–85: You appear to be very independent already.

2c With your partner, look again at the problems listed in 1d. Try to think of the most resourceful way of solving them independently. Discuss your ideas, giving reasons why you think your solutions would be effective.

Decision-making

Later in this unit you will give a presentation and then write a short essay on your chosen decision-making assignment title.

By now you have already started gathering information about the topic from the notes you took in the listening (Unit Task 4 Part A), as well as the reading (Unit Task 4 Part B). However, these are rather general introductions to the topic and you will need to find other sources of information which are more relevant to the assignment title you have chosen.

a Before the next lesson, search for material about decision-making which is specifically relevant to your assignment title. When you find possible sources, read them critically and take notes, then synthesize them together with the other information you have.

b Try to keep a record of bibliographic information for the sources you find in the space below. Doing this as soon as you find a source is easier than going back to look for the information after you have finished your essay.

1	
2	
3	
4	
5	
6	
7	

Go to the checklist on p.203. Look again at the tips relating to Unit 4 Parts A–B and tick (✓) those you have used in your studies. Read the tips relating to Unit 4 Part C.

Reporting in speech

By the end of Part D you will be able to:
- draw suitable conclusions in a presentation
- speculate on findings
- make recommendations
- prepare and rehearse for a presentation.

1 Drawing suitable conclusions in a presentation

1a Work in pairs. Decide what elements might be included in a 'good' conclusion for a presentation. Make a note of your ideas in the space below. Then compare your ideas with another pair of students.

> **'Good' presentation conclusions**

1b Read this plan of a presentation about resource allocation. Identify the speaker's main idea. (The plan continues on p.178.)

Assignment title: Give an overview of the factors involved in resource allocation decisions

Introduction:
Resource allocation describes the way in which an individual or organization makes decisions about how to use and distribute finite resources such as money, time, machinery and human and natural resources. Decisions about how to allocate resources feature in almost every field of human inquiry or endeavour, though the factors which must be considered tend to differ widely between different fields; it is therefore difficult to make generalizations. For this reason I will be limiting this presentation to a consideration of the factors involved in the decision about how to allocate that most basic of resources: money.

I will give an overview of the factors which the person making the resource allocation decision must take into account, then consider some external factors which can influence the decision. I will conclude with a short discussion of psychological research which looks at how completely individuals consider these factors when facing complex resource allocation decisions.

Main body:

1 Factors to be taken into account in financial resource allocation
   a Number of alternative uses
   b Priority of alternatives
   c Relative abundance of resource available
   d Opportunity costs of options not chosen
   e Schedule of use
   f Risks and benefits involved in any choice

2 External factors which can influence the decision
   a Bias towards a lower priority alternative
   b Time pressure

3 Research results of resource allocation psychology
   There is an expectation that people will make rational resource allocation decisions based on the factors above. However, research indicates that not all such choices are made rationally.

4.7

1c Listen to two alternative conclusions to the presentation. Decide which of the two conclusions is better and why.

1d Check your answers with a partner. Can you add any more points to your ideas about what constitutes a 'good' conclusion, based on what you have heard?

1e Read a plan for a presentation about the choices students make when they allocate their time outside lectures. Identify the speaker's main claims.

Assignment title: Examine the factors affecting student time allocation decisions

Introduction:
According to educationalist Pauline Frears, there is a tendency to view students as poor managers of their own time. The belief persists that students must make a simple decision when outside the classroom to 'either' engage in study or pursue leisure and that time spent not studying is wasted. However, there are a number of competing demands on the average student's time. This is a classic resource allocation problem. In this presentation I will try to outline some of the factors which must be taken into account when managing time spent outside the classroom and suggest that students are, in fact, more skilled managers of their own time than they are often given credit for.

Main body:

1 This is a typical resource allocation problem, the key factors involved being:
   a Number of alternative ways to spend time
   b Priority of alternative time choices
   c Relative amount of time free

2 How this relates to the situation of students:
   Most students must balance some or all of these alternative ways of spending time outside class.
   a self-study
   b socializing with friends
   c eating
   d sleeping

e hygiene
f exercise
g 'beneficial' activities (e.g. volunteering, learning a language, reading)
h working part-time
i childcare (mature students)

3 Studies suggest that many students make 'rational' time allocation decisions for their situation. However, 'rational' does not necessarily mean that the student spends their time on self-study unless this is one of their priorities.

4 The results of one study (Hirsh, 1986) reveal that the majority of students tend to be less skilled at making decisions about how to allocate their time for long-term project work.

1f Write a suitable conclusion for the presentation in this space.

2 Speculating on findings

2a Review what you have learned about speculation in Unit 3 Part A2. In what circumstances would it be suitable to include speculation in a presentation?

> A certain amount of speculation may be acceptable towards the end of a presentation, as it shows that you have been thinking of consequences or possibilities arising from the topic that you have been speaking about. Speculation is normally appropriate as long as it is clearly signposted and hedged.

4.8

2b Listen to two students introducing speculations into the final part of their presentations. Make a note of the topic of the presentation, and the speculations they make.

2c Listen again. Work in pairs. Decide which student introduced speculation more successfully. Explain your reasons.

2d Look back at the presentation about student allocation of time resources in 1e. Use the space on p.180 to try writing some speculations that might be suitable to include at the end of this presentation. Speculate about:

1 the reasons why students tend not to prioritize long-term projects
2 the reasons why many teachers assume students are poor time managers
3 what methods might be effective to help students improve their time management skills.

2e Compare your ideas with another pair. Decide whether the speculations they have proposed are reasonable.

3 Making recommendations

3a Look at the script of the conclusion from a presentation on student decisions about how to allocate time. What recommendations does the speaker make?

> 'In conclusion, the evidence I have presented here suggests that students must make a sophisticated series of decisions about how they divide their time when they are not in lectures. Disregarding time spent sleeping, self-study competes with pure leisure activities such as socializing with friends, as well as self-maintenance such as eating and hygiene, exercise and possibly working a part-time job or doing childcare. It may be the case that students are far better time managers than teachers give them credit for when all these different factors are taken into account. An interesting question which is worthy of further study is the possible difference in the way that the most successful students use their time when compared with their less successful classmates.'

3b Check your answers with a partner.

> Many academic presentations include a number of recommendations in their conclusion. A number of different types of recommendation are possible.
>
> 1 Recommendations about the way that a future researcher could improve the work in the current presentation. The presenter may identify weaknesses in their own research and suggest ways to improve it in the future.
>
> 2 Recommendations for other research about issues which have not been covered in the present study. The presenter may identify unresolved questions arising from the current research and make recommendations for how to investigate them in future.
>
> 3 Recommendations for actions to be taken by governments or organizations based on the findings presented in the research.

3c Look at the transcript for the first conclusion from 1c in **Appendix 6**. Identify the type of recommendation that the speaker made.

Your recommendations are made directly to your audience, in the hope that they will be able to act on your suggestions. Therefore, the recommendations should be appropriate – practical and realistically achievable. It isn't appropriate to make general recommendations that your audience would be unable to act upon.

3d Work in pairs. Decide if each of the recommendations made below is suitable to the audience.

1 **Presenter:** 2nd-year student presenting results of a small research project

Theme of presentation: A study of the way that students decide to allocate their time between study and leisure

Audience: Classmates

Conclusion and recommendation:
'In conclusion, the results of my study suggest that, contrary to the complaints of parents and teachers, most students are capable of making adequate decisions by themselves about the best way to divide their time between study and leisure. However, my study is based only on a very small number of questionnaires given to students on this course, so it would be interesting to see if the same results could be obtained in a wider study involving more students.'

2 **Presenter:** 3rd-year student presenting results of a small research project

Theme of presentation: An investigation of the factors affecting students' decisions about which university to apply for

Audience: Classmates

Conclusion and recommendation:
'I'd like to summarize by restating my main points here. Overall, students contemplating whether to cease education and enter the workforce, or continue their education at university, are faced with a number of serious choices about forgone earnings and future career prospects. These are very difficult choices for people of undergraduate age to make alone so universities should offer better advice.'

3 **Presenter:** Postgraduate student presenting results of research

Theme of presentation: A comparative investigation of high- and low-achieving students' study time choices

Audience: Other postgraduates and academics

Conclusion and recommendation:
'In conclusion, the results I've presented here suggest that there are some significant differences in the way that students at opposite ends of the achievement spectrum choose to use their non-lecture time, with the lower-achieving students predictably choosing to spend more time on pure leisure activities overall. However, the results do also indicate that a large number of low-achieving students spend an equal amount of time on study as their more successful peers. Possible reasons for this include differences in the approach taken while studying, as well, perhaps, as the time when such study is done. However, this is far from clear and further research is needed in order to shed more light on this.'

3e Read this overview of some research about study time allocation choices. Answer the questions below.

Study aim	To understand how students reach decisions about the way to arrange their time.
Sample and method	• 40 first-year students on an undergraduate physics course. They were all volunteers and were not paid for participating. • Students were asked to write detailed diaries recording the time they spent outside lectures over the course of a week during the early part of term, then repeated the diary during the week before exams. • Each student was interviewed about how they had decided to use their time.
Findings	• In the early part of the term, around 60% of students tended to leave work until shortly before important deadlines. • In the latter part of the term, students prioritised study at the expense of leisure time.
Conclusion	As expected, most students tend to prioritize study when deadlines are imminent.
Problems encountered	Not all students kept the diaries consistently.

1 Is the number of respondents in the survey sufficient to conclude that the finding is definitely true?

2 What could be done to improve the methodology so that the findings are more strongly supported?

3 How seriously did the problem encountered affect the study? Is there any way that the problem could be avoided in a future study?

3f Imagine that this was your research. Make a note of the recommendations that you could suggest to your audience in this space.

4 Preparing and rehearsing for a presentation

The best way to ensure that your presentation is a success is to rehearse it until you are confident that you know the subject and can express it clearly to your audience. Group presentations can be easier to rehearse for, as you have the motivation of working in a group and are able to give each other feedback. An individual presentation, however, still needs rehearsal, so it is beneficial to ask a friend to help you prepare by listening and questioning you.

Preparation for the question and answer session of a presentation can be critical to persuading your audience to accept your ideas.

Questions and comments from the audience normally fall into these categories:

1 Requests for more information or clarification of information given

2 Comments or questions calling attention to weaknesses or omissions in your argument or research

3 Questions concerning the future development or implications of your argument or research.

4a Read the following outline of a presentation. Work in pairs. Identify any apparent weaknesses in the presentation and anticipate what questions and comments are likely from the audience.

Slides	Presentation content
1 **The Tyranny of Choice** • Introduction and background • Research evidence for the 'choice overload' theory • Implications • Applications • Conclusion	The student presents her first slide and defines 'the tyranny of choice', explaining that it becomes difficult to make a decision when one is presented with too much choice. She explains that in her presentation she gives research evidence on the tyranny of choice, then considers its real-world implications and finally suggests some things that can be done to ease the process of making decisions.

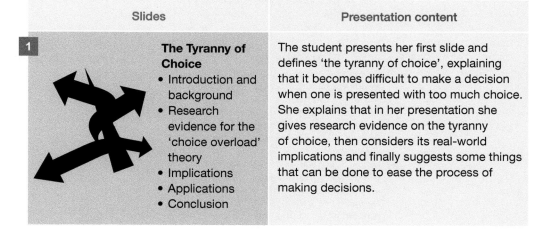

<table>
<tr>
<td>

2

Background

"Although some choice is undoubtedly better than none, more is not always better than less." (Schwartz, 2004:70).
    1. 'The Tyranny of Choice' / 'The Paradox of Choice' (Schwartz, 2004).
    2. 'Choice Overload' (Iyengar and Lepper, 2000).
People have difficulty making a decision when they are faced with a large number of options.

</td>
<td>

The student explains that the phrase 'Tyranny of Choice' was coined by psychologist Barry Schwartz to describe the difficulty that people have making decisions when they have too many options to choose from, but that the phenomenon has also been called by other names.

</td>
</tr>
<tr>
<td>

3

Research evidence

- People faced with a choice of flavours of jam or varieties of chocolate were more likely to make a choice when the range of options was limited (Iyengar and Lepper, 2000).
- Online grocery shop sales increase when product range on offer is halved (Boatwright and Nunes, 2001).
- People struggle to make a decision when too many attributes are involved (Fasolo et al., 2006).

</td>
<td>

The student introduces some evidence for the phenomenon, arguing that it demonstrates clearly that people are unable to make decisions when presented with too many options.

</td>
</tr>
<tr>
<td>

4

Implications

Marketing Sales can be affected by the number of alternatives offered to consumers.

Mental health People faced with too many choices are likely to suffer stress (Schwartz, 2000).

Safety An inability to make timely decisions may have an impact on safety, e.g. airline pilots, drivers, operators of dangerous machinery, or others working in high-risk environments.

</td>
<td>

The student argues that this has implications for a number of different situations, some of them quite serious.

</td>
</tr>
<tr>
<td>

5

Conclusion

- Stores should offer a smaller range of products in order to increase sales.
- Our societies should deliberately simplify themselves in order to reduce anxiety and depression caused by the tyranny of choice.
- More research is necessary to discover how the tyranny of choice affects the efficiency with which people operate dangerous machinery.

</td>
<td>

The student concludes with a summary of the main points, saying that the tyranny of choice is a serious problem in a number of ways. She makes a number of recommendations.

</td>
</tr>
<tr>
<td>

6

References

1. Boatwright, P. and Nunes, J.C. (2001). Reducing assortment: an attribute-based approach. *Journal of Marketing, 65*, 50–63.
2. Fasolo, B., McClelland, G.H., and Todd, P.M. (2007). Escaping the tyranny of choice: when fewer attributes make choice easier. *Marketing Theory, 7*, 13–26.
3. Iyengar, S. and Lepper, R. (2000). When choice is demotivating: can one desire too much of a good thing? *Journal of Personality and Social Psychology, 76*, 995–1006.
4. Schwartz, B. (2004). The Tyranny of Choice. *Scientific American, 290*(4), 70–75.

</td>
<td>

The student shows a slide containing her references.

</td>
</tr>
</table>

4b Compare your ideas with another pair of students.

4c Use this checklist to help you prepare and rehearse for presentations.

Item	Tick (✓) if OK	Check this section for more advice
Are you clear about your own purpose for making the presentation?		• SS3 Unit 3 Part D1
Are any visual aids suitable?		• SS3 Unit 1 Part D2
Are the graphics you are using suitable?		• SS3 Unit 2 Parts D1–D2
Is the content of your presentation logically organized, clearly argued, persuasive and well supported?		• SS3 Unit 1 Part D3
Is the delivery of your presentation clear and persuasive?		• SS3 Unit 1 Part D4
If you have used information from other sources, are these sources acknowledged properly?		• SS3 Unit 2 Part D3
Have you anticipated questions that your audience might ask?		• SS3 Unit 2 Part A3

➤ UNIT TASK Decision-making

In this unit task, you will prepare and deliver a group presentation on the decision-making assignment title that you have chosen. Your tutor will tell you how long the presentation should be.

a Form a group of three or four students who have all chosen the same assignment title.

b Discuss these questions to help you plan your presentation.

1 What is your purpose in this presentation?

2 What is the main idea of your presentation?

3 What kind of evidence will you present to support your ideas?

4 How will you structure the content of the presentation for best effect?

5 Will you include visual or graphic data of any sort?

6 What roles will each member of the group take?

c When you have prepared the main body of your presentation, review Unit 2 Part A3, about asking questions. Work as a group. Try to anticipate the questions that you might be asked by the audience or your teachers.

d Practise asking each other and responding to the questions.

Go to the checklist on p.203. Look again at the tips relating to Unit 4 Parts A–C and tick (✓) those you have used in your studies. Read the tips relating to Unit 4 Part D.

Reporting in writing

By the end of Part E you will be able to:

- write a suitable conclusion
- proofread written work
- review written work for logical flaws
- edit written work for logical flaws
- reflect on completed work.

1 Writing a suitable conclusion

1a Think back to what you have learned about writing conclusions in the past. Work in pairs. Make a list of features that might appear in a conclusion to a piece of academic writing.

1b Look at the list of possible conclusion features in the box below. Make sure that you understand each feature. Then read the example conclusion below. Underline any features that you find.

Possible features of a conclusion

1 Summary of key points

2 Discussion of implications from key points

3 Recommendations for further research

4 Suggesting broader applications of the thesis or findings

5 A restatement of the original thesis

6 Weaknesses of the research

7 Answering a question introduced in the introduction

> The evidence presented above suggests that we are faced with serious questions about the | 1
> best way to manage our natural resources in the coming half century. Increasing population
> will put more stress on existing water, food, energy and industrial supplies. While these
> problems are undoubtedly significant, they can nevertheless be overcome through planning,
> preparation and coordination of government with industry and local communities. Further | 5
> applied research is necessary to test the 3-stage Resource Planning model presented here
> in a real-life resource allocation situation. The model potentially offers an invaluable tool
> for government and business decision makers faced with the problem of how to handle
> increasingly scarce resources.

> Not all of the features mentioned above need to be included in every type of conclusion. They may vary with the type of subject being presented, as well as by the academic level of the text.

1c Underline any features in 1b that you find in the conclusions below.

1

Precise information on the state of resources is vital for effective ecosystem management. [1]
Ecosystems are complex and constantly changing environments and, though their effective
management depends on accurate and reliable decision making, their complexity, paradoxically,
makes reliable decision making very difficult. Resource allocation is a particular issue and
decision makers involved in this process have previously relied on professional experience alone [5]
to help them make resource decisions. This paper has compared a number of computerized
decision-making systems which can support this process and lead to greater decision-reliability.
Though both GIS and DSS decision-support software are effective, their combination into an
integrated system helps the decision maker to best allocate resources, where the goal-function of
the software is to optimize resource allocation and reduce wastage. This combination of software [10]
has other applications outside the field of ecosystem management, including emergency relief
and government environmental policy.

2

In conclusion, it is apparent that difficult resource allocation decisions are as common in the provision [1]
of medical care as in any other type of field. Resources such as medical supplies, staff and money for
investment or purchase of equipment are finite, so decisions must be made about how to distribute
these for the care of needy patients. There are obvious ethical dilemmas involved in how to allocate
scarce medical resources and, though cost-effectiveness is an unpalatable issue in medicine, with [5]
competition between medical departments for available resources, many medical authorities argue
that it must nevertheless be considered.

3

The results presented here suggest that resource allocation decisions made by consumers are [1]
influenced strongly by considerations of value, cost and prestige. Shoppers appear to allocate
financial resources based on intuitive feelings about whether an item is 'positive', rather than a
careful consideration of the benefits involved. Because of the exploratory nature of this study,
we were unable to collect data from multiple respondents, therefore a number of variables have [5]
been derived from only a single respondent. Though the reliability of these answers from a
single source is uncertain, the results provide some evidence that shopping behaviour follows
other types of affect-based decision making. The model of shopping behaviour used in our study
does not incorporate considerations of opportunity costs, which is a factor that has a significant
impact on the resource allocation decisions studied here. Further research needs to be done [10]
on developing a more complete model of shoppers' financial resource allocation behaviour. It
would also be beneficial to try to apply approaches from cognitive psychology to understanding
how incentives affect allocation decisions.

4

This paper has introduced factors involved in student time allocation decisions, and the effect [1]
that this can have on academic performance. Course attendance and self-study are balanced
against competing non-academic pursuits including leisure time, health maintenance and
improving pursuits such as 'volunteering'. Students optimize their time when they are subject to
a time constraint such as a deadline. This implies that students can be capable managers of their [5]
own time, but that this does not always mean that they manage their time in order to maximize
study potential: instead, it depends on the student's own priorities.

1d The conclusion should logically follow from, and be supported by, the arguments,
reasoning and evidence presented in the main body of the work. Read the essay
outline on p.189, then evaluate each possible conclusion that follows it to decide
how suitable they are.

Assignment title:
To what extent are concerns that finite natural resources (such as fossil fuels, fresh water and agricultural land) are running out justified?

Overall argument:
'Many natural resources on which the human population relies for survival and economic growth are finite. Population pressure and continued economic growth make it very likely that these resources will run out unless careful decisions are made about how to manage them sustainably.'

Supporting arguments:
1 Many finite resources are being rapidly depleted.

2 The Earth's population is growing rapidly, requiring more resources to support larger numbers of people.

3 The seriousness of the situation is clear from the fact that many governments are making detailed plans for future resource management.

Conclusion 1

There is evidence that the Earth's finite natural resources are becoming depleted. After decades or even centuries of use, people have come to think of these resources as abundant and limitless. This is unlikely to be the case, however, as evidence from a range of studies into fresh water, agricultural land, fisheries and forestry make clear. The situation with fossil fuels, particularly oil, is more difficult to assess due to widespread doubt about the size of official oil reserves. The balance of our natural resources is put under even more pressure by a combination of increasing population and the demand for perpetual economic growth, leading to greater, and ever faster, consumption of the resources which do remain, despite government attempts to plan for resource management. Unchecked, this situation is likely to lead to serious resource depletion; it is likely that we will face difficult decisions in the years ahead about how best to balance our desired living standards with the limits of our resources.

Conclusion 2

Natural resources such as woodland, fisheries, fresh water and fossil fuels are necessary for continued economic growth. In order to ensure a high standard of living for the Earth's population, both in developed countries and in the developing world, careful use of these resources is vital. However, some evidence suggests that overuse is leading to the depletion of these resources, making economic growth particularly difficult, especially in the developing world. However, through technological development, the possibility exists that alternatives to these resources can be found (for instance, fish farming, or the use of biofuels). International organizations must work together with the government to ensure funding for research in order to safeguard our economic prosperity.

2 Proofreading written work

Having completed your final draft of a piece of work, the next step is proofreading. It is possible to do a certain amount of proofreading yourself, but it is normally more effective to give your work to a friend whose advice you trust and ask them to look over it as well. Editing via computer is fast and effective, but printing out a hard copy of your work which a proofreader can then mark up with pen is a more thorough way of making sure that you catch as many errors as possible.

2a Which of these things would be appropriate to ask a proofreader to do?

Action	Appropriate	Inappropriate
Check for formatting errors		
Identify spelling and grammar mistakes		
Correct spelling and grammar mistakes		
Raise questions about parts that they don't understand		
Substitute inappropriate vocabulary for something more academic		
Re-write sections that don't make sense		
Comment about whether the progression of ideas seems logical		
Improve expressions which, while not grammatically incorrect, are awkward		
Correct your work and then print the document for you		
Write sections that you are finding difficult to explain		

2b Compare your answers with a partner.

2c This table contains some common proofreading symbols which could be used to mark a text. Look at the example of how these symbols are used. Then practise annotating the sample text which follows.

Meaning	Symbol in text	Symbol in margin
Insert missing word	⋀Moscow children in this study …	The ⋀
Delete	The main reason ~~is~~ is that …	ℓ
Insert a space	Known⁄as the normalcy bias	#
Close space	Five diff ͝ erent modules were …	͝
Wrong font	The decision-making process is …	wf
Begin a new paragraph	… is possible//Another factor is …	¶
Run on (don't make a new paragraph)	… is permanent. ⌒ Though Bell (2009) claims that …	No ¶
Upper-case	… organized by nasa in 1968.	cap
Lower-case	It is Unlikely that they will …	lc

Italicize	used an <u>ad hominem</u> argument.	*italic*
Make roman	There are only *fifteen* possible …	rom
Insert comma	… includes water oil and fisheries.	˄,
Insert apostrophe	It won't be a significant …	˅
Insert full stop	… which are desirable However, it …	⊙
Insert quotation marks	Which Smith calls a fuzzy process.	˅ ˅ or ˅ ˅ quotation marks
Query to author	… computer designed in <u>1473.</u>	ok/?
Spelling	… a further 12 <u>sujbects</u> were given…	sp.
Subject/verb agreement	… many <u>people</u> is involved…	s/v
Tense	… was <u>create</u> in Moscow in 1976.	T
Leave unchanged (after proofreader makes a mistake)	Omer (2006) refers to it as latency.	✓

Example

Sustainable management of natural resources is vital ⌐ , and depends on cooperation between government (or business) and local <u>comunities</u> which may **sp.** s/v depend on the resources in <u>its</u> area for subsistence. <u>it</u> is the responsibility of **cap.** government or other agencies (such as <u>ngos</u>) to make policies designed to **cap.** safeguard natural resources, though this must ƀ be harmonized with local ⌐ ⊙ community needs ˄.

1. Scarcity of goods time and money mean that resources need to be allocated with care

2. Most people agree that scarcit yof time makes peoples decisons less effective.

3. Galotti et al. 1986 showed that time pressuresignificantly affects the ability to solve problems.

4. Time is a vitsl element in human decision making. people adapt their decision making process when time is limited in order to arrive at the best available opiton that the circumstances will allow.

5. a principal step in engineeting projects is optimal resource allocation.

6. This paper will studied the impact of resource scarcity on choice optimisation .

2d Read this excerpt from an essay about resource dilemmas. Use the proofreading symbols to correct any errors you find.

Many of the world's most precious natural resources are finite. Fisheries; land for agriculture; wood for forestry; fresh water; minerals; and fossil fuels such as oil, gas and coal are all naturally limited. Their exploitation cannot continue indefinitely without careful management. While the tendency throughout most of human history has been to act as though these resources were boundless, recent events such as the near collapse of the North Atlantic fisheries ((Pauly et al., 2002) or tension over fresh-water supplies (Poff et al., 2003.) have helped to make us more aware that they need careful management and will not last if they are overexploited. a combination of growing population and lifestyle choices is putting serious strain on the Earth 's ability to provide for all of us. Clearly, this is now the most significant environmental problem that we face. This essay will offer some examples of resource emanagement problems. The only solution to these problems is to ban commercial fishing and use fish farming instead.

Acrodding to Foran and Poldy (2002), in a report about natural resource problems facing Australia in the coming decades, societies strain their natural resources through their focus on economic growth. The growth of the economy is the cause of all environmental problems: more resources is used, more consumption demands more products, and yet more resources must be used to satisfy further growth. From an economic point of view, this is attractive idea and appears to make sense in terms of growth and the raising of living standards, particularly in developing nations.

however, this model of growth is only sensible in the short to medium term. If one looks at the longer term , then it hardly makes economic sense to promote growth if that will lead eventually to serious resource depletion, which will ultimately undermine the prosperity of all nations. Foran & Poldy (IBID), make the claim that the manner in which modern societies consume resources is excessive and wasteful, and is consequently unsustainable.

The first world economies are often criticized for overconsumption, with some authors claiming that the average individual in a developed nation produces about 30 times as   much waste as those living in developing nations. However, many developing nations are rapidly industrializing so they are creating more waste which adds to the problem.

References

Foran, B. and Poldy, F. (2002). *Future Dilemmas: Options to 2050 for Australia's Population, Technology, Resources and Environment.* Working Paper Series 02/01, Canberra: CSIRO Sustainable Ecosystems.

Pauly, D., Christensen, V., Guenette, S., Pitcher, T.J., Sumaila, R., Walters, C.J., Watson, R. and Zeller, D. (2002). Towards sustainability in world fisheries. *Nature*, 418, 689–695.

Poff, N.L., Allan, J.D., Palmer, M.A., Hart, D., Richter, B., Arthington, A.H., Rogers, K.H., Meyer, J., Stanford, J.A. (2003). River flows and water wars: emerging science for environmental decision making. *Frontiers in Ecology and the Environment, 6*, 298–306.

2e Compare your answers in small groups.

3 Reviewing written work for logical flaws

3a This table contains a list of the logical flaws that you have learned about throughout this book. Write a short definition of each flaw in the space provided.

Type of flaw	Definition
Necessary conditions	
False premises	
Sufficient conditions	
Correlation	
Arguments 'against the person'	
'You too' arguments	
Weak analogy	
Circular arguments	
Limited options	

> A writer may use an argument that they know is logically flawed as a deliberately dishonest attempt to persuade their reader. However, it is likely that most logical flaws enter work through mistakes in the writer's reasoning. As most of us assume that our own thinking is logical, these mistakes can be difficult to spot.

3b Read through the essay in 2d again. Carefully consider the logic of the claims that the author makes. Try to identify any logical flaws.

4 Editing written work for logical flaws

4a Different people have various ways of editing work, so it is advisable to find what works best for you. Read the suggestions for ways to improve your editing below. Work in pairs. Discuss which ideas you have tried, or think would be useful.

Suggestions

1 Ask yourself these questions as you read through a piece of work for editing.

  a What is the writer's overall aim in the piece of work?

  b Are there clear linking sentences between paragraphs and sections?

  c Does each paragraph have a single clear topic?

  d Are the introduction and conclusion logical?

  e Is there anything which is repeated unnecessarily?

  f Is enough evidence presented to support the writer's point?

2 On a piece of spare paper, write a one-sentence summary of each paragraph. If you are unable to do this, it probably means that the paragraph is unclear or contains more than one topic.

3 Look at the list again and ask yourself these questions.

  a Are the paragraphs arranged in the most logical sequence?

  b Could anything be rearranged in order to make better sense?

  c Could any paragraphs be merged to prevent repetition or improve the line of argument?

  d Do any paragraphs contain more than one topic? If so, could they be split?

4b Work in pairs. Use the suggestions above to analyze the essay in 2d.

4c Look at this new draft of the student essay about resource dilemmas. A friend of the author has already read it and made some editing suggestions. Read the essay and decide if you agree with the suggestions or not.

Outline the dilemmas involved in maintaining the Earth's natural resources

Many of the world's most precious natural resources are finite. Fisheries; land for agriculture; wood for forestry; fresh water; minerals; and fossil fuels such as oil, gas and coal, are all naturally limited. Their exploitation cannot continue indefinitely without careful management. While the tendency throughout most of human history has been to act as though these resources were boundless, recent events such as the near collapse of the North Atlantic fisheries (Pauly et al, 2002) or tension over fresh-water supplies (Poff et al, 2003) have helped to make us more aware that they need careful management and will not last if they are overexploited. A combination of growing population and lifestyle choices is putting serious strain on the Earth's ability to provide for all of us. This essay will offer some examples of resource management problems, and conclude by considering the decisions facing those who must management our resources for the future.

According to Foran and Poldy (2002), in a report about natural resource problems facing Australia in the coming decades, societies strain their natural resources through their focus on economic growth. As the economy grows, more resources are used, more consumption demands more products, and yet more resources must be used to satisfy further growth. From an economic point of view, this is an attractive idea and appears to make sense in terms of growth and the raising of living standards, particularly in developing nations.

However, this model of growth is only sensible in the short to medium term. If one looks at the longer term, then it hardly makes economic sense to promote growth if that will lead eventually to serious resource depletion, which will ultimately undermine the prosperity of all nations. Foran and Poldy (ibid.) make the largely uncontroversial claim that the manner in which modern societies consume resources is excessive and wasteful, and is consequently unsustainable.

This problem is exacerbated by the likelihood of continuing population increase. Though some nations may experience an overall decline in birth-rates, global population is likely to continue to increase, and even developed societies are likely to see contractions in the native population offset by increased immigration. As a result, national as well as global resource consumption levels are likely to increase. If the patterns of resource consumption do not change, analysts warn that future population pressure will have an extremely serious impact on the world's resources.

This needs evidence to support it. Also, could put it earlier in your argument.

Governments, businesses, and individuals face difficult choices in the years ahead. It is likely that sustainable management of the Earth's resources will require

5 Reflecting on completed work

5a Work in pairs. Discuss any strategies you have used after producing an assignment for reflecting on and improving your academic writing skills and consolidating your subject knowledge.

5b Compare your ideas with the suggestions in the information box below.

Any written work you do is designed to help you develop your knowledge of a subject, as well as improve your written academic skills for future work. After you finish writing and editing, reflect on what you have learned about the topic. These questions may help you to do this.

Developing subject knowledge

1 How confident do you feel that you have understood the subject fully?

2 What connections exist between this topic and other subjects that you have learned about?

3 How does what you have learned in this assignment help you in your chosen subject?

4 How can you store your notes so that they may be useful for future assignments or revision?

Improving writing skills

1 What did you find easiest in the writing process? Why?

2 What did you find most difficult? Why?

3 Which parts of your written assignment are you happiest with? Why?

4 Which parts are you least happy with? Why?

5 What could you have done differently to improve on your weakest points?

6 What are your strongest points as a writer? How will you improve these points still further next time?

> **UNIT TASK** **Decision-making**

Draw together all the work you have been doing in this unit on decision-making to write an essay on your chosen title. Your tutor will tell you how long your essay should be.

a Use this table to help you plan.

Title:		
Your main idea:		
Background information:		
Your supporting ideas:	**Evidence or citations:**	
	For	**Against**
1		
2		
3		
4		

b Write your answer to the essay title. Remember:
- use information from other sources to support your ideas
- use citations and a reference for each source you use.

Go to the checklist on p.202–203. Look again at the tips relating to Unit 4 Parts A–D and tick (✓) those you have used in your studies. Read the tips relating to Unit 4 Part E on p.203.

Review
Thinking in higher education

Now that you have completed Skills for Study Level 3, consider how your understanding of thinking in higher education has changed. Work in pairs. Without looking at your original answers to the quiz at the very start of the book, take the quiz again. Decide how strongly you agree or disagree with each statement by ticking (✓) the column (1–5) which best describes your opinion according to this scale. Do not worry about giving 'correct' answers, as this exercise is designed to help you reflect on the way you approach your studies.

1 = strongly disagree
2 = disagree
3 = neither agree nor disagree

4 = agree
5 = strongly agree

	Using and interpreting data	1	2	3	4	5
1	The most important skill for success in an English-speaking higher education institution is being fluent in the language.					
2	Critical thinking is not important for my subject.					
3	Memorizing facts, concepts and details is essential to my success in higher education.					
4	Critical thinking is much more important for subjects in the social sciences and humanities than for those in STEM (Science, Technology, Engineering and Mathematics).					
5	The most important task for a higher education student is to learn the information that the tutor or lecturer gives them.					
6	I should critically evaluate the information I hear when listening to lectures.					
7	I should carefully consider the accuracy of the information in every text I read.					
8	I should question the logic, methods and claims in everything I read or hear.					
9	I should be able to generate original ideas when completing projects and assignments in my subject.					

When you finish, turn back to the start of the book and compare your answers above with your original ideas. To what extent have you changed your mind?

Good study practice checklists

There are many ways you can practise the skills you have learned in these units on your own. Here are some suggestions. Use the suggestions as a checklist to help you develop your skills independently.

Tick (✓) if you have followed suggestion

Unit 1 – An electronic world

Part A Listening		
1	Recognize the type of subject you are studying and consider how your teachers expect you to listen in lectures.	☐
2	When you listen, think about the speaker's purpose – is the speaker trying to persuade you of something? If so, consider the strength of their idea. Do you agree with it or not?	☐
3	After lectures or classes, review your notes. Identify points that you do not understand fully and plan to research them by yourself.	☐
4	Spend time reviewing the ideas, methods and evidence that you have listened to. Review your notes critically.	☐
5	Try using Cornell notes to help you prepare for exams and develop a deeper understanding of the subject.	☐

Part B Reading		
1	Find out what text types are common in the discipline you want to enter.	☐
2	Become familiar with different text types and become familiar with the functions of each section.	☐
3	As you read a section of a text, ask yourself what its function is.	☐
4	Try to recognize ways in which the author is persuading you.	☐
5	When you do find persuasive techniques used in writing, ask yourself if the writer has done enough to persuade you.	☐

Part C Investigating		
1	Consider the degree you are studying for – how will critical thinking help you to succeed with it?	☐
2	Consider your future career – in what ways will critical thinking skills be useful for you?	☐

3 When you read any new source text, do not accept it without questioning and carefully evaluating the evidence, theories and methods.

4 Do enough background reading so that you can come to your own conclusions about a topic.

**Part D
Speaking**

1 Think about who your audience is and what can persuade them.

2 Look for examples of good PowerPoint slides and assess their strong points.

3 After planning your presentation, question the content and think of ways that you can increase its impact.

4 Make sure that your visual aids and speech complement, but do not unnecessarily reproduce, each other.

5 When working in a group, get to know each other's strong points at the outset.

6 Practise together and give each other honest, useful feedback.

**Part E
Writing**

1 Brainstorm alternative structures when making an essay plan. Think about how your information might fit into each of these structures. Choose the most suitable structure for your thesis and argument.

2 Think about your purpose in using a citation when writing.

3 Try to find examples of student essays in your subject (online or in your college library). Pay attention to the typical features that appear in them.

4 When you do find persuasive techniques used in writing, ask yourself if the writer has done enough to persuade you.

Unit 2 – New frontiers

**Part A
Listening**

1 Research a topic well enough before attending lectures so that you are able to identify the speaker's position on it.

2 Listen carefully for evidence and logic. Try to detect anything illogical or biased.

3 Question everything you hear and prepare to ask questions.

4 Compare the information you hear with other things you know on the topic. Synthesize this information and use it to create new questions.

5 Be wary of obvious attempts to force your agreement. Focus on deciding if you agree with the content of what you hear.

Part B
Reading

1 When reading, don't take the author's position for granted. Try to identify the argument and any reasons that support it.

2 Think about the premises which the writer has based their argument on. Do you accept them?

3 Spend time evaluating the author's argument.

4 Try to identify any assumptions which are not clearly stated in the text. Do you agree with the assumptions?

5 Be open-minded – reflect on what you read and be ready to change your own position as you encounter more information.

Part C
Investigating

1 Consider several points of view before you decide your own stance on a topic.

2 When you read any other source, think about the premises and conclusions offered by the writer. Are there any alternative explanations for a claim that the author has not considered?

3 Take the same approach to your own work – question your own conclusions and consider whether they can be explained by anything else.

4 Consider the relevance of sources or other information to your argument, not simply because they are concerned with the same topic.

Part D
Speaking

1 When creating a presentation, think about ways that you could represent textual information in an effective graphic form instead.

2 Use the checklist to help you avoid common mistakes when you are making graphics.

3 Before using other types of media in a presentation, think carefully about how necessary it is to support your main idea.

4 Always acknowledge sources of information in a presentation with citations and a reference list.

Part E
Writing

1 When planning a piece of writing which requires an argument, try to consider counterarguments and how you will refute them.

2 Build an argumentative essay not just by giving evidence which supports your own main idea, but also by arguing against opposing views.

3 Consider several alternative ways to structure your argument.

4 Choose evidence which is directly relevant to your topic.

5 Give citations for any evidence which you use.

Unit 3 – The individual in society

**Part A
Listening**

1 When a speaker makes a claim, ask yourself how reasonable the premises are, and if they have given enough evidence for you to accept it.

2 Ask yourself whether the claims you hear are reasonable, or just speculation.

3 If you notice that a speaker is speculating, consider their motive for doing this.

4 Do not accept speculation as it is – make questions to try to get more evidence or explanation from the speaker.

**Part B
Reading**

1 When reading, carefully consider whether claims about the relationship of information are logically correct.

2 If you detect a logical flaw in a writer's argument, consider whether it is simply a mistake or a deliberate attempt to persuade you about something which isn't accurate.

3 With any claim that is made, ask yourself if the claim has met the necessary conditions to be accepted as true.

4 When a claim is made for the sole cause of a phenomenon, consider whether this is a sufficient condition to explain that phenomenon.

5 Carefully examine any claim linking correlated phenomena. Consider whether anything else might explain the link between the two things.

**Part C
Investigating**

1 Think carefully about the assignment before taking notes so that you avoid writing anything unnecessary.

2 After taking notes on individual sources, synthesize what you have collected so that you can compare and contrast ideas and information from different sources more easily.

3 When synthesizing notes, ensure that you write citations so that you know where the information has come from.

4 Review your notes after you have synthesized them to help you clarify your ideas on the topic.

**Part D
Speaking**

1 Bear in mind the purpose of your presentation and plan the presentation in a way that is appropriate for that purpose.

2 Consider incorporating your own primary research as support for a presentation.

3 If you do include information based on your own research, this must include a clear explanation of your methods.

4 When planning a presentation with a clear argument, consider including (and refuting) alternative viewpoints as a way to strengthen your claims.

5 When refuting alternative views, make sure that you give a strong enough argument or evidence to do this. Refutations should not be superficial.

Part E Writing

1 Synthesize information from different sources in your writing by comparing and contrasting ideas from other authors and adding your own comments.

2 Avoid using long quotations in your writing.

3 When you use quotations, use introductory phrases and comment on their significance in your own words.

4 Try expressing ideas in your own words whenever possible. Comment on other writers' claims, but do not simply paraphrase them without adding anything of your own.

5 Be aware that patchwriting is considered to be poor scholarship and strive to express as much as possible in your own words.

6 Avoid making inappropriately strong claims by using hedging.

Unit 4 – Choices

Part A Listening

1 Question the logic of the speaker's claims.

2 Pay attention to the speaker's conclusions and decide if they follow logically from the main body of the talk.

3 Make your listening more effective by preparing, listening critically and reflecting on what you have heard.

Part B Reading

1 As you read, be aware of *ad hominem* arguments aimed at the writer rather than their line of reasoning.

2 Avoid accepting 'you too' arguments and judge writers' claims on their logical merits instead.

3 Question the justifications for claims to decide if they follow a logical 'line', or whether the author has presented a circular argument.

4 When you read analogies, consider how similar the two things compared really are.

5 Always question the range of options which a writer presents. It may be that there are other options which have been ignored.

Part C **Investigating**	1	Evaluate your own level of independence. What more could you do to improve this?	☐
	2	Find out what sources of information are available to you and use the ones which are most effective.	☐
	3	Ask yourself how confident you are to learn independently. Identify the things that stop you feeling confident and work to change them.	☐
	4	Find out what study skills resources are available to you online or in your library.	☐
	5	Be a 'self-starter' – learn how to become knowledgeable on a topic through your own research.	☐

Part D **Speaking**	1	Look for examples of good conclusions in academic presentations online.	☐
	2	Consider using reasonable speculations about the implications of your topic when you conclude your presentation.	☐
	3	Make practical recommendations that are suitable to your audience.	☐
	4	Rehearse your presentation until you are confident that you can deliver it well.	☐
	5	Anticipate questions and comments from your audience.	☐

Part E **Writing**	1	Write a conclusion that is logically supported by your essay.	☐
	2	Ask a friend who you trust to proofread for you.	☐
	3	Proofread by printing a hard copy of your work and marking it up.	☐
	4	Accept only advice from proofreaders. Don't allow a proofreader to change or write anything on your behalf.	☐
	5	Don't just stop as soon as you have completed a first draft of your work. Edit it as many times as necessary.	☐
	6	Take time to reflect on your work after editing. Use this as an opportunity to consolidate your knowledge and skills and plan for future improvements.	☐

Appendices

Appendix 1: Recording script

Lecture One

Internet use is growing rapidly, and with it comes an increasing demand for more content delivered online: web pages, documents, graphics, audio and video content. This all results in a corresponding jump in demand for electricity. Now some of these things, like TV and radio, were previously delivered to the home using other devices, but since 2007 there has been an enormous rise in the number of people using the Internet to watch TV shows that they could have watched on their home TV set, or likewise listening to radio shows online rather than switching on a dedicated home radio. The evidence is clear that using the Internet for this kind of content actually requires more power consumption than if the user were to use a regular TV or radio. Looking at the figures for TV, we see here that average power consumption for a desktop computer is between 100 and 150 watts, with a laptop being rather less than half of that. By contrast, TVs stand at 74 watts. Now it may seem that there is little difference between the two, but it's important to consider that the energy consumption does not stop with the end-user's computer. There are also the cabling systems, and finally the data centres which the service providers use. The data centres are the enormous 'server farms' where firms run and maintain their computer hardware round the clock, and these use a phenomenal amount of power. According to data released last year by the Lawrence Berkeley National Lab at UCLA, data centres in the US used 61 billion kilowatt hours of energy in 2006, and this number had risen above 80 billion by 2010. Partly this increase is from simple web use, and the explosion in people using the web over the last few years. It doesn't automatically mean that these billions of kilowatt hours are being used for TV.

There are, of course, many other uses for the Internet. However, if we look here at the difference between looking at a web page and watching video content, we see that the video content requires approximately ten times as much power as it does to view a document. So it is clearly evident from the data we can see here that energy-intensive applications like streaming video, TV and radio on the Internet use an incredible amount of power. So in terms of national or even global energy consumption it's probably fair to say that using the Internet for these purposes is worse, in energy terms, than using a TV or radio, which show a lower overall energy demand than computers do, if we include the massive energy use at computer data centres. If we think about the level of household energy consumption, and costs to the consumer, the data also strongly suggests that it is more cost-effective, and certainly more energy efficient, to use a dedicated TV set or radio for that kind of content than it is to watch or listen to it via a computer.

Lecture Two

The past couple of years or so have seen increasing claims that the kind of content that people view on the Internet can cause excessive electricity consumption. Today I want to compare Internet use for viewing things like video and TV with the electricity demand from viewing the same type of content on a regular TV, and to throw some light on claims that the Internet is causing some kind of electricity 'drain'. Certainly, the number of Internet users is growing quickly – it's increasing at a phenomenal rate, in fact. Recent estimates put the number of Internet users around the world at just under two billion. Clearly, with an increase in the number of users, there is also an increase in the energy which they consume while using the net. It is undeniable that more energy is used by the Internet and associated technologies now than, say, ten years ago, or even two years ago, for that matter. This is undeniable. It is also true enough that certain kinds of content require more power than others. Thus, viewing video or TV online, using the kinds of services which have recently become available, does indeed require more power than viewing a document, or typing an email and so on. Again, this is undeniable.

But it is important not to misinterpret this information. Though we can see a massive increase in the use of online TV and radio services, and a trend towards higher electricity consumption as a result of increasing Internet usage overall, this does not mean that watching TV or video content online is itself more energy intensive than using a dedicated television set, or radio or DVD player or things of that sort. It is, in fact, almost certain that using the Internet to view this kind of content is more energy efficient than using a separate, dedicated machine, and that this efficiency will continue to improve. If we look, for instance, at TV, we find that on the surface of it, watching it online tends to require more power as a result of running the computer itself, as well as the energy used to power the servers of the company providing the service. TVs, by comparison, use less energy overall, both the machine itself and the broadcasting infrastructure. However, consider that with a home computer you have but a single machine which can play DVDs and CDs, link to online radio, streaming video and TV services. All of these things would in the past have required a separate machine, which would have required a lot of energy to create in the first place. You can comfortably watch a lot of TV online before you would ever equal the amount of energy required to produce a television set in the first place.

Another point I want to make is that of increasing efficiency. Computers and the Internet are cutting-edge technologies, and there are strong continual improvements in the efficiency of all of the equipment associated with them. For instance, laptops these days are already three times more efficient than they were even four years ago. Older data cables required just under four kilowatt hours of electricity per gigabyte transmitted. The most modern fibre cables, however, can transmit the same amount of data at just 0.77 of a kilowatt hour. In fact, we can see the same trend in reverse with televisions. The most modern TVs are using more efficient parts, but they are incredibly expensive, which means fewer people buy and use them, and when they do, increasingly large screen sizes mean that energy demand from modern household TV sets is increasing by comparison with the gains made in computer hardware. These improvements are obviously set to continue so that we'll see things like online TV and video content become increasingly viable over the next few years.

Appendix 2: Internet privacy

A Internet commerce in the UK has expanded rapidly since the turn of the century. This has been fuelled by a combination of factors, including better broadband connectivity enjoyed by a growing number of users, as well as an easing of early fears about the safety of online shopping which were prevalent in the 1990s (Gopnik, 2008, p.357). Using the Internet not just for casual browsing or communications, but also for shopping, banking and other financial transactions, such as the purchase of services, has come to be generally accepted as a safe and efficient means of handling one's personal affairs. Recent research suggests that online shopping now accounts for 11% of all consumer sales in the UK (Howell, 2007, p.14) and there is no sign that this rate of growth will slow in the near future.

B Against such a background, it is instructive to revisit the question of Internet privacy. As Internet sales and the volume of personal information moving online have grown, so has the possibility of abuse of this data, despite the fact that more people accept that the Internet is a convenient method of shopping. Many people who say that they are happy to do online shopping nevertheless also indicate that they are concerned about Internet privacy (ibid.). This paper will identify some of the key issues involved in Internet privacy in relation to online commerce and conclude by identifying ways in which some of these issues may be addressed in future.

C The key point around which all privacy issues for online shoppers revolve is what happens to one's Personal Identifying Information (PII). This includes demographic data such as age, gender, socio-economic status, as well as address (both real-world and IP) and telephone contact details and also potentially financial, legal and health records (Kerswell, 2009). The following section will outline significant factors affecting the protection of PII.

D The first area in which privacy may be threatened is the very act of collecting and storing PII in the first place. This is a routine matter for most online businesses, which keep certain types of PII on record for a period of several months after contact with any given customer (Gopnik, 2008). Internet Service Providers (ISPs) similarly maintain records about sites visited by any given computer for anything between six and ten months (ibid.). There are moves afoot by the British Government to require businesses and ISPs to store this information for a much longer period of time – anything up to a decade, according to some claims (Richardson, 2009, p.104). This would dramatically increase the amount of time that personal data resided on databases, but the fact remains, however, that there is currently no legal limit to how long the information may be stored, and it tends to differ between different organizations. The threat here is that the simple existence of such data makes it open either to deliberate abuse (such as hacking), or accidental release in a manner which will injure the person to whom the data relates.

E The UK Online Privacy Commission has indicated that this enormous store of data is open to abuse in a number of ways. The danger of third-party theft is an obvious and well-recognized concern. The data itself has the potential to be highly valuable for criminals, who could use it for outright extortion or resale within the criminal underworld. However, much as this is a real threat, public anxiety about this type of crime has meant that ISPs and companies doing business online have, on the whole, instituted very strong technical defences against this kind of theft. The instances of such theft are, correspondingly, rather small (Kerswell, 2009, p.1322).

F A far more troubling issue affecting personal privacy is the onward sale of one's personal data by the company to which it has been entrusted. This is a lucrative temptation for many businesses, which can profit by selling on bulk client data to marketing or other associated companies (Abbott, 2009, p.118). However, it is a practice which almost no organization is keen to admit to doing and so data about the extent of this type of activity is scarce.

G Deliberate actions, whether criminal or merely ethically questionable, inhabit one end of the continuum of risks to which one's privacy is exposed on the Internet. A problem which has proved to be equally damaging, and in fact may be more so in light of the frequency of its occurrence, is accidental loss. The Online Privacy Commission has identified 30 cases in the last five years in which significant amounts of personal data were lost, either by accidental online transfer, or while being carried on a different media such as a USB file or even a laptop (OPC Privacy Report, 2009). It is impossible to determine what happened to this data after its loss, but the potential for abuse should not be underestimated.

H In conclusion, online privacy, particularly the protection of personal data while performing transactions with companies online, has improved in the years since the initial phase of e-commerce in the late 1990s. Nevertheless, it is apparent that there are a number of issues affecting privacy and the safety of consumers' personal data. These stem from the fact that PII is stored online for months after use, opening it to the possibility of theft, unethical resale, or accidental loss. Further research is required in order to estimate the degree to which these represent a real threat and also to determine the damage caused both at an individual and social level in recent events of the type outlined above.

REFERENCES

Abbott, D. (2009). How private is 'private'? A study of the resale of consumer personal data. *Ethics in Management, 22*(1), 110–119.

Gopnik, P. (2008). *Paces of Change: The Internet in the 21st Century*. London: Mulberry Tree.

Howell, A. (2007). Tracking the boom in Internet sales. *E-commerce Quarterly, 12*(4), 11–27.

Kerswell, M. (2009). What constitutes PII? *Surveillance Issues Quarterly, 26*(2), 1309–1337.

Online Privacy Commission (2009). *3rd UK Privacy Report*. Basingstoke: CSC.

Richardson, J. (2009). *Data and the State in 21st-Century Britain*. Liverpool: Active Press.

Appendix 3: Assessing stress impacts associated with workplace email

A   The psychological stress impact associated with email has received a great deal of   1
academic interest, with classic studies of emotional stressors from non-response
(Kuhn, 2003) and reduced job satisfaction resulting from 'email overload'
(Denman, 2004) to stress effects from perceived rudeness (Gorman, 2003; Siedel &
Wilson, 2008; Trang, 2008). In the following paper, I will attempt to draw together 5
the most salient findings from work done in this field over the last five years,
and propose some of the most common stress triggers associated with email. The
definition of stress adopted here follows Kuhn (ibid.), including both physiological
and mental symptoms, whether real or imagined by the sufferer.

B   It is fair to say that modern business as we know it would be almost entirely   10
impossible without the conveniences that email offers: swift communication with
co-workers; the time and space to think through rapid communications in a way
that is impossible in real time over the phone; the ability to send and receive large
documents without the need for expensive and time-consuming printing or hand
delivery.   15

C   However, it is clearly apparent that email has also introduced a range of serious
stress triggers into the workplace. One of the first studies on the subject (Brandeis
& Ho, 1998) questioned whether these were in fact damaging stressors, or
merely an inconvenience, arriving at the conclusion that email did not introduce
measurable stress into the workplace. A contrasting position has been taken by   20
most other researchers (see for instance Denman, 2004; Norman, 2008; Siedel
& Wilson, 2008), who claim that email is evidently one of the most significant
causes of workplace stress. Denman's study was particularly broad, gathering
results from a total of 9000 workers in 200 US businesses, which demonstrated an
overwhelming feeling among US office staff that email was a primary workplace   25
stressor. Other studies in Europe have echoed the results of Denman's work and
it now seems irrefutable that email, despite its many benefits, is also a cause of
significant workplace stress, rather than a mere inconvenience. From the range
of studies presented here, and a growing body of evidence, it might even be
reasonable to propose that it is in fact quickly becoming by far the most stressful   30
aspect of modern workplace life.

D   Before looking at the particular stress triggers themselves, it is instructive to
consider what function email serves in the modern workplace and what method of
communication it is, exactly, that email is replacing. Email has often been likened
to an instant, electronic memo, a kind of electronic Post-it note. By framing email   35
in this way, it is possible to misunderstand how stressful it can be. Post-it notes left
stuck on a colleague's desk do not need, or have space for, overly polite salutations,
after all, which is what might be found in a formal letter or even a phone
conversation. Nixon (2008) argues that claims of stress resulting from terse email
language are irrelevant because the email recipient is simply misinterpreting the   40
type of communication that email is: short, terse, work-related communications.
However, in contrast to Nixon, I would argue that it is more accurate to view
email as a kind of letter, albeit not requiring a stamp or paper. This is due to the
fact that the email stressors most commonly identified are precisely the things
that one would expect to see in a letter but which often get left out in an email.   45
Email at work, therefore, is perceived by its recipients as being a letter form of

communication, and there is an expectation that the standards of formality and care which apply in formal letters should also apply to email. Clearly, when these standards are broken, stress results. As almost every office worker in the developed world now has an email-capable computer, it is likely that email has silently become the single greatest cause of workplace stress. 50

E Email-associated stress factors can be divided into two types: essentially quantity factors and quality factors. Denman (2004) has clearly demonstrated that quantity factors – the sheer number of emails that one receives on a daily basis – contribute strongly to feelings of stress. An interesting parallel can be found in a case study 55 by Oktay (2004) of a single junior manager at a busy customer care centre in Des Moines. The individual concerned received well above 300 emails a day and was exhibiting symptoms of clinical depression resulting from work stress, which he identified as being caused mainly by his email (Oktay, 2004, p.109).

F Stress arising from email content, which we may term 'quality factors', is also a 60 significant issue. Gorman (ibid.), in a study of 700 lecturers, identified a range of content-related factors which contribute to stress. The principal stressors, according to Gorman, appear to be negligent grammar and spelling, the use of overly casual emoticons in official mail, and lack of clarity from rushed or overly abrupt emails. However, the most significant stressor by far was the lack of common greetings or 65 salutations. This would tend to support the view that email is perceived as being somewhat like a letter, with the expectation of proper politeness formalities. A large number of other, though similar, results have been revealed in other studies, all pointing to the lack of letter-like politeness as a significant stress trigger.

G Another interesting point, which has so far received only a little attention, is what 70 may be termed the 'temporal issue' (Roberts, 2006, p.417). There is a suggestion that email-related stress can arise from misunderstandings, or at least a different understanding, between sender and recipient of the way email works in time. Email is, of course, absolutely not an instantaneous form of communication, in the way that a phone conversation is. After sending an email, the author can only 75 be sure that it has arrived in the recipient's inbox; they have no way of knowing when, or indeed if, the recipient has read it. Email exchanges therefore require time for the recipient to read and possibly act on the content of the mail before replying. Many email users nonetheless perceive email to be instantaneous, possibly because it is a modern electronic technology. Roberts' study demonstrated that one party 80 in an email exchange is behaving as though email were instantaneous, while the other feels that it is not.

H The evidence overwhelmingly indicates that email is a significant cause, perhaps the primary cause, of modern workplace stress. It is important that the evident benefits of email do not cause us to overlook this fact, or minimize its impact on 85 workplace wellbeing, job satisfaction and the dreadful consequences of stress-related illness.

REFERENCES

Brandeis, W., & Ho, L. (1998). The place of email in modern working life. *Computers and Communication, 14*(1), 12–19. Retrieved from: http://www.sciencedirect.com/journals.

Denman, I. (2004). *Psychology in the Modern Workplace*. Austin: AUP.

Gorman, K. (2003). Content, politeness and formality: stressors arising from unorthodox communications at work. *Psychology and Language Journal, 3*(6), 134–152.

Kuhn, A. (2003). The perception of delay in email response as a stress trigger. *Language and Community, 9*(3), 1105–1119.

Nixon, J. (2008). Language and motive: interpreting email. *Language and Community, 14*(7), 243–245.

Norman, M. (2008). Workplace stress: the role of email. In B. Pope (Ed.), *Communication at Work: Studies in the Modern Office Environment* (p.103–129). London: Mendip Press.

Oktay, P. (2004). Clinical stress effects of ICT in a high-volume call centre. *ICT and Psychology Review, 13*(1), 101–111.

Roberts, I. (2006). The effect of time-lag in email communications. *Bulletin of the Communication Technology Society, 4*, 403–422.

Siedel, D., & Wilson, G.B. (2008). Assessing environmental and communication stressors in the modern office. In B. Pope (Ed.), *Communication at Work: Studies in the Modern Office Environment* (pp.407–414). London: Mendip Press.

Trang, V. (2008). 'What's he getting at?' An inquiry into politeness levels and the misinterpretation of electronic messages. In B. Pope (Ed.), *Communication at Work: Studies in the Modern Office Environment* (pp.391–402). London: Mendip Press.

Appendix 4

Text A: Communications technology and culture

The rapid spread of the Internet in the last years of the 20th century saw a renewal of the fear, in some quarters, that it would mean a creeping spread of westernization and the further erosion of local cultures around the world. In this essay, westernization is taken to mean, essentially, that culture originating in northern Europe, including therefore the US and Australia–New Zealand. Although two of these are geographically not western, few would dispute their rightful place in the 'western' club. At first glance, it seems easy to be sympathetic to the claim of a one-way flow of western culture through the medium of the Internet when one considers the apparent evidence of this westernization: teenagers the world over drinking Coca-Cola, listening to global brand-name bands from the US, Australia and Europe, as well as mimicking dress styles and behaviours that are fundamentally alien in their own cultures; politicians and business leaders from all nations using common, often US-led, models of 'best practice'. However, it is important not to confuse globalization – which is undoubtedly being assisted in its development by the Internet and other advanced communications technology – with westernization. In this essay I will attempt to show that the spread of globalization through the Internet is having a paradoxical effect: far from being a vehicle for western values which is overwhelming non-western cultures, the Internet is actually helping to strengthen those local cultures and indeed prevent globalization from being merely a 'westernizing' phenomenon.

The idea that the Internet is the medium for the one-way spread of western values is derived in large part from the fact that the vast majority of its content is in English (Crystal, 1997). To add to the dominance of English on the net, until very recently all domain names have been assigned by a US government body which of course required that they be typed using the English alphabet. The logical conclusion that follows from this is that such English-language domination has resulted in a culturally western Internet, which has permeated societies around the globe and is undermining their own local cultures. However, this view ignores the fact that the Internet gives all of its users the opportunity to upload their own content. It is an overwhelmingly English medium at present, perhaps, but that does not mean that this is a one-way transmission of western culture. It is increasingly apparent that people all over the world are using the freedom of the Internet to contribute their own news, opinions and cultural information. Wikipedia is an excellent example of a project which depends on contributions from users who may be based in any nation creating a shared store of knowledge. Similarly we can see the popularity of uploads from essentially every nation on Earth on sites such as YouTube. To take one example of cultural fusion rather than westernization, we have the two Chinese students lip-synching to the Backstreet Boys who became an Internet hit around the world in 2006. This is a somewhat trivial example but it demonstrates that the Internet is, essentially, free to all people who wish to upload content and that content from places other than the West has the possibility of becoming popular the world over.

The Internet is also helping diaspora communities to maintain their own cultures. Be they Chinese, Pakistani, Turkish or Yemeni, people from these, or any other culture, who have moved to foreign countries such as the UK for work are able to hang on to their cultural identity by using the Internet to download news and entertainment in their own language. This is a radical departure from even two decades ago, when contact with the home culture was limited to a small selection of newspapers and magazines. The Internet allows ordinary citizens to continue to participate in their own community without needing to actually be present in the home country. This arguably helps to maintain the vitality of communities spread around the globe and ensure that the home culture is not lost by second and later generations growing up in a different country. Far from causing the loss of cultures to western values, the Internet is helping, in this way, to ensure their continuation even in cases where people have chosen to live in a western nation.

In fact, the very necessity of moving to the West for work may itself be weakened by the Internet. Previously, the hope of a high salary or other economic comforts pushed skilled workers, or those seeking to acquire high-paying skills, to emigrate to Europe, Australia–New Zealand, or North America. While it is clear that this is still the case, there are equally clear examples in which the spread of the Internet has meant that this emigration is no longer necessary. Friedman (2007) cites the example of skilled computer workers in India. Arguing that they would have previously been required to pursue their dreams of economic and career advancement by moving to the US, Friedman observes the rapid growth of the computer services industry within India itself. The ease of online communications between nations has seen a massive increase in high-tech work being outsourced to the newly energized BRIC nations. This serves to strengthen the economies and support the cultures of non-western nations.

The debate about western cultural imperialism spreading via the Internet has in fact spurred a backlash against the very idea of western / English-language dominance of the Internet. The period since 2005 has seen a rapid increase in the number of non-English language websites, and these are increasingly fracturing the Internet into a collection of culturally differentiated zones – thus in China we can see the enormous popularity of Baidu, a home-grown and Chinese-language search engine, compared with the relative insignificance of its western counterpart Google. In 2009 it was declared that the US body which oversees domain names would cease to control this right, allowing domain names to be entered in non-English alphabet characters for the first time.

In conclusion, far from being a western, and uniformly westernizing, phenomenon, the spread of the Internet is clearly showing that it is a convenient technology for non-western cultures to use to strengthen and promote their own cultural values. It allows non-westerners to distribute and upload their own content and helps to spread this content to the wider world, where its popularity may go beyond their own disparate communities. To see the Internet as being a westernizing medium simply due to its existence is to misunderstand that non-western peoples are not passive objects of western domination. They are perfectly capable of grasping the potential of the Internet to serve their own cultures.

REFERENCES

Crystal, D. (1997). *English as a Global Language*. Cambridge: Cambridge University Press.

Friedman, T. (2007). *The World is Flat: the globalized world in the 21st century*. London: Penguin.

Text B: The Internet and western cultural domination

If it is true that the Internet is an 'information superhighway', then it is becoming increasingly clear that it is a one-way highway. The vast majority of information carried on the Internet is in the English language and inevitably flows from the English-language cultural centre out to the non-English regions of the world. As it does so, it carries with it not just the language but also popular western cultural values and western liberal politics and philosophy. Communications technology such as satellite television, mobile technology and, in particular, the Internet is the medium through which cultural homogeneity is spreading and this is ultimately a homogenization that reflects western values. It has both positive and negative consequences. This essay will suggest some examples which clearly demonstrate the western (and westernizing) character of the Internet, before considering the implications, both good and bad, of that homogenization.

The Internet itself does not, of course, cause homogenization of cultures in favour of the West. This is a consequence of a variety of historical, economic and indeed military phenomena. However, given the global aspects of western culture, it is reasonable to assume that the Internet, an incredibly powerful vehicle for ideas, is responsible for making these ideas spread further and faster than ever before. This increasing westernized uniformity of culture can be seen in popular, political and business culture around the world.

At a popular level – movies, music, branding and consumer goods – the overwhelming popularity of western culture is perhaps most evident. It is something of a cliché now to note that teenagers the world over share tastes in video games, soft drinks, music styles and even dress sense. This reflects an enduring fascination with western, often American, consumer goods and cultural icons. It is certainly true that local variations on these types exist. For instance, Japanese-style blue jeans have enjoyed popularity with youths across Asia in the last ten years, but the fact remains that these are all variations on blue jeans, which are an essentially western fashion item. This local variation on ultimately western items is clear throughout most global industries. The Internet assists in this: in fact, it positively supercharges this trend by making it easier for people in any nation to go online and find out what the latest trends are. The Internet helps youths around the world to create a sense of community that is not national, but is based on shared interests in fashion, gaming, music and so on, with other young people in other nations. In a similar way the enormous popularity of football, and European football teams in particular, is maintained through dedicated fan websites which are run by people across the globe who may never have even visited the home country of the team which they support.

However, the fact is that popular culture is a relatively trivial expression of the power of the Internet to spread western values. At the political level we can see the gradual acceptance, followed by adoption, of certain basic notions of political conduct, human rights and democratic freedom which are arguably western in their origins (Howard, 1995). The contribution of the Internet to this phenomenon becomes clear when one considers human rights and other protest movements around the world which have used websites, Internet and mobile communications technology to promote their causes (Gibson et al., 2003). Invariably these are popular, grassroots democratic movements. The publicity they achieve through the Internet helps to strengthen a global consensus about what constitutes basic human and political rights.

The Internet supports, and drives, a similar westernization in global corporate culture. Albirini (2008) has noted the diffusion of certain business practices that had their origins in US business. The continued perception of such Ivy League institutions as Harvard and Yale as the global leaders in business management practices supports this trend. Internet technology facilitates this by allowing transnational corporations to operate efficiently with business premises spread throughout the world, using standardized business software developed, by and large, by US companies, to communicate with head offices which are often located in the North-America–Europe region. The phenomenal success, and global reach, of such powerful transnationals as BP, Coca-Cola, Microsoft and McDonalds has helped to convince business leaders the world over that the western way is the 'right' way. Whether this is the case or not is somewhat beside the point here, as it is the popular belief in this fact which supports its continuation.

It is not within the purview of this essay to argue whether this trend towards cultural homogenization along western lines is right or wrong. The fact is that it has both positive and negative sides. The positives are surely the consensus on fundamental human rights. Western aid and political organizations which have global reach, such as Amnesty International and the Red Cross, have been able to use the Internet to promote their causes and highlight abuses around the world. They now draw their membership not only from concerned citizens of the western democracies, but from people of all nations who are united in common beliefs about their rights, or 'decent' behaviour by their political rulers. Few would dispute that a greater sense of the world as a community is a good thing.

However, there are clearly negatives in this as well. As Crystal (1997) and others have shown, much of value is lost in the creeping trend towards homogenization of values and cultures along western lines. Local non-western ways of seeing the world, and certain traditional skills which could feed back into creative industries, are lost as a result of increasing globalization (Balick, 2003). A veneration of all things western also carries with it, unfortunately, the western tendency towards over-consumption and waste – the desire to raise their citizens to a materially western lifestyle, rich in consumer goods, is a dearly held dream in many Third-World societies, and this desire is kept alive by the Internet. This is clearly a problem when people aspire to a lifestyle that cannot be supported by the planet's resources.

In conclusion, I would argue that the Internet supporting a global trend towards westernization of cultural, political and business values is undeniable. What is open to question, certainly, is the extent to which this is beneficial or not. Though there are clearly problems with the wholesale adoption of western cultural values, I would cautiously suggest that it is on the whole advantageous, giving as it does a greater sense of a global community with shared values.

REFERENCES

Albirini, A. (2008). The Internet in developing countries: a medium of economic, cultural and political domination. *International Journal of Education and Development Using ICT, 4*(1), 49–65.

Balick, M. (2003). *Traditional knowledge: lessons from the past, lessons for the future*. Paper presented at the Conference on Biodiversity, Biotechnology and the Protection of Traditional Knowledge. Saint Louis: Washington University School of Law, Retrieved from http://law.WUSH.edu/centeris/pages.aspx?id=1836.

Crystal, D. (1997). *English as a Global Language*. Cambridge: Cambridge University Press.

Gibson, R., Ward, S., & Lusoli, W. (2003). The Internet and political campaigning: the new medium comes of age? *Representation, 39*(3), 166–180.

Howard, R. (1995). Occidentalism, Human Rights, and the Obligations of Western Scholars. *Canadian Journal of African Studies. 29*(1), 110–26.

Appendix 5: Recording script

So, the nature of identity is itself flexible – it depends to a large extent on the situation that we are in. Let's look at what the future holds for the three different concepts of identity – physical, psychological, and behavioural.

All of us have at one time or another changed some aspect of our physical identity. We've all probably changed our hairstyles or clothing fashions at one point or another. Maybe you have had the experience of looking at an old passport photo of yourself and thinking that the person there is somehow no longer 'you', because your appearance has changed so much. But these days we can take physical changes much further, changing ourselves in ways that were impossible for earlier generations. Maybe some of you have changed your eye colour with coloured contact lenses, for instance. Some people choose plastic surgery in an effort to remake themselves, while others who are profoundly uncomfortable with their identity at birth may choose a sex change – perhaps one of the most fundamental physical, and emotional, changes of the self. Technological advances, and also ideas within society about what is acceptable, offer us increasingly profound ways to change who we appear to be to the rest of the world. In the future, we are likely to see even more extreme forms of self-expression become normal. Plastic surgery will probably become more widespread. According to figures from consumer attitude surveys published by the Hughes Institute in the USA, the percentage of adults who would be prepared to have some form of plastic surgery has risen from 12 % in 1995, to around 35 % today, and it seems likely that this trend towards seeing such surgery as a positive thing will continue ever upwards. As the technology develops, and such surgical procedures become cheaper, more socially acceptable and routine, it is possible that we might change between several radically different appearances throughout the course of our lives. For the police and border control agencies who rely on each of us having a constant physical identity, this will present incredible challenges. DNA testing will become a more important method of identification than photographs, and so we will see a greater social acceptance of the idea of national databases, where all citizens' DNA is stored. Passports will include DNA samples rather than photographs. From the point of view of security, think of how this will affect the use of Closed Circuit TV, or CCTV, cameras, that we see in buildings and all over our towns these days. Will these become useless if everyone is able to make radical changes to their appearance? Not so: in the future, CCTV will be combined with sophisticated computer software which will recognize people caught on camera, not by their facial features, but by the unique way in which each of us walks, and extremely accurate measurements of things like height, shoulder width, the shape of your cheekbones, and so on. So, from a physical point of view, the future will see us able to change ourselves beyond all recognition, while at the same time we will be scrutinized more closely than ever before by security technologies.

Behaviourally, as well, our identities will be opened up to public view in new ways. Previously, for instance, your shopping habits were your own business, because nobody knew what you were buying with your own cash unless you told them about it. But soon most of us will be living in societies where cash has been replaced by cards, electronic transfers, and online shopping. It is possible for other people to find out just about anything about how we spend our money these days, and marketing companies use this valuable information to build a picture of your 'identity' as a consumer. We will enter an age where technology is so common in aspects of our lives that we will leave a digital trace of everything we do – a sophisticated electronic picture of how each one of us lives.

This will allow a wide range of organizations – governments, the police, employers, commercial companies, advertisers – to build a profile of who you are based on where you go, what you do when you are there, and what you like to spend your money on. Your identity will be opened to public view as never before.

This has implications for the psychological aspects of identity. What will it mean to live in a world where everything about you is so clearly open to view? Privacy is a basic human need, and it is unlikely that we will allow our most private identities to be visible to outsiders in this way. We are likely to see fewer people willing to share information about themselves online. Social networking sites like Facebook, which are so popular now, will actually decline in popularity in the coming years, as privacy, and the protection of our basic identity, becomes more precious to us.

Appendix 6: Recording script

In conclusion, we can see that there are a number of general factors that need to be taken into account when making a decision about how to allocate resources such as money. These include estimations of the risks and benefits involved in any choice, as well as considerations of the amount of the resource available, and also the priorities with which it might be needed. However, there are a number of external factors, such as bias and time pressure, which can influence this decision. The research evidence which I've presented here suggests that many people do not make such choices by rationally considering every factor. An interesting question that this raises is whether people who rationally consider all the alternatives actually make better decisions than those whose decision-making process is irrational, or intuitive. It might be the case that people do not need to consider every possible factor in order to make a good decision about how to allocate the resources available to them. However, the answer to that question is outside the scope of my presentation. Thank you very much for listening. Are there any questions?